PRAISE FOR

The Lessons of the American Civilization

"A deep blend of American history and economics. Once upon a time in America, and not so long ago, we were on our way, striding, purposeful, and succeeding. Del Beccaro's *Lessons* shows us how to break out of modern habits and resume our journey toward freedom, peace, and, above all, prosperity."

—ARTHUR LAFFER, PhD, founder and chairman of Laffer Associates

"Picking up where he left off with *The Divided Era*, Del Beccaro continues his writing in the tradition of Will and Ariel Durant with *The Lessons of the American Civilization*. His sweeping study of the American civilization places America's past in the historical perspective too often missing from American classrooms and political discussions today."

—JOHN GIZZI, political correspondent at Newsmax Media

"Thought provoking . . . well worth reading."

—BETSY MCCAUGHEY, former lieutenant governor of New York

"Tom Del Beccaro's *Lessons of the American Civilization* demonstrates a keen understanding of economics and history. It is a must-read by anyone concerned about the long-term future of this country."

—STEPHEN MOORE, senior visiting fellow in economics at the Heritage Foundation

"This book reminded me why I am so proud to have become an American. And it reminds all of us why being an American means much more than nationality. It means inheriting a set of ideas that represent both opportunity and obligation: opportunity to live our lives in the greatest nation on earth, obligation to fight to keep it so—especially today, when the American idea is under assault, even from within. This is an essential book for *now*."

—**STEVE HILTON**, former director of strategy for British Prime Minister David Cameron

"Del Beccaro's must-read *Lessons of the American Civilization* is a wide-ranging and incisive analysis of American culture, economics, history, and politics covering the waterfront of forces affecting America's future."

—**DAVID MCCUAN**, PhD, professor and chair of political science at Sonoma State University

"*The Lessons of the American Civilization* once again demonstrates Del Beccaro's deep understanding of the nexus between government policy, economics, and human behavior. He is a big thinker in the mold of Charles Krauthammer."

—**TONY STRICKLAND**, former mayor of Huntington Beach, California

"Benjamin Franklin described America as 'a Republic, if you can keep it.' Thomas Del Beccaro outlines beautifully what forces have been at work both to keep and to destroy that republic. Americans would do well to read this book so as to learn how to repeat our past successes and, perhaps more so, avoid the harbingers of our downfall."

—**E. J. ANTONI**, PhD, public finance economist

"Del Beccaro's *Lessons* is reminiscent of Toynbee and Durant, with the analytical skills of a Bill Buckley—rendered in an approachable and digestible manner. A triumph of research and thoughtfulness for the Everyman."

—**STEVE COHEN**, media executive

"Many ask what is happening in American culture today. Del Beccaro's *Lessons of the American Civilization* vividly answers the question with his incisive historical perspective."

—**SHELBY SCARBROUGH,** author of *Civility Rules!* and former protocol officer for the US Department of State

The LESSONS *of the* AMERICAN CIVILIZATION

The LESSONS of the AMERICAN CIVILIZATION

Its Confident Rise & the Warning Signs of Its Decline

THOMAS G. DEL BECCARO

RIVER GROVE
BOOKS

The views expressed herein are solely those of the author and do not imply endorsement by Greenleaf Book Group or discrimination against other points of view.

Published by River Grove Books
Austin, TX
www.rivergrovebooks.com

Copyright © 2024 Tom Del Beccaro

All rights reserved.

Thank you for purchasing an authorized edition of this book and for complying with copyright law. No part of this book may be reproduced, stored in a retrieval system, or transmitted by any means, electronic, mechanical, photocopying, recording, or otherwise, without written permission from the copyright holder.

Distributed by River Grove Books

Design and composition by Greenleaf Book Group and Teresa Muñiz
Cover design by Greenleaf Book Group and Teresa Muñiz
Cover photograph of Washington, DC, courtesy of Tom Del Beccaro. Portrait of Abraham Lincoln courtesy of the National Portrait Gallery. Image of immigrant women courtesy of the Library of Congress. All other images (© Tony Baggett, xiaoliangge) used under license from Adobe Stock.com.

Publisher's Cataloging-in-Publication data is available.

Paperback ISBN: 978-1-63299-857-6

Hardcover ISBN: 978-1-63299-874-3

eBook ISBN: 978-1-63299-858-3

First Edition

To my parents, Annette Del Beccaro and Edward Del Beccaro, as well as to Will and Ariel Durant. God rest their souls.

Contents

Introduction 1

    Chapter 1: How Civilizations Rise and Fall 9

    Chapter 2: The Foundation of the American Civilization 25

    Chapter 3: The Ethic of the Early American Civilization 33

    Chapter 4: The Purposes of the Early American Civilization 47

    Chapter 5: The American Ideal 61

    Chapter 6: From Revolution to Revolution—America Comes of Age 75

    Chapter 7: America at War with Itself 89

    Chapter 8: America as a Superpower 109

    Chapter 9: America in Doubt 125

    Chapter 10: America, Capitalism, and Socialism 143

    Chapter 11: America's Modern Morality, Religion, and Culture 175

    Chapter 12: The State of the American "Empire" 191

    Chapter 13: Ten Vital Lessons of the American Civilization 201

Epilogue: What Lies Ahead 221
Appendix: Key Points from the Book 231
Notes 237
Index 269
About the Author 283

Introduction

*If you want the present to be different
from the past, study the past.*

—**Attributed to Baruch Espinoza**

The American civilization is unique to history. Never before, and not since, has a nation of its size been born of such fresh ground and cultivated so deliberately by ideals. America's earliest settlers, despite landing on nameless shores, without any guarantees and under the most trying of circumstances, nevertheless triumphed and set the stage for the future United States to become the world's most dominant civilization to date. This book is the story of America's confident and purposeful rise through the centuries.

The America of today, however, is not the America of its first four centuries. As with other great civilizations that have matured, America's economic, governmental, and societal institutions, along with its ethics and morals, have changed. *The Lessons of the American Civilization* tells that story as well, including the weakening doubt America finds itself in today.

★ ★ ★

At the dawn of the American civilization, there was already an Old World in Europe and even older civilizations in the East. The North American expanse, by comparison, was a New World. Yes, it was populated with vibrant indigenous populations but it was largely undiscovered by those older worlds—let alone defined by them. Over the last five hundred years, the North American portion of the New World has been the destination of an unprecedented number of diverse peoples from around the globe to its shores to pursue, not the cultures or systems of their pasts but, rather, the religious, economic, and political fortunes of their futures.

At the time of the Founding of the United States, almost three hundred years after settlers first began arriving, fewer than two and a half million colonists, what amounts to a single city today, populated the 430,000 square miles of the thirteen colonies on the Eastern shore. In time, however, through unrelenting immigration, births, war, the spreading of disease, and economic and political Manifest Destiny, immigrants and their progeny, displaced much of the existing indigenous population. In doing so, they would turn North America into a single nation from sea to shining sea with more than 331 million people.

The dramatic differences of the United States of today goes far beyond its population and land mass. Its economic activity, once limited to trade with a few nations and ships along that Eastern shore, now traverses the globe by boat, air, wire, and satellite. The American culture, once developing, is now exported to as many places as its goods.

Its governments, once limited and largely local, and its freedoms nearly unlimited, have been replaced by governments of numerous levels, which now make up, by far, America's largest industry, and, with that, freedoms won so dearly have been curtailed proportionally. Meanwhile, Americans have shifted from the calm of an agrarian society dominated by farms and small villages to a society often defined by its large cities and an omnipresent mass media.

America has had its wars as well. They have been abroad and at home, led by presidents and generals. Even so, the country is better known for its captains of industry. The American Industrial Revolution spawned mass industries and mechanized farms helped feed the world. Today, the evolution of machines spurs the technology of communication that, in turn, supplies messages to a world hungry for information.

Through it all, despite its errors and travails (which are the subject of much discussion today), the American civilization became as dominant as any in history. But America is not a story unto itself; nor does it exist alone. So, while it is true that America is unique, nevertheless, it was born of the laws of nature and what I call the "understandings of time." There are Americans, but they remain part of a greater humanity and subject to history's laws, maxims, and lessons.

This book is also about those lessons played out across the American expanse of time and land—how America came to be, its rise, and yes, what appears to be the beginning of its decline.

As for those laws, maxims, and lessons of history, over time there has been a discussion as to what they are—as well as debate about the characteristics of civilizations as they rise and fall, regardless of their people or their locale. It is a field of thought known as *historical philosophy*—the process of placing the "part in light of the whole" of time, as the American historical philosopher Will Durant explained to us.[1]

The Rockefellers and Carnegies of that field, in addition to the American Durant, include Friedrich Hegel, Johann Wolfgang von Goethe and Oswald Spengler from Germany, Thomas Carlyle of Scotland, Arnold Toynbee of England, and Saint-Simon of France—just to name a few. Before them, in 1725 Giambattista Vico of Italy published his *Scienza Nuova* (*The New Science*) on the subject. It was largely unappreciated in its time, but it laid the groundwork for the discussion about historical philosophy to follow. Before Vico, Plato had an important say in the matter two thousand years earlier. Each of them advanced theories, to one degree or another, of how civilizations come together, what they are like as they rise, and what they share as they fall.

Despite their extended discussion over thousands of years, what has become familiar now, the notion that history repeats itself, has in fact only gained a wider currency in the last 250 years. That seminal understanding is based on the trials and errors of humanity and the work of those gifted philosophic minds.

Among them, there is a consensus that civilizations come together and rise almost with a unifying, guiding principle, in an energetic, productive, and organic phase of growth—a common belief. They also fathomed that such an ascendance begins to be lost when that unifying dynamic becomes questioned amid societal skepticism and then is often abandoned as part of a general decline in a period of unbelief. They believed that history repeats itself in the sense that societies demonstrate remarkable similarities in their youth, middle age, and as they wane.

The Lessons of the American Civilization first helps us understand those laws of history that they considered for all of humanity. As we do, rather than pass judgment, we shall endeavor to follow Oswald Spengler's directive that "it is the historian's business not to praise or to blame but to consider morphologically"[2]—in this case, the progressions civilizations make as they rise and fall. Using the historical philosophers' guidelines, distilled by my views, we shall then explore the roots of the American civilization and its rise from the 1500s through the 1700s. We shall pay great attention to the ideals that were America's cohesive forces, which included declaring that the common man had rights bestowed on them from God, in direct contradiction to the history of the divine right of kings. When those ideals were combined with its practices, America extended freedom and democratic institutions well beyond any place and time before it. That unprecedented level of democratization is one of the main historical storylines of the American civilization.

We shall note that, despite the fractious and quite divisive second half of the 1800s, including a decisive war over the injustice of slavery, nascent capitalism, and other difficulties of an emerging civilization, America continued its Manifest Destiny of thought and physical growth—its productive and organic phase—all the way into the 1950s en route to becoming the World's dominant power and preeminent culture.

We shall then come to see how the initial seeds of doubt, some of which were planted in the 1890s and 1930s, gained wider currency in the 1960s. From there, the gathering signposts of the skepticism in America today, which likely herald its period of unbelief and its potential, if not its actual, decline, are explored.

Lest the reader become distressed, it is more than worth noting that *history is no more a straight line than the emotions of our days*. What may appear, in any one moment, to be evidence of decline may only be a pendulum swing to be undone. Moreover, almost without notice, changing technologies or trade routes, wars, disasters, or great leaders can change the course of history and reinvigorate a population.

So, as varied as history is, there is no assurance that the future of America will take any particular path. Meanwhile, the nation's geography, nuclear weapons, and technological capabilities provide a security unknown to Rome (which took four centuries to decline) or any other place in history. Therefore, please be cautioned from thinking that the American civilization has a particular expiration date. Even so, we must understand that, like a sunset, no civilization, has lasted forever except in its influence.

In other words, we understand that the Greece of Plato and Solon is no more—in the same way that the Roman Republic is of our collective past. Yet every day some aspect of their achievements is played out in our present, in the form of our governments, in our art and language, our diet, and so much more.

Overall and in the final analysis, we shall find that history does repeat itself—but only "in the large," as Will Durant would say. This book takes a look at America from that wider perspective and provides a greater understanding of America's place in history, as well as what might lie ahead.

★ ★ ★

As you read along, I ask you to keep the following in mind.

Obviously, there is much to cover in this book, given the task of comparing America's five centuries to that of other civilizations throughout history. To assist with that effort, before we consider the American story, in chapter 1, I rely on some of those great historians who specialized in what is called "historical philosophy." That branch of historical writing seeks to find order in our varied pasts. By comparing civilizations, those philosophers—from Plato 4,500 years ago to Will Durant of the last century—analyzed the patterns in human behaviors as civilizations came together, rose, and fell, as well as the pendulum swings in between.

Also, earlier in this introduction, I refer to what has been variously called the lessons of history, the laws of history and its maxims—what I call "the understandings of time." Those are references to the more dominant commonalities that civilizations share along the continuums of their histories. For instance, civilizations of the past tended to be born in an agricultural phase and then progress to a commercial society. They exhibited greater religious devotion in their beginnings than in their decline. They tended to be more militaristic in their youth than in decline as well. Those are but a few "lessons" or "laws" of history we shall reference and explore.

Chapters 2 through 12 then tell the story of the American civilization in light of those many understandings and lessons. Throughout that journey, I refer to other times and places to illuminate the American experience.

After that survey of the American civilization, we will reach chapter 13, which is titled "Ten Vital Lessons of the American Civilization." That self-explanatory chapter covers such topics as America's place in history and where the current trends in America place it in comparison not only to other countries but also to America's founding principles. In the epilogue, I consider what lies ahead for the American civilization.

I am hopeful that you will not only enjoy this book but also consider it as an entrée to more books on this subject.

Finally, I must note that my parents introduced me to the historical philosophy field of study. At the age of ten, I started reading my father's copies of the *Economist* and *Foreign Policy* magazines. I watched the Sunday morning political shows with them as well. My studies started in earnest at sixteen, when I sat down to read their set of Will and Ariel Durant's

The Story of Civilization—an eleven-volume, nearly ten-thousand-page set of books that survey the history of civilizations. That was followed by *The Lessons of History*. Those Durant books are a monument to historical philosophy. So, if there are numerous references to Will Durant, my first teacher on how to think about this subject, that is why.

Altogether, their works and guidance inspired so much of my endeavors, intellectual and otherwise. So much so that I conceived of this book in my late teenage years and have worked on and off it since then—first through study and then writing. I note that Will Durant once said that a sixty-year-old "historical philosopher" is still "young." That is likely true. But now that I have passed that age, it is time to publish my thoughts on the lessons that are this book.

With that background, let us begin to understand how we have come to believe that history repeats itself. We shall do that before we focus on how the American experience falls within the guidelines that the likes of Plato, Giambattista Vico, Goethe, and others devised for all time.

CHAPTER 1

How Civilizations Rise and Fall

*Civilizations "develop in conformity...
by a constant and uninterrupted order of causes
and effects present in every nation."*

—**Giambattista Vico**, *The New Science*

It will be important for us, before we can take stock of the American civilization, to answer two basic questions: Does history repeat itself? Do civilizations rise and fall? As we answer yes to both questions to varying degrees, with the help of the great historical philosophers, we should first recognize the difficulties those philosophers faced in bringing such understandings to us.

We must always remember that while the history of the world is quite old, the written version of its history is comparatively quite young. At the time Gutenberg invented his printing press, around 1440,* and for many hundreds of years afterward, books were a luxury item for the few, not a common or useful possession of the masses. Even long after books became an item of production for the masses, instead of just the patient art of monks or the useful implements of commerce, literacy rates remained well below half of any given population.†

Not surprisingly, therefore, for most of time, the study of history was confined to a select few and did not begin to reach the public at large until the last three hundred years. Within those comparatively few years, the thorough knowledge of history, let alone its acceptance as a guide, was even more limited. Even today, few can be said to have a widespread knowledge of history. As for an understanding of the works of those attempting to place the history of billions of people into a few predictable patterns—the work of the historical philosophers—well, obviously, that forms the smallest of those subsets.

Even so, today many accept the notion that history "repeats" itself to some degree—a variant of a very basic tenet of the historical philosophers. They do so now because of the amazing triumph of those thinkers not only over a lack of books but also over a second hurdle they and every historian faces—that in every age, for most people, the dust of the past has never been as appealing as the allure of the present. That second hurdle was perhaps best described by Will Durant's lament that we are "choked with news, and starved of history."[1]

Nevertheless, the likes of Vico, Goethe, Hegel, and Carlyle overcame not only those two hurdles but also a difficult third hurdle—the notion

---

* Centuries before Gutenberg, "printed" books appeared in China.

† Professor S. Dorey Armstrong estimates literacy in the European medieval world following the Magna Carta (1215) to be between 10 percent to 20 percent of the general population. Dorsey Armstrong, "Years That Changed History: 1215," Great Courses, accessed April 17, 2024, https://www.thegreatcourses.com/courses/years-that-changed-history-1215.

that history was unworthy of considerable study. Indeed, throughout the ages, many—often those in power or those seeking it with a desire to remake society—have posited that because each time and place was so unique, the stories of long ago could not possibly yield useful understandings regarding the tribulations of the present. Those same social engineers have also recast history to make their case to create or force societal change—a process that further or purposely confuses the quest for the true lessons of history.‡

Such disregards for the past and false representations were not limited just to the ambitious. Indeed, those sentiments have been so widespread throughout history that one of the greatest historical philosophers, Friedrich Hegel, lamented in his early 1800s *Lectures on the Philosophy of History*—his contribution to bringing order to our varied past—that "what experience and history teach is this,—that peoples and governments never have learned anything from history, or acted on principles deduced from it."[2] One hundred years later, George Santayana extended that sentiment in the now more familiar understanding that "those who cannot remember the past are condemned to repeat it."[3]

Even today, those sentiments impede what should be our greater understandings. Nevertheless, let us begin to understand some of the lessons of history and their place in our lives. As we do, let us also be cautioned that there are exceptions to every rule of history. Not all of the moments in time, let alone the reactions to them by the multitudes, can be so easily fit into the order we naturally seek in life. Nevertheless, we hazard our way forward in thought.

---

‡ France's Jean-Jacques Rousseau (1712–1778) for his own reasons is believed to have lamented that "the falsification of history has done more to impede human development than any one thing known to mankind."

HISTORY AND THE QUESTION OF REPETITION

Does history repeat itself?

It does—but we know not literally, despite the great Roman poet and philosopher Virgil's expectation that one day, history would repeat itself in literal detail.[4] Instead, we should understand that the United States senators of today and tomorrow will face and will respond to the challenges of war, poverty, and corruption, which has afflicted every civilization and always will, with the same basic human nature as did the Roman senators for whom they are named. What happened in Rome, however, is surely of different detail than of the Washington, DC, of today.

If that is so, then what do we really mean when we say history repeats itself?

The answers are all around us.

Biologically, we are surrounded by renewal. With each spring, the earth comes to life after our cold, lifeless winters. We mark the seasons with regularity and the sun relentlessly rises and sets while we orbit skies that dictate our predictable calendar. Millennia of such rebirths and their precision have seeped into the consciousness of countless generations and have made us predisposed to believing that we too are subject to some degree of regularity.

So we cannot be surprised to find that some of our earliest religions incorporated some form of renewal. Indeed, eternal return or eternal recurrence, the idea that the universe, if not all things within it, are part of a recurring cycle, has been part of Indian religions for thousands of years. It was a part of the ancient Egyptians' belief in life after death and why Virgil, just before the birth of Christ, wrote of such themes in his *Fourth Eclogue* and in his immortal *Aeneid*. Of course, Christianity's core belief in the Resurrection and eternal life after death reflects a similar view.

Even before Virgil, let alone Christ, we find in the Book of Ecclesiastes (c. 450–200 BC), which is part of the Hebrew Bible and the Christian Old

Testament, this passage: "What has been will be again, what has been done will be done again; there is nothing new under the sun."§

Returning to the study of the historical philosophers, Giambattista Vico (1668–1744) named a chapter on such predictability in his ground-breaking work *The New Science*. He called it "The Course the Nations Run." He surmised that nations were subject to "principles of universal history" that cause them to "develop in conformity . . . by a constant and uninterrupted order of causes and effects present in every nation."[5] Not long after, Friedrich Hegel (1770–1831) wrote, in his work *Lectures on the Philosophy of History*, that

> a community that is acquiring a stable existence, and exalting itself into a State, requires formal commands and laws—comprehensive and universally binding prescriptions; and thus produces a record as well as an interest concerned with intelligent, definite—and, in their results—lasting transactions and occurrences.[6]

If we look to history as lived, as opposed to philosophies discussed, and while there are many more characteristics of civilizations than can be summarized in thousands of pages let alone this short book, we can find that nations have been born, struggled to survive, flourished, and then declined, repeatedly. They have done so with remarkably consistent attributes and weaknesses.

Let us begin by noting that, most often, the rate of internal growth and progression of a nascent civilization, not to mention its survival, is dependent on security from external dangers and the relative absence of internal division. A nation is likely not to form in the absence of secured borders, let alone progress. Excessive internal division can also prevent natural

---

§   Ecclesiastes 1:9 (NIV).

boundaries from forming the outlines of a nation or hamper the progress of a nation, as demonstrated by the brief history of the Qin Dynasty (221 to 207 BC, now part of modern-day China), which was plagued with assassination attempts and revolts.

We can also note that the Italy of today, geographically compact though it is, took many centuries and brute force to be "united" after the Fall of Rome created a wilderness of decentralized and competitive independent city-states. Meanwhile, the political division within the Italian city-state of Genoa, in the 1300s, greatly hampered its progress and made it susceptible to foreign intervention and influence. During the Renaissance, the Italian city-state of Sienna periodically suffered a similar fate, limiting its trajectory.

Once formed, it should be no surprise that nations tend to be more militaristic in the beginning than at their end. Not infrequently, they are born of victory on the battlefield. Consider the Swedish War of Liberation (1523) or the history of the thirteen American colonies. Later, when security is not jealously guarded—or when it is taken for granted, usually after wealth and skepticism weaken the martial spirits of a people—pacifism rises. Pacifism's rise often hallmarks the decline of a civilization and any empire it once flaunted. Alternatively, or perhaps at the same time, an empire may crumble because of its weakened economic abilities, brought on by the burdens and debts of government or the declining will of its people—eventually to fall to more stoic or martial forces. Consider the fate of the Assyrian Empire (fourteenth to seventh century BC) and that of ancient Rome.

THE FAMILY, COMMERCE, RELIGION, AND THE ARTS

Civilizations most often begin with an agricultural phase and later, if conditions allow, they incorporate a commercial and then industrial society. They usually start along the shores of their oceans or the strategic corners of their rivers. In those beginnings, the family is the center of economic activity, especially when farms are the economic centers of a civilization.

When that civilization migrates to the allure of the culture and jobs of the city, and as wealth and education delay marriage, the family declines in favor of the individual as the center of economic activity. Children, once viewed as economic assets on the farm, become more costly in an urban setting, and, altogether, those dynamics lead to declining birthrates. Witness how the birthrates of today in the comparatively poorer and less industrialized countries of the southern hemispheres, and of those near the equator, outpace the birthrates of the richer northern countries such as the United States and those of Europe.

With relatively free commerce, the accumulation of wealth accelerates and spreads, likely as unevenly as the distribution of ability among a people. By contrast, the stagnant economies imposed by excessive government controls are characterized by relative equality among the masses (not their rulers)—at the price, however, of significantly lower standards of living and less personal freedom. Consider the economic and political records of the United States versus those of Soviet Union–turned-Russia or Cuba as evidence of those dynamics.

Civilizations are born in faith. For instance, the towns of the Etruscan civilization were designed by the dictates of religious rituals. We also shall find that the early towns of the American colonies were mini-theocracies with churches at the center of the town square. For centuries upon centuries, Western kings took power through the divine right of kings. Half a globe away in what would become China, ancient and imperial kings and emperors took their power through a Mandate of Heaven. Each fought wars in the name of their gods. Their civilizations initially thrived with a stern moral code buttressed by religious codes and a strong faith and a supportive education system.¶

In time, however, if a civilization prospers and lasts long enough, it

---

¶ It is said of Ancient Eturira, that "religious rituals govern the founding of towns, the laying out of walls, and the placement of gates." Susan Wise Bauer, *The History of the Ancient World* (New York: W. W. Norton, 2007), 435.

tends to decline amid wealth, moral laxity, and widespread religious doubt, which doubt almost always walks hand in hand with growing wealth and the advance of science. With the advance of science, the realm of religion forever declines. Early man once prayed to the sun and moon; but when their orbits became subject to scientific explanation, their religious allure waned.

The state also plays a role in the fate of a people's religiosity—their level of devotion. If a religion is persecuted by the state, its believers will tend to hold it more dear. Consider the history of Judaism, whose adherents have for centuries upon centuries faced discrimination if not persecution, including at the hands of the Crusaders, in Germany under Hitler, and even today. If a religion becomes a state religion, it often becomes culturally pervasive. The religious histories of Italy and France provide examples in that regard. If, however, the state is indifferent to religion, if it neither sponsors nor persecutes a religion, in time that religion loses its cultural currency and wanes. What isn't taught in the schools of a nation's youth eventually becomes forgotten in its culture. We shall find that true of the United States today.

History also has a lesson to teach us on the decline of the family, the fate of religion, and the rise of the state. It is not merely coincidence that the family and religion often decline together. The loss of family as the central unit of society, which occurs with the transition from the family farm to the cities of individuals, diminishes natural, hierarchical authority. In the same train often comes expanding wealth and then the easing of morals, if not moral laxity. That often tends to place spiritual decisions in the hands of those of an impressionable age—all of which make very difficult the tasks of priests and rabbis let alone parents.

Throughout history, we also find that with the rise of cities comes accelerated increases in government. Another lesson of history is that limited government is more plausible in a countryside of strong families and self-reliance than in cities of commerce, individuals, and temptations. As that latter dynamic unfolds, the commandments of religion diminish and the laws of the state tend to rise in their place. Then, when government becomes large enough, and as dependence on the state rises, religion comes under attack from ambitious politicians who disdain the competition religious doctrines, such as self-reliance, hope, and charity, pose to the state.

Overall, history strongly suggests that no civilization can endure without a moral code, and moral codes cannot survive long without structure and constant affirmation. That most often comes in the form a structured religion for everyone and a supportive education system for a civilization's youth. They too decline in tandem under the relentless pressure of wealth and science. As societies luxuriate in the present, they tend to consider the afterlife with indifference, if not disregard it. *Paganism and atheism tend to be the thoughts of the rich, not the life of the poor.*

For their part, art and science flourish along with commerce and wealth—not often before. Compare the artistic outpouring that was Renaissance Italy of the 1400s and 1500s, whose commercial wealth financed artists and scientists alike, to the poverty of their medieval ancestry. Today, America features far more artists per capita, whether in music, painting, the graphic arts, or otherwise, than at the time of its founding.

THE PROGRESSION OF GOVERNMENTS

Turning to our governments, they form in simplicity and grow in complexity and reach—and then in complicated tax schemes and debt. Paradoxically, authoritarian governments, with tightly controlled structures, can have a lesser reach and fewer tentacles than elected governments and their ever-burgeoning bureaucracies. Alexis de Tocqueville (1805–1859) hinted at that dynamic by referencing the nature of the French monarchy versus the reach of the English Parliament. In the process, societal innovation begins to wane as the natural desires of bureaucracies to proliferate regulations and to sustain themselves limit the abilities of the creative to succeed.

Oswald Spengler, author of the seminal work *The Decline of the West*, likely would have referred to that as part of his dynamic of "rigidity following expansion."[7]

As for the impositions of governments, the world has known tax revolts in almost every age, from the Delian League Revolt (Greece) in 431 BC, to the American Revolution, to the 1978 Californian property tax revolt known as Prop 13. Overall, *at the beginning of a civilization's government, particularly if it is freely elected, there is a competition of ideas for the betterment of all. Toward the end, there is a competition for government spoils at the expense of ideals, economic growth, and the less fortunate.*

In his *Republic*, circa 375 BC, Plato described a progression of governments in cyclical and, perhaps, in cynical terms. Civilizations, he thought, progressed from aristocracy degenerating into timocracy (a militaristic state accentuating honor, such as Sparta). Timocracy would be followed by oligarchy (rule by a few of great wealth and land ownership). Oligarchy then evolved to democracy (rule by many) and, finally, to tyranny (rule by fear, without just laws, as in despotism). We can agree with Plato, more than four millenniums later, if we acknowledge that the transition from democracy to unjust laws usually includes the marriage of large governments and powerful special interests, whether they be large business interests/corporations, public employee unions, or others. Those interests profit from government spending at the expense of voters who lack the funds to compete for government spoils and whose votes, correspondingly, become ever less effective. Within that dynamic, a ruling class can emerge. Then, those larger governments and their ruling classes seek to protect themselves and their power from the electorate. In those ways and many others, democracies pass to authoritarianism. Such a dynamic exists in America today.

None of those many dynamics just recited are new under the sun—and, in significant part, it was the regularity of those happenings that convinced Plato in the fourth century BC, Italy's Giambattista Vico in the 1770s, Germany's Johann Wolfgang von Goethe in the 1800s, and America's

Will Durant in the 1900s, along with others, that, as Vico wrote, nations "develop in conformity . . . by a constant and uninterrupted order of causes and effects present in every nation."[8]

So, yes, history repeats itself—but not in every detail or manner. France is not the United States, and neither of them is Japan. We eat, but we don't eat the same meals. We have artistic painters, but they tend to paint different subjects. We pray, but our rites and even gods differ. The variance in the details of those progressions led Will Durant to conclude that "history repeats itself, but only in outline and in the large."[9] We too should come to that conclusion.

Before we move on, let us dwell awhile longer among the genius of those philosophers who believed that civilizations rise and fall with regularity. If we read further into their works, we find they often believed that nations had the traits similar to those of people. So Georg Wilhelm Friedrich Hegel, the German philosopher of the late 1700s and early 1800s, thought that "the nation lives the same kind of life as the individual when passing from maturity to old age."[10] Similarly, Thomas Carlyle, the nineteenth-century Scottish historian, believed that "culturally, both nations and individuals pass through the phases of childhood, youth and manhood."[11] For his part, Plato asked, "Can we possibly refuse to admit that there exist in each of us the same generic parts and characteristics as are found in the state?"[12]

We should not literally believe civilizations are like children or eventually an aging grandparent, although both are more vulnerable at birth and near death, and both tend to have more energy and fight in their youth than they do at the end. Instead, it seems more logical to conclude that civilizations are the sum of their parts and as they rise and fall, they have similar characteristics and phases, just as people do.

On that last very important point: there appears agreement among the great thinkers that there are two broad phases of a civilization. Simply stated, in the first phase, a civilization comes together. In the second, it pulls apart. Organization becomes disorganization. The English historian Arnold J. Toynbee (1889–1975) blithely wrote in his *Study of History* about "the growth of civilizations"[13] and then their "breakdown"[14] and eventual "disintegration."[15] Spengler likened the process to the seasons, from spring to winter. America's Durant would write of Spengler that he envisioned "a period of centrifugal disorganization in which creed and culture decompose in division and criticism, and end in a chaos of individualism, skepticism, and artistic aberrations."[16]

The French philosopher Claude Henri de Rouvroy, comte de Saint-Simon (1760–1825), described that unification as a phase "in which all human actions are classed, foreseen, and regulated by a general theory, and the purpose of social activity is clearly defined."[17] The Republic of Venice (700–1400s), which was almost singularly dedicated to becoming a commercial empire, is a clear example of that dynamic. On the other hand, the second period Saint-Simon described was one "in which all community of thought, all communal action, all coordination have ceased, and the society is only an agglomeration of separate individuals in conflict with one another."[18] We see elements of that in America today.

The great historical philosophers also described those two periods as periods of belief and unbelief. Johann Wolfgang von Goethe (1749–1832) believed that history was an "unceasing oscillation between Faith and Negation."[19] Thomas Carlyle vividly described the dynamic: "As in a long-drawn systole and long-drawn diastole, must the period of Faith alternate with the period of Denial; must the vernal growth, the sum luxuriance of all Opinions, Spiritual Representation and Creations, be followed by, and again follow, the autumnal decay, the winter dissolution."[20]

If we delve deeper into that dynamic and their thoughts, the philosophers are far more complimentary of the initial phase and much less so about the human dynamic of the second phase.

Thomas Carlyle, in his "Characteristics," describes periods of when faith can "remove mountains," and then, when it's in decline, "heroic Action is paralyzed" as "Divinity [is] withdrawn."[21] Hegel believed that "a Nation is moral—virtuous—vigorous—while it is engaged in realizing its grand objects, and defends its work against external violence during the process of giving to its purposes and objective existence."[22]

Saint-Simon wrote that "critical epochs—periods of debate, protest, . . . and transition[—]replaced the old mood with doubt, individualism, and indifference to the great problems. . . . In organic periods men are busy building; in critical periods they are busy destroying."[23]

Goethe wrote that "all epochs wherein belief prevails . . . are splendid, heart elevating, fruitful for contemporaries and posterity. All epochs, on the contrary, where unbelief, in what form soever, maintains its sorry victory, should they even for a moment glitter with a sham splendour, vanish from the eyes of posterity, because no one chooses to burden himself with a study of the unfruitful."[24]

THE FATE OF PUBLIC VIRTUE

With that in mind, we must also consider, as a civilization progresses along its historical continuum, the fate of what Edward Gibbon called "public virtue" along with nationalism. Here we shall define "nationalism" as *Merriam-Webster* does: "a sense of national consciousness exalting one nation above all others and placing primary emphasis on promotion of its culture and interests as opposed to those of other nations."[25] According to Gibbon, in his *Decline and Fall of the Roman Empire*, "public virtue . . . among the ancients was denominated patriotism" and was characterized by participation in public life."[26] The Roman historian Sallust wrote of Rome before its decline that "the people and the Senate shared the government peaceably and with due restraint."[27] In such settings, nationalism runs high as a people coalesce and build their civilization.

In a nation's decline, however, such virtue is often lost in favor of "greed, corruption, pride, general decadence, and other fruits of prosperity"[28]—as Susan Wise Bauer wrote of Rome in her work *The History of the Ancient*

World. Further, amid such loss of public virtue, due restraint is often lost as well. In those critical periods when they are busy destroying, division also reigns (often among classes), and patriotism and nationalism become nostalgic thoughts among a declining number of citizens more than the current animating and uplifting passions of a civilization on the rise.

★ ★ ★

We must and will apply those thoughts as we consider the history of the American civilization. We shall survey its rise and the general consensus about its purposes, on which it flourished. We shall then see how and when the seeds of doubt and dissent were planted, even during the nation's ascent.

One last note about the philosophers on the very start of civilizations. How is it that they begin to form? Toynbee wrote of the influence of prior civilizations and between civilizations. By contrast, Spengler took the view that civilizations were more distinct than Toynbee allowed. It seems difficult to accept that, amid the migrations of the centuries and exchange of thoughts, that civilizations have not influenced one another. Certainly, the melting pot of the United States is closer to Toynbee's view than Spengler's.

In light of all of that, let us conclude with the understanding that, if a civilization is afforded the luxury of security, at the start of it, streams of people, thoughts, and circumstances come together in a pool of dynamics that give birth to that civilization. As the civilization moves forward, if it is to last, it tends to flow in a concerted direction of dominant, common beliefs, values, and habits, which, when tempered by time, become the more rigid morals and traditions of a culture.

Think of that progression much like a great lake or several of them that transition into a high banked, majestic river rushing with such haste that even societal differences are swept along by the more prevalent norms. Over time, as a result of a variety of factors, from gathering wealth to rising skepticism, from changing demographics to burdensome governments and the slowing economies they engender, that energy dissipates and the river begins to slow. No longer banked by unquestioned views, it flows into a delta of diversity, peoples, and ideas perhaps hardly reminiscent of its beginnings. As to the American civilization, think of the Great Lakes flowing into the Mississippi, which hurries along at great length until it reaches its delta. *This book is about where along that Mississippi of time America flows.*

Of course, not all civilizations are afforded the luxury of time. Perhaps an unmet challenge—geological, bacterial, military, or social—hastens a decline. In his book *1491: New Revelations of the Americas before Columbus*, Charles Mann details how the great Indian civilizations of the land east of the Appalachians, the land that would make up the bulk of the thirteen colonies, were likely and greatly diminished by the spread of disease.[29] Of course, that is of great historical importance because it was on that less populated land that the American civilization began.

It must also be remembered that no civilization has an expiration date. Even among difficulties, civilizations have been known to rally and extend their life and influence. Durant was right to point out that it took Rome four hundred years to decline. Not to mention that there can be great contributions to history from a culture in its decline much like elders provide wisdom to the generations to come.

Finally, regardless of how a civilization declines, few disappear altogether.[30] Their remnants are often carried off in many directions in the streams of time where they influence posterity, much like the ancient Greeks and Romans still define how we live—from the way we build our roads, the manner of our sculptures, and the formation of our governments. In those ways and countless others, thoughts become potentially timeless, even as the morals and traditions of a culture, and the outlines of its society, become lost on the rapids of time.

With all of those thoughts in mind, let us begin to consider the rise, middle age, and then what could be the warning signs of the decline of the American civilization.

CHAPTER 2

The Foundation of the American Civilization

Civilization, as we know it, is a movement and not a condition, a voyage and not a harbor.

—**Arnold J. Toynbee,** *Civilization on Trial*

North America, geologists will tell you, was made by the collision of massive continental plates millions of years ago. In turn, those blind, powerful forces gave birth to fruited plains, beautiful amber waves of grain, and the majesty of the American mountains. Underneath them lay the riches of vast natural resources, the amount of which, even to this day, are immeasurable. As for the coastlines of North America, they were sprinkled with harbors and river mouths of immense beauty, but those were not their only traits. They also held the promise of endless commerce carrying not only the bounty of this continent but the trade of many others. Many years later, a young surveyor named George Washington would spy many of those rivers that wound their way inland as holding the promise of connecting a great unified nation.

AMERICA'S GEOGRAPHICAL ADVANTAGES

Hundreds of years before Washington, the Vikings found their way to North America and then, as the 1400s were coming to an end, Columbus sailed west from Spain in search of the silk and spices and, therefore, the riches of India. The world now knows Columbus landed not in India but, instead, in the islands of the Bahamas, in October of 1492. He never made it to what would become the American mainland. In time, however, the Old World from whence Columbus came would find the North American continent in earnest. They also would find out, over time, what was known to its inhabitants, if only their knowledge could have been unified.

Yes, North America was beautiful with bountiful potential. Beyond that, though, the immense continent was uniquely situated between two vast and protective oceans. Combined, the strategic nature of the continent and its resources, along with sparsely populated lands, provided more potential to birth a civilization than any place ever known to the Old World.

Keep in mind that, as the American civilization came into being, no country of Europe was free of external danger—at least for very long. Even the islands that now make up Great Britain provided only limited strategic buffering to and from its enemies—so little that it would fight numerous wars with France, including a Hundreds Years' War. What is now mainland France, bordered by water and land, clashed with the other countries around it as well, as did what is now Spain, Germany, and, of course, Ancient Rome. There were Gothic Wars, Saxon Wars, Gallic Wars, the Sicilian Wars, Byzantine wars, Norman conquests, world wars, a Ukrainian War, and literally countless others—not to mention the invasions by armies who originated more than a continent away, including the Umayyad conquest of Hispania and Mongol invasions of the thirteenth century. As a result, and throughout the centuries, peace and security for the European continent has been a precarious matter of constantly changing leaders and alliances and even more constant vigilance. Such a history garnered the European continent its moniker among historians, such as professor of history Kenneth R. Bartlett of the University of Toronto, as the "violent" continent.[1]

Comparatively speaking and geographically, the American continent carried no such risk. Although at the outset of the American civilization there was competition for its land among the European powers and its indigenous population, which is explored in greater length in chapter 3, in a rather short period of time England, France, and Spain would retreat to their Old World. Thereafter, the American continent enjoyed relatively secured borders and unchallenged shores unlike any major Western civilization in history. Combined with its other natural resources, that inherent and most important cornerstone of advancement—lasting security—provided by the oceans, would foster and greatly accelerate the rise of the American civilization in relative peace.

No civilization, however, comprises just land or the riches it holds. Civilizations are forged out of those resources by a people. Civilizations come about, as Saint-Simon said, because a people were "busy building."[2] Not just building though. It rises in the hands of people, as Hegel would say, "giving to its purposes and objective existence"[3]—all of which occur in a period of a common belief.

FAITH, COMMERCE, AND OPPORTUNITY

So, who were those people that came to what would become the American continent, what did they build, and what did they believe? It is now time for us to consider who laid the foundation of the American civilization.

If we consider the continent as a whole, we are well aware that it was first settled by the forerunners of what we would come to know as American Indians—a misnomer likely based on Columbus's mistaken belief he initially found India.* For his part, Columbus sailed under the auspices of the Monarchs of Aragon, Castile, and Leon in Spain, which later would make claims to parts of modern-day Florida.

England would begin to send ships and settlers in the late 1400s and early 1500s. The first colony of Roanoke, in modern day Virginia, would literally be lost to time. Jamestown, also in modern-day Virginia, would be settled, struggle, and eventually become a success by cultivating the cash crop of tobacco. In time, of course, England would take control of thirteen colonies at the heart of the new American civilization.

England's great competitor on the European continent, France, for the most part, chose to go around those coalescing English settlements. France started with unsuccessful settlements on the East Coast and in modern-day Canada, and then they reached the other side of the Appalachian mountains with founding settlements in Detroit, Green Bay, and St. Louis. They also went to Florida, New Orleans, and Baton Rouge, as well as Biloxi and Mobile in the South.

Of course, we cannot forget the Dutch, who in 1609 created the settlement, then city, that became the financial center of the world, New York City. Germans settled throughout North America before settling in great numbers in what would become Pennsylvania. Those from Sweden initially tended toward what would become New Jersey and Delaware. The Scottish found their way to Carolinas and New Jersey, while Norwegians made their way to Pennsylvania and Massachusetts. In the mid-1800s,

---

* This book cannot possibly do justice to the first inhabitants of North America. Many worthy books have been written on the first civilizations of what is now North America. This book focuses only on the American civilization that arose after them in North America.

America's Jewish population increased from 3,000 to 250,000,[4] often settling in large cities. Of course, amid those movements, indentured servitude and slavery, which are discussed at greater length in chapters 7 and 8, were brought to America as well. Both played a pivotal role in the rise of the American civilization, as did the free Blacks who came to North America.

Those were just some of the many peoples who started the American civilization. With that knowledge, it is important to recognize several things at this juncture. First, those early immigrants that came across the Atlantic and populated the continent came to a place where there was no entrenched, long-standing class culture. There was no aristocracy, no local lords or references to peasants and commoners. The absence of those social constructs and their economic and political limitations, with the eventual serious exceptions of slavery and indentured servitude (which often resembled slavery), meant that there was a much more open and level economic playing field for most of the arriving immigrants—far more so than in any European country. That relatively level playing field permitted greater opportunity and incentives for taking risks, which, in turn, promoted increased commercial activity and wealth for the burgeoning civilization.

Second and quite obviously, they did not all come from one country. Even more to the point, they were not of a single nationality. They were English, French, German, Dutch, Spanish, and otherwise. They did not have a common DNA or a single culture. Nor did they always seek to live among each other. To the contrary, early America was a patchwork fabric of enclaves of immigrants who sometimes took the names of their country for towns, such as Germantown, Pennsylvania. Even to this day, hundreds of years later, there are areas within American states, cities, and townships that remain rather culturally distinct, such as Chinatown in San Francisco, Koreatown in Los Angeles, and countless Little Italys across the United States.

What most of those immigrants did share at the outset of the founding of America were complementary *purposes*. Those purposes were the free exercise of religion and opportunity, and ultimately the democratization of rights—economic and political.

Many settlers were animated by opportunity and trade. That would become a central aspect of the American DNA—perhaps *the* major foundational aspect of the American civilization that has endured through the centuries. As Hegel might have analyzed, opportunity and commerce were a great part of their "purposes" and "objective existence."[5]

That was not all that can be said of those varied cultures. The early American civilization fostered competition among its inhabitants. At times, that competition would result in war. For instance, the French and Indian War fought on American soil was another episode in the long-standing competition between England and France and, after two years, would become a theater in their Seven Years' War. Most often, however, it manifested itself in a fount of ideas, economic activity, and cultural expression that enlivened the American continent and helped weave the fabric of its civilization. The overall effect of that dynamic cannot be understated.

A comparison to the Italian Peninsula could be helpful at this juncture. The modern-day country of Italy did not become a unified country, with respect to its borders, until the latter half of the nineteenth century. In the centuries before, especially as the Renaissance got under way in the 1400s, the Italian peninsula was a honeycomb of economically and politically competitive city-states that did not consider themselves to be of one culture—however similar they were. To the contrary, they were proud of their long-standing separate identities. The Milanese were not Venetian, and neither were Roman or Neapolitan. Their food was distinct, their forms of government different, as were the bases of their economies. Politically, they were fiercely independent, unless and until an alliance suited their current political or economic interests—and when they didn't, they were dissolved with dangerous ease.

Those dynamics, at times, led to armed conflict among them. They battled over trade routes, such as the Genoese and the Venetians, over religion, among those that supported the Pope and those who allied with Holy

Roman emperors—and even over claims to artists. More significantly, however, the rather close and small city-state dynamic led to a cauldron of activity that produced a torrent of economic trade, advanced international banking, a rush of scientific inquiry, the deep study of intellectual thought, and a total transformation in art. Not surprisingly, some of history's greatest and most dynamic leaders, minds, and artists were produced during that period of time, such as the Medici (Cosimo, Lorenzo, and Catherine), Pope Julius II, Isabella and Beatrice d'Este, Michelangelo, da Vinci, Copernicus, and Machiavelli.

Some of that same competitive dynamic was present at the outset of American civilization. Over time, that competitive aspect steeled the early American spirit, as did hardships of the often-lawless frontiers. In the centuries that followed, that dynamic would remain and continue to define the American civilization, and it would find expression in the sciences and art after America recovered from economic costs and debts of its break from Great Britain.

But there was far more to the foundation of the American civilization than commerce and opportunity. There was intense faith as well—faith that dominated the early American civilization and guided its resolve.

The world knows the story of the *Mayflower* landing at Plymouth Rock on the Northeastern seaboard, now Massachusetts. Some one hundred people boarded it in 1620 seeking religious freedom—from England. In their wake, thousands upon thousands would make their way to America over the centuries to pursue a life where they could live according to their chosen church. In that way, the careful reader must be cautious to say that America was founded on religious freedom. It is more correct to say they sought religious freedom *from England*, whose leaders had constrained religious freedom and expression, sometimes by death. When they arrived in America, those religious pilgrims established villages and towns wherein their chosen religion was paramount and governed their lives with great fervor. Even after the First Amendment to the Constitution, which guarantees religious expression, into the 1800s Southern states regulated the exercise of religion within their state consistent with the beliefs at the time of their inhabitants. The difference with England, however, was that there was not to be one required religion for all in America. Given the size of the colonies to be, and the knowledge immigrants had of where their countrymen and religious kin had settled, they could find their like kind and live as they wished—relatively free from coercion of other settlements and colonies.

Thus, the founding of the American civilization was not limited to commerce and economic opportunity. Its first immigrants, and countless thousands after them, also had a deep Christian faith. For many, those aspirations were rather complementary and became recognized as the Protestant Work Ethic. Further, we know that civilizations, in their youth, most often are dominated by an economy based in agriculture and a moral structure buttressed by religious institutions. The outset of the American civilization was not just an example of that—it was a prime example of it.

Indeed, faith, farming, trade, and the self-reliant work ethic found in the youth of a civilization were, as Hegel would say, the "comprehensive and universally binding prescriptions"[6] of the American civilization. We can add to that economic and political democratization. All combined, they were America's "general theory," borrowing this time from Saint-Simon,[7] and it was a quite unique blend in history.

In time, it would become, as Goethe described, an epoch "wherein belief prevails . . . splendid, heart-elevating, fruitful for contemporaries and posterity."[8] Obviously, that did not occur overnight but only after great risk and even greater work, as the next chapter reveals.

CHAPTER 3

The Ethic of the Early American Civilization

A nation is born stoic.

—Will Durant, *The Story of Civilization*

The American historian Will Durant philosophized that "a nation is born stoic."[1] He did so in conjunction with decades of study, along with his wife, Ariel Durant, that resulted in his twelve-book, 9,700-plus-page masterpiece *The Story of Civilization*. So just what did Durant mean by saying civilizations are born *stoic*?

One modern definition of stoic is "a person who is able to suffer pain or trouble without complaining or showing what they are feeling."[2] Two millennia before that, in the early third century BC, *Stoicism* was a philosophy founded in Ancient Greece by Zeno. It was not simply a theory, however, for the Greeks to study. Instead, it was a life-philosophy of action that focused on living a virtuous life. Indeed, adherents of Stoicism believed that "virtue is necessary and sufficient for happiness,"[3] if not the highest good. Recalling that the other historical philosophers we have discussed described the outset of civilizations with such adjectives as "moral—virtuous—vigorous," (Hegel) and heroic (Carlyle), a fair reading of Durant's extensive works safely leads to the conclusion that he believed that civilizations were born stoic in both of those senses we have described—and so it was for the emerging American civilization in its ethic (the subject of this chapter) and in formulating its ideals (the subject of the next two chapters).

We can start by considering the voyage of the *Mayflower* as an example of Durant's thinking. The *Mayflower* was originally part of a two-boat flotilla that included religious separatists—religious devotees who, at first, left England for Holland seeking religious freedom. After a relatively short stay in Holland, and "willing to endure almost anything if it meant they could worship as they pleased,"[4] they were to cross the Atlantic in August of 1620 to begin life in North America. They did so likely knowing that attempts to establish settlements in America, before them, had either failed or endured horrific initial results such as Jamestown.[5]

As the *Mayflower* got underway, the second boat in their flotilla, named the *Speedwell*, proved unseaworthy.[6] As a result, both boats turned back to their original point of departure, Plymouth, England. A month later, the most determined passengers crowded onto the *Mayflower*, 102 passengers in all, including numerous young families.[7] The *Mayflower* was an eighty-foot merchant ship that was designed to carry cargo. It had low five-foot ceilings below the decks and compartments meant to house cargo, not people, let alone for trips that could exceed sixty days on rough seas. Nevertheless, the *Mayflower* left Plymouth, England, with its cargo of people for its three-thousand-mile Atlantic journey. The delay in their departure meant that along the way they endured fierce storms and frightful seasickness on a boat that was not designed to cross the Atlantic.[8] Incredibly, despite insufficient supplies and food, they lost only one person, a boat hand, and that was to waves crashing over the decks. That human loss, however, was replaced by the birth of a young boy appropriately named Oceanus.⁹

HARDSHIP IN THE EARLY COLONIES

Enduring that trip, across the second-largest ocean on the globe, was just the beginning of their hardships—hardships that would come to define and temper the early American civilization. Upon their arrival in America, farther north than they intended, in what we now know as Plymouth Rock in modern-day Massachusetts, there were no welcoming relatives or governments to safeguard them. To the contrary, they faced an unknown shore of tides and rocks, with "a gloomy unbroken forest"[10] in front of them inhabited with "Indians" who were possibly savage—or so they would have been told.[11] Understandably, when they arrived, the *Mayflower* settlers did not immediately attempt to live ashore. Mindful of the danger that lurked, slowly but surely, the Puritans built fortifications on that shore—a process which took months. Meanwhile, until they felt sufficiently secure, they continued to live aboard the *Mayflower*. Despite their progress, their plight remained more than difficult because they had arrived in November. Although yet to clash with Indians in any meaningful way, the harsh elements of their first isolated winter in New England, along with their limited and poor diet, claimed the lives of *almost half* of those pilgrims.[12]

More than a decade before them, a similar fate awaited the first settlers of Jamestown. They came to what would be America for largely commercial reasons when compared to those on the *Mayflower*. According to historian Alan Taylor, 104 colonists landed in April 1607. However, fate treated them even worse than those of the *Mayflower*—only 38 survived that first winter.

Then it got worse. Between the winter of 1609 and May of 1610, just sixty of the prior year's four hundred survived in Jamestown. George Percy, one of Jamestown's earliest settlers wrote, at the time, about his fellow settlers, that they were "so leane that they looked lyke anotannes [skeletons] crying owtt, We are starved, We are starved. Others goinge to bed as we imagined in healthe weare fownd deade the nexte morneinge."[13]

Even more stark was the fact that of the first ten thousand who immigrated to Jamestown, only two thousand were still alive in Jamestown fifteen years later. Decades later, by mid-century, the mortality rate of the settlers remained shockingly high. In Maryland, for example, an "estimated 34,000 people . . . arrived . . . between 1634 and 1680, but the colony's total population in 1680 was only 20,000,"[14] even after accounting for the children born there.

For those who survived the earliest landings and winters in North America, the new inhabitants endured what historian Bernard Bailyn termed "the barbarous years."[15] Of those early Jamestown settlers, Bailyn writes that "Indian attacks were multiplying, the outer settlements were destroyed, and stragglers, foragers, and exploring parties were routinely killed."[16]

Later, Indians would slaughter 347 colonists during the Jamestown Massacre of 1622, including men, women, and children. It was in retaliation for the settlement's execution of an Indian suspected of murder[17] and followed the passage of the Virginia's General Assembly's Act for "perpetuall warre" with the Indians.[18] That was a fitting title for the fate of the endless number of settlers who came to America and became engaged in the often savage and nearly continuous American Indian Wars from the 1500s to the late 1800s.[19] The early wars ranged from Rhode Island, in the Northeast, west to Ohio, south to Louisiana, and in every territory in between.

The wars between the Indians and settlers, the latter of whom often fought without government help, took such names as the Pequot War of Connecticut, fought over land and trade between 1636–1637. In that war, the Pequot tribe, once sixteen thousand in number, was reduced to five hundred by the settlers.[20] King Philip's War took place between

1675–1676. "King Philip" was actually the chief of the Wampanoag tribe. His war was typical of the wars between the early settlers and the Indians in the sense that some twenty thousand Indians of various tribes of Southern New England were in dangerous proximity to over thirty thousand settlers of New England or vice versa, depending on your origins. Although the New Englanders had purchased land from the Indian tribes, such as the Narragansetts, the Nipmucks, and King Philip's Wampanoags, disagreements over rights and territory still arose. As grievances accumulated, a single incident let loose the Indians' overriding fear–turned–fighting zeal, so that the "very presence" of the settlers "threatened everything that had been theirs from time immemorial."[21] During that war, "of the 90 English settlements in New England, [King Philip's] alliance destroyed 12 English towns, and burned parts of 40 more."[22] Nevertheless, it can be said that the settlers prevailed, given that while 5 percent of the region's white population was killed, a stunning "40 percent of the Indian population," including King Philip himself, perished.[23]

In North Carolina, in 1711, a coalition of Indian tribes "burned English towns with impunity for three days. The best estimates are that around 140 whites were killed and 30 captured."[24] In 1729, the Natchez Indians killed some 150 soldiers and colonists at the French Fort Rosale, in Mississippi, while on the attack before a coalition of French and Choctaw Indians brought "overwhelming force against the Natchez villages,"[25] which eventually led to the demise of that tribe by 1736.

The First French and Indian War, or King William's War, was fought over territory and trade in Connecticut, Massachusetts, New Hampshire, and New York, between 1689–1697. Along with the French and Indian War of 1754–1763, they became proxy wars and preludes to international incidents because of the French support of the Indians against the interests of Great Britain in America.

Those are just a few examples of the dozens of wars between settlers and Indians. Those deadly wars, and the danger which lurked before and after them, were a fact of life, along with the weather that claimed so very many lives of those building the early American civilization. Over time, as history well knows, the European settlers of North America overwhelmed the American Indians, pushing those who survived the warfare ever farther west. They overwhelmed them not only in population but also in weaponry and, at times, brutality. Whether considered right or wrong in the eyes of Americans today, it was a warring process that hardened the resolve and the fortitude of the early American civilization along with the harsh elements we have seen.

A GROWING POPULATION, SERVITUDE, AND SLAVERY

As for the life of the American family outside those wars, the hard and dangerous lives they led were strained even more by the high mortality rate of children and their mothers who risked their lives in childbirth. In New England, some 35 to 40 percent of children did not reach adulthood, lost to disease, malnutrition, or worse. With such a high child mortality rate, combined with stern moral and Christian codes of the times, women literally hazarded childbirth on average five to eight times in their relatively short lives. They did so despite enduring their own childbirth mortality rate of 1 in 8.[26] Perhaps no greater indication of the determination of the early American civilization to live and prosper can be cited.

Despite all of those daunting numbers, word of which migrated back to their homes in Europe, settlers continued to come in droves to America, some freely and, of course, many not—some well to do, others not at all. By 1700, of those coming from Europe, the largely Eastern seaboard population of America had grown to an estimated 250,000. As the new civilization expanded west, but still 95 percent east of the Appalachian Mountains, the population of settlers rose to an estimated nearly 1.2 million in 1750 and then more than tripled to 5.3 million, according to the census taken in 1800. Prior to 1790, those numbers may not fully account for those brought to America as slaves. By one count, during the 1700s, between 250,000 and 300,000 slaves were brought to North America,[27] and then, by 1820, by some counts, nearly four times as many slaves were forcibly crossing the Atlantic than willing Europeans.[28]

On the other hand, those numbers likely account for those who came as indentured servants. They were people, most often men, who contracted to work in the New World, typically, but not uniformly, for four to seven years at a time. The cost of their crossing the Atlantic was paid by their "master." In exchange, they received room and board, along with protection—for some. For many others, as we shall see in chapter 7, their servitude devolved into slavery. England alone is said to have sent over seventy thousand such "servants" in the seventeenth century.[29] Some believe that initially "half of the settlers in the southern colonies came to America as indentured servants."[30] Over time, however, the economic "costs" of that practice would result in the diminishment of that practice in favor of the lower economic "costs" of outright slavery—excluding slavery's inhuman toll.

Those European immigration numbers also likely account for the thousands of "vagrant" children sent to America—many of whom were indentured servants despite their tender age. They were literally collected from the streets of London and "public institutions," sometimes at the forceful urging of the government. They were to be "apprentices" in America with the promise of land, up to fifty acres, upon maturity.[31] Although, as we shall see, ill fortune, disease, and greedy and ruthless masters provided no guarantee of success.

There were, of course, those of greater means who came to America. Rarely, however, were they among the first settlers.[32] Once the risks associated with the early settlements had lessened by the mid-seventeenth century, and settlements like Jamestown had become more established, they came in greater numbers. Of those that came, it could be said that many came despite their family titles. At the time, English society, rich in history and aristocratic families, was based on the concept of primogeniture. Under that strict social system, first sons inherited a family's land and titles—second sons and beyond rarely did. Virginia became the destination of many who were second and third in line. With diminished hopes of inheritance in England, they accepted land grants in America. Among them were a class of "gentry" known as the First Families of Virginia,[33] of which there were dozens, with names such as Lee (the ancestors of Robert E. Lee) and Washington.[34]

Their lands and eventual larger farms and plantations were almost exclusively in the South. Despite their advantages, however, the seminal historian Gordon Wood, in his work *The Radicalism of the American Revolution*, points out that "Few members of the American gentry were able to live idly off the rents of tenants as the English landed aristocracy did."[35] Overall, the disparity in the economic makeup of over two million settlers in America, prior to the Revolution, was historically very small[36] compared to their ancestral homes.

AGRICULTURE AND SELF-SUFFICIENCY AS A WAY OF LIFE

As to what those many immigrants in their adopted homeland did for a living, true to our understanding of the start of civilizations, agriculture was the primary livelihood for nearly 95 percent of the settlers in 1700. One hundred years later, by some counts, 90 percent of the America's colonial population was still directly involved in farming,[37] with 75 percent making their living as farmers.[38] With an estimated population of over two million, "at the time of the Revolution . . . there were perhaps 300,000 farms."[39]

The majority of the remaining population was employed either as commercial traders or small businesses that supported the farming industry, their local communities and trade (local and international). Even so, most often they farmed for their own purposes as well. Thus, it could be said that "Every man was a farmer, even if he was also a shoemaker or blacksmith or a carpenter or a miller or a weaver. Everybody worked with his hands, even if he was well to-do."[40]

The majority of farmers and their families farmed for their own needs and, usually, marketed any available surplus for income. It is estimated that somewhere between 50 percent and 75 percent of the colonial gross national product was "produced and consumed at home."[41] The word homespun, which in modern times refers to a nostalgic simplicity, was the *actual* manner in which the settlers lived, making their own homes, clothes, tools, and growing their own food.

As in other earlier times and places, agrarian-based economies featured the family as the central economic unit—not the individual as in modern times. It would not be until the commercialization of the American economy had occurred (the development of trade and commerce) and then its industrialization (the development of industries and manufacturing) along with the urbanization of society, and the corresponding decline in the percentage of those involved in farming, that individuals would make their rise as the central economic unit of the American economy.

Until then, a farming society meant that the family was at the center of the economy and children were economic assets that increased the output of the family economy. Self-reliance was their way of life. Children were tasked with farm and household work, often starting at the break of dawn and lasting to dusk. "Farm men and boys worked in their own barnyards and fields. . . . Women and girls cooked and preserved in the house and the garden."[42] As the frontiers became colonies and the trades arose, a child as early as eight or nine would be "bound out" to tradesman to learn a trade of their own.[43]

It is worth noting that historically we find child labor prevalent at the start of civilizations, in agrarian-based economies and in places of limited wealth. It is not until a substantial rise in wealth, and the substantial commercialization of an economy, that child labor diminishes and is later regulated, such as in the late fifteenth-century Venice and America today, to name just two examples. As for the widespread farm economy of America, during the 1600s and 1700s, that meant that child labor was the norm. Overall, the "blending of family and the economy applied to virtually everyone. . . . Family, household production, and education for life were synonymous."[44]

The family, in those early American times, as it had been for thousands of years, was most often patriarchal, the "unquestioned assumption that authority resided rightfully in the father, and all were required to follow him."[45] Women, generally, did not own property and tended more to domestic matters than financial. Overall, "a family was viewed as a little kingdom . . . providing sustenance, shelter, job training, religious instruction, and care for the young, sick, and elderly . . . The family was considered to be both a microcosm and a building block of society."[46]

Even so, the families of early America quite often were not the simple nuclear family that dominated America's twentieth century. The mortality rates that we have seen deprived many a child of a parent or two and remarriage and/or the joining under the same roofs of relatives were quite common. George Washington, for instance, despite marrying at twenty-six, did not have children of his own, and when he married Martha Dandridge Custis, he became the father of that merged family before he became the Father of the Country.

As for their style of living, it was common for settlers, especially on the frontier, to live in one-room homes with earthen floors through much of the 1600s and not much more than two rooms by the early 1700s. Those early single-room homes were most often made of limited wooden frames, and "walls" made of sticks, mud, and clay with thatched roofs. Furniture was rather limited to bare necessities like a table, perhaps a bed that could be rolled up and a chest for storage. "A family might own a few pewter plates and spoons that they had brought from England. Most of the dishes, however, were made of wood. In the average household there were no forks, no china, and no glass."[47] In time, their homes were made of logs. Lofts were added above and were accessed by ladders. Fireplaces stood at the end of the room and provided warmth as well as the flames for cooking. As the frontier was pushed back and as wealth rose, so too did the height of those homes with the familiar look seen in the New England colonies, now states, to this day.

Amid all of those stark realities, and limited wealth, the stoic Americans slowly but surely built an enormously successful economy leading up to its Revolution.

Given the varying geography and weather of America and of the differences of those who came, we cannot be surprised to find that farming developed differently throughout the colonies as the 1600s and the 1700s unfolded. Larger farms, with a greater interest in trading crops like tobacco, were more prevalent the farther south one traveled and where longer growing seasons fostered larger farms and plantations—which populated what came to be called the Tobacco Colonies. By contrast, the North and its shorter seasons featured farms meant to sustain individual families. Overall, "soil types, length of the growing season, the farmer's European background, proximity to dependable markets, even chance (as in the case of the discovery of indigo in South Carolina) influenced the character of agriculture in the scattered American settlements."[48]

For some it was a difficult and lonely existence. Consider this description from Bernard Bailyn about seventeenth-century Maryland farmers:

> Slowly, in small parcels, they took over promising lands along the main riverways and streams, settled into rigorous seasonal routines, and learned ways of coping with the vagaries of distant tobacco markets, the periodic upheavals of nature, and the isolation and lack of community life in this borderland world. In hundreds of modest farms, the planters, their families, and one or a few servants lived alone, there only regular contacts the commercial agents or more prosperous planters who managed the marketing of their tobacco crop, and there are few closest neighbors five or ten miles distant.[49]

So central was farming to the lives of those early Americans, that the historian T. H. Breen wrote that "The quality of one's crop—be it rice, tobacco, wheat, or livestock—was a central element in a complex agrarian moral system. Producers measured the worth of other men as well . . . by the appearance of the plants, by the prices they received, by the ability to manage a farm or plantation."[50]

TRADE AND PROGRESS

Of course, the colonial economy was not just based on the management of farms and plantations. Blessed with ample coastlines and willing buyers, the colonies built a thriving trade with Europe, the Caribbean/West Indies, and even Africa. From the northern colonies, fish, forest products, shipping, and mercantile services dominated trading. There were "grains and grain products from New York and Pennsylvania," while "the exports of the upper south were dominated by tobacco" and then wheat. From the Deep South also came "foodstuffs; rice, indigo, and deerskins."[51]

With regard to England alone, "exports from the thirteen colonies grew from an annual average of £289,081 in 1697–1700 to £1,452,476 in 1771–5," fivefold, as kept by English customs records.[52] The less advanced American colonies did not keep similarly comprehensive records at the time. Imports, by contrast, rose to over four million pounds in the late 1700s.[53] Early on, tobacco dominated American exports (83 percent of the Exports to England around 1700) and then, as the economy diversified, and with the rise of other exports such as rice, tobacco exports fell to 35 percent of the exports to England just before the Revolution.[54] Export earnings to rest of Europe, Africa, and the West Indies initially trailed the earnings derived from trading with the English before surpassed it leading up to the Revolution.[55]

Altogether, it could be concluded by the economic historians Gary Walton and James Shepherd, in their book, *The Economic Rise of Early America*, that "economic progress in the colonial period stemmed from growth in the stock of land [westward expansion], labor [through birth and importation], and capital [from trade] . . . and from increases in productivity."[56] All of that economic activity also led to a rising standard of living such that Benjamin Franklin would be able to fairly write, "The first drudgery of settling new colonies, which confines the attention of people to mere necessaries, is now pretty well over; and there are many in every province in circumstances that set them at ease."[57]

So it was for the first centuries of the American civilization.

★ ★ ★

Our journey so far, through the beginnings of the American civilization, has revealed a story of great courage, determination, and perseverance. The daunting, if not deadly, obstacles faced by the early settlers, who came from so many countries, and their triumph over those obstacles as a group, not necessarily as individuals, justifies Durant's assessment, at least in this case, that civilizations are born stoic.

How else can we explain the many young families that came to America, for their beliefs, not their comfort, well knowing the dangers that lay ahead for them? The same could be said for those who came here to establish trading enterprises through arduous work in dangerous territories. As for those who pushed westward, they did so knowing that behind them lay territories often disputed and many times conquered in bloody wars. Ahead of them lay the continued uncertainty of a lawless frontier they often had to face on their own.

Amid all of that, with their bare hands, they established homesteads, farms, plantations, and many of the cities with which we are familiar today. They also built the foundations necessary to make the colonies the economic juggernaut they would become during the 1800s and beyond.

It was a remarkable accomplishment, given the obstacles they faced. They were, indeed, stoic. In the chapters ahead, we shall come to understand the ideals that also defined the early American civilization and that completed the "heroic" nature of the early Americans.

CHAPTER 4

The Purposes of the Early American Civilization

[In the beginning of a civilization,] all human actions are classed, foreseen, and regulated by a general theory, and the purpose of social activity is clearly defined.

—**Claude Henri de Rouvroy, comte de Saint-Simon,**
quoted in Durant, *The Lessons of History*

Recall that, in the views of the historical philosophers we have discussed, civilizations are born in *faith* and decline in *doubt*. The faith and doubt to which they were referring, however, are not limited to religious faith—although they include it. The faith they describe encompasses a larger dynamic, which starts with the strong belief of the populace in the very purposes of their civilization. Doubt, on the other hand, refers to a loss of faith, not only in religious devotion but also in the foundational purposes of a civilization.

Consistent with that definition of faith, the French historical philosopher, Claude Henri de Rouvroy, comte de Saint-Simon, described the cultural unification of civilizations at their outset as periods "in which all human actions are classed, foreseen, and regulated by a general theory, and the purpose of social activity is clearly defined."[1] In that initial phase, which Saint-Simon described as the "organic" period, he believed that "men are busy building." In decline, which he characterized as the "critical" period, he thought that "they are busy destroying" the foundations of society. Similarly, Thomas Carlyle characterized that building phase as a civilization "engaged in realizing its grand objects" with the ability to "remove mountains" along the way.

As for religious faith, we know that at the outset of civilizations, people tend to be more religious than toward the end of a civilization. That is due in part to the influence of living in an agrarian-based society. Agriculture, which usually dominates the beginning of civilizations, reinforces religious faith for the reasons we discussed in chapter 1, the fundamental renewal of life and the seasons.[2] By contrast, the advances of commerce, industrialization, urbanization, science, and wealth, always and everywhere and usually acting together, have tended to erode religious beliefs.

In chapter 3, we learned that the early Americans were courageous, to say the least. They persevered through dangerous and difficult times while building the foundations of a lasting culture and economy. Those dynamics helped define the early American ethic.

FOUNDING PRINCIPLES: RELIGIOUS AND ECONOMIC FREEDOM

We now must come to fully understand the unifying purpose of their social activity, what they believed, and just as importantly, why they held those beliefs. In doing so, we shall find that the initial animating principles of the early American civilization were twofold. First, many were engaged in the pursuit and founding of "just societies." They founded small communities where they could practice their religions, with like-minded settlers, free of English restrictions and persecution. Simultaneously, many of them and many others undertook the complementary pursuit of a relatively unfettered economic opportunity in America, based on individual responsibility and initiative. Later they sought the same with respect to political expression. All combined, and over time, those purposes forged what would become the animating principles of America, self-governance in practice that invested enormous power in the people. Those principles reached a pinnacle unknown to history in the form of the American Revolution, its Constitution, and the Bill of Rights. As Hegel likely would have concluded, working together, those principles and dynamics gave the early American civilization its "purposes and objective existence."

If we first consider America's religious founding, on both sides of the Atlantic, it was accepted that "the religious foundations of colonial life were a powerful factor in American development."[3] That was the conclusion of the historian Sydney H. Ahlstrom in his book *A Religious History of the American People*, published in 1975. In Scotland over one hundred years earlier, in 1844, the Reverend Robert Baird wrote, in his exhaustive work *Religion in the United States of America*:

> Of the greater number of the early colonists it may be said, that they expatriated themselves from the old world, not merely to find the liberty of conscience in the forests of the new, but that they might extend the Kingdom of Christ, by founding states where the truth should not be impeded by the hindrances that opposed its progress elsewhere.[4]

Of course, the "hindrances" of which Rev. Baird wrote were more than just that. Religious differences, sometimes violent, had defined an era in Europe and beyond.

Indeed, for centuries before, the European continent and beyond had been plagued with religious wars and discontent. Eight major Crusades occurred between 1096 and 1291. Those were the religious wars sponsored by Western kings and popes primarily to recover from Muslims the rights and ownership of the Holy Land, as well as the trade routes along the way. The Crusades were seminal events and were generally known to the greater populaces of their participants. Later, starting in the 1500s, religious strife and wars accompanied the Reformation, the structural and economic challenge to the authority and actions of the Catholic Church centered in Rome. As the number of religious sects/faiths proliferated as an outcome of that doctrinal break with Rome, social instability followed, with bloody consequences in the name of leaders and their beliefs.

We must also remember that, at the time settlers began coming to America, the European continent had only recently emerged from the Middle Ages—the Age of Faith, as Will Durant described it, referring to the rather religious nature of the times. During that era, religion was the dominant force in people's lives and remained that way and culturally ubiquitous for many years after. Consider the fact that although the Magna Carta, written in 1215, is remembered in history for its effect on common law and due process (clauses 38–40), the very first clause states **"FIRST, THAT WE HAVE GRANTED TO GOD,** and by this present charter have confirmed for us and our heirs in perpetuity, that the English Church shall be free, and shall have its rights undiminished, and its liberties unimpaired."[5] Centuries later and of England in the 1500s, the historian Peter Marshall wrote in his book *Heretics and Believers* that "religion was woven inextricably into the fabric of . . . society, politics, culture, gender, art, literature, [and the] economy."[6]

When the Reformation reached the shores of England, it came in the form of the heavy hand of Henry VIII. His outlawing of Catholicism in the mid-1500s, at least initially for the sake of divorcing a wife, brought religious persecution within a single country to unparalleled state-sanctioned heights. Quoting Marshall again, the "English Reformation was . . . unusually and bloodily prolific in its creation of martyrs, through successive decades, and across the entire spectrum of religious belief."[7]

Overall, Henry VIII is said to have condemned to death some 57,000 people who were in opposition to his mercurial and brutal rule.[8] In connection with Henry VIII's outlawing of Papal authority in England, with the help of a compliant Parliament, authorities stripped Catholic churches of their crucifixes, their stained-glassed windows, other personal property, and even their lands. The exact number of how many died purely because of their suddenly outlawed religious beliefs is not known. It is thought that the number is less than a thousand by most counts. Today, the Catholic Church alone recognizes three hundred such martyrs.[9] Short of death, the imprisonment, silencing, or banishment of those in disagreement were not infrequent.[10] Altogether, the terror felt by religious dissenters from those persecutions, including the very public burnings at the stake of those who strayed from Henry's newly fashioned requirements of religious "uniformity," was painfully real.

It was not until 1689, with the Toleration Act, that England finally outlawed religious persecution, ending centuries of religious persecution and strife within England. Before then, in very plain terms, the colonies of America offered religious settlers refuge far away from English persecution and a chance to live and worship freely—and come they did. We have seen that the Puritans settled throughout New England as did a limited number of Baptists, Presbyterians, and Quakers before they moved to Pennsylvania. In the Middle Colonies, Quakers and Anglicans settled. Catholics and other Protestants went to Maryland. Baptists, Presbyterians, Huguenots, and Anglicans populated the South.

In doing so, "John Winthrop, the governor of the Massachusetts Bay Colony, told his fellow travelers that "We have been singled out by God to serve as a 'modell of Christian charity.'"[11] They "were on a religious mission, or what later became known in Puritan circles as an 'errand into the wilderness.'"[12] Meanwhile, the "Quakers, or Friends, as they called themselves, eventually forsook New England for Pennsylvania, a colony established in 1681 by William Penn as a 'holy experiment.'"[13] Of the founding of Connecticut, it was said that the settlers "made religion the basis of their institutions."[14] The initial charter of Virginia, granted by the King of England, urged the "propagating of the Christian religion" to the Indians,[15] while the charters of the Southern states sought the "propagation of the gospel."[16] Even the Dutch, who settled New Amsterdam, later New York City, for commercial trading reasons, established a church there in the early 1600s.[17]

The cultural nature of those religious settlements extended well beyond their initial charters and landings. Indeed, for the most part, there was no separation between church and state for many years after. Rather than separation, the "church was not only the geographical and social focus of town life, but its spiritual center as well, formed at the earliest possible time."[18] Many "laws mandated that everyone attend a house of worship and pay taxes that funded the salaries of ministers."[19] The New England colonies were dubbed the Bible Commonwealths, and in those places, "scripture was cited as authority for many criminal statutes."[20] Even in the commercial founding that was Jamestown, the enforcement of the rules imposed to govern those early settlers, known as the "Lawes Divine, Morall and Martiall," required guards to "publicly read a seven-page prayer twice each day" and "required every person to attend church twice every Sunday."[21] In other words, religion provided needed structure throughout America in addition to giving settlers *purpose*.

It was very evident that those early settlers sought freedom of religion *from* English restrictions, *not freedom of religion within individual settlements or colonies*. In fact, "eight of the thirteen British colonies had official, or 'established,' churches, and in those colonies dissenters who sought to practice or proselytize a different version of Christianity or a non-Christian faith were sometimes persecuted."[22] Indeed, the founders of New England were "intolerant to those who differed from them in religion. . . . They persecuted Quakers and Baptists, and abhorred Roman Catholics."[23] That is why the Quakers, who had been subjected to whippings, imprisonment, and worse,[24] left New England for Pennsylvania, where they were welcomed. Of Virginia, early on, it was reported that "attendance at parish worship was . . . required under severe penalties . . . [and] Dissenters, Quakers and Roman Catholics were prohibited" from settling there.[25]

In most colonies, "civic privileges were confined to members of the established faith,"[26] and the Massachusetts Constitution in 1780 authorized support of "public Protestant teachers of piety, religion, and morality":

> As the happiness of a people, and the good order and preservation of civil government, essentially depend on piety, religion, and morality; and as these cannot be generally diffused through a community but by the institution of public worship of God, and of public instructions in piety, their happiness, and to secure the good order and preservation of their government, the people of the commonwealth have a right to invest their legislature with power to authorize and require and the legislature shall, from time to time, authorize and require, the several towns, parishes, precincts, and other bodies politic, or religious societies, to make suitable provision at their own expense, for the institution of the public worship of God, and for the support and maintenance of public Protestant teachers of piety, religion, and morality, in all cases where such provision shall not be made voluntarily.[27]

Maryland, on the other hand, granted toleration of the practice of all Christian religions,[28] and became the home to "papists"—Roman Catholics—among other faiths.

The multiplicity of those "establishment"-related laws made clear that the individual settlements believed they had a clear purpose. So too did the length that those laws were enforced. Consider also the fact that nearly two centuries after the initial colonial foundings, Article VI of the Constitution was written in response to the existing "established churches" and "religious tests for offices" prevalent throughout the colonies.

Article VI of the Constitution includes this language: "No religious test shall ever be required as a qualification to any office or public trust under the United States." At the time, that law applied only to those seeking federal offices. Despite the adoption of the Constitution in 1789, inclusive of Article VI and the Ratification of Bill of Rights in 1791, which guaranteed "freedom of religion" at the federal level, "New Hampshire kept its establishment until 1817; Connecticut kept its establishment until 1818; and Massachusetts did not abandon its state support for Congregationalism until 1833."[29]

Further evidence that religion was woven inextricably into the fabric of the early American civilization was the fact that George Washington's first inaugural address was predominantly an ode to the providence of God, and as president he issued a Thanksgiving Day Proclamation that stated, "Whereas it is the duty of all Nations to acknowledge the providence of Almighty God." For his part, well after the adoption of the Bill of Rights, John Adams attended church services in the US Capitol, and state laws sanctioned particular Bibles over others into the 1800s. When the US Capitol was rebuilt after being burned down in the War of 1812, a relief of the law-giver Moses was installed to look down on the Speakers' rostrum in the House of Representatives Chamber. Perhaps surprising to some, it was not until 1961 that the Supreme Court struck down Maryland's law that required officeholders to affirm their belief in "the existence of God."[30] In doing so, the Supreme Court cited the Fourteenth Amendment, which had been ratified nearly one hundred years earlier, in 1866, and which applied the First Amendment to the states.

Another cultural aspect of America's religious founding was how children were taught in those early years. We must remember that schools were not initially commonplace and that even as they became more prevalent, the often distant, rural nature of the lives of settlers meant that those schools were not accessible to all. As a result, children were most often initially "schooled"—taught values and how to read—by their parents at home.[31] Of course, that was done with the help of the most prevalent book of the times, the Bible.[32] Indeed, the historian Dr. Lawrence Cremin wrote that the Bible was "the single most important cultural influence in the lives of Anglo-Americans."[33] Thereafter and not surprisingly, "the establishment of compulsory school attendance resulted largely from religious requirements."[34] Religious-based schools were founded throughout the colonies, including the Collegiate school of commercial center New Amsterdam (now New York City) that was chartered by the Dutch Protestant Church in 1628. The Collegiate operates privately to this day. South of that, the Jesuit priests in Maryland founded numerous schools, including Saint Mary's (1650), Newtown (1670), and at Bohemian Manor.[35] Even after "public" schools—that is, schools that received funds from public sources—came into being, they were often subject to fights for control by religious institutions and churches.[36]

Looking back at all of those dynamics, it is inescapable but to conclude that the early American civilization of the 1600s and 1700s was forged not only on the edges of an uncertain wilderness but also with religious values and the Bible firmly in the hands of many Americans and their leaders. Those cultural beginnings were reinforced by the nature of the early economy as well.

COLONIAL ARTISANS AND THE MERCHANT CLASS

We already know the extent of the agricultural basis of those early centuries. For hundreds of years, Americans lived almost exclusively in farm country. Keep in mind that in 1700, only three American "cities" had populations in excess of 3,000 people: Boston (approximately

6,700), New York (approximately 5,000) and Philadelphia (approximately 5,000). By stunning contrast, London had a population of nearly 600,000 souls in 1700.

Today, the Boston of 1700 would be considered a very small town. Even by the time of the Revolution, the number of "cities" over 10,000 in population was just six, with Philadelphia leading the way at just over 44,000—leaving over two million colonials living outside of those towns. Given the rural nature of America and the fact that the overwhelming majority of Americans farmed at least to some extent, certainly the renewal of the seasons, which played a role in the religious beliefs of farmers throughout history, played that same role in the early American civilization. Thomas Jefferson, a farmer himself, expressed a sentiment tying agriculture and religious beliefs together that was representative of the thoughts of many colonial farmers. In his 1785 *Notes on the State of Virginia*, he wrote that "those who labor in the earth are the chosen people of God, if He ever had a chosen people, whose breasts he has made his peculiar deposit for substantial and genuine virtue."[37]

Obviously, the colonies of the 1600s and 1700s were not rich commercial societies. Those early years were periods of limited wealth and hard work. Commerce, as opposed to farming, was but a small part of the economy and industrialization had yet to occur. Advances in science and education were quite limited. So we should not be surprised that, altogether, religious fervor was alive and well in the Colonial period.

America's founding, however, was not just based on religious motives. The opportunity that America presented to the religious also extended to those who saw the commercial possibilities of the colonies. The loading docks of Jamestown came before the pews of Plymouth.

When those seeking economic opportunity arrived in America, they found not only wide-open horizons but commercial opportunities almost without restriction. Whereas Europe was socially stratified with a rather distinctive class structure, the colonial settlements of the 1600s and the 1700s were not. Guilds that restricted access to trades and were the forerunners in many respects to modern-day unions were known to Europe centuries before Jamestown. However, they did not make their first organized appearance in America until almost two centuries later, in 1794, with the formation of the Federal Society of Journeymen Cordwainers (shoemakers) in Philadelphia. Here, as we have seen, second sons not expecting inheritances, vagrant children, indentured servants, and hungry entrepreneurs could come together for the opportunity that was America in far greater numbers than the well-to-do.

In addition to the countless independent farmers, Edward Perkins explained in his book, *The Economy of Colonial Americas*, that toward the end of the 1700s and into the 1800s,

> The successful colonial artisan was an independent, self-employed worker who owned his own tools and furnished his own materials. Work was performed in the home or on the job. On occasion two craftsmen joined together to create a small shop. The artisan was also a small business entrepreneur, for he usually had a sizable investment in equipment and tools, managed his own work and kept his own account book.[38]

The wide-open nature of the economic landscape, according to the historian Thomas Doerflinger, in his descriptive book of the nature of the early American entrepreneurs, entitled *A Vigorous Spirit of Enterprise*, meant that:

> Entry into the merchant community was not inordinately difficult. An ambitious person possessing modest capital, proper contacts, or commercial talent had a fair chance of becoming merchant. . . . As a result, a great many merchants were upwardly mobile strivers—intense entrepreneurs who were tough, grasping, and willing to take large risks.[39]

Those and others like them were the foundation of what Doerflinger believed would become Americans' "strong commitment to economic success," a commitment that he believes was so deep and successful that it has existed in just a handful of other places and times in world history, such as Florence in the 1400s, Holland in the 1500s, and Great Britain of the 1700s.[40] We should add to his list the Republic of Venice, whose government was deeply committed to its commercial success. Perhaps most importantly, it is readily apparent that the commitment Britain had to economic success was exported in earnest to the American colonies in those early years.

★ ★ ★

As we finish this chapter of the early purposes of the American civilization, we cannot understate the character of the settlers in those early years. Harlow Giles Unger, in his book *Lion of Liberty: Patrick Henry and the Call to a New Nation*, sums up the period well with this passage:

> Settlers isolated in the hamlets and woods of New England had lived free of almost all government authority for more than 150 years. They had cleared the land, felled great forests, built homes and churches, planted their fields, hunted, fished, and fought off Indian marauders on their own, cooperating with each other, collectively governing themselves, electing their militia commanders and church pastors and turning to assemblies of elders to mediate occasional disputes. . . . Like Patrick Henry, they had lived in freedom, without government intrusion in their lives and saw little need for it.[41]

As the American colonies grew in economic strength and started down the path to revolutionary independence, they did so in significant part because of the independent and entrepreneurial manner in which the settlers lived their lives in the 1600s and the 1700s. That entrepreneurial spirit was often closely aligned with the religious beliefs of many Americans at the time. Indeed, in what became known to history as the Protestant Work Ethic, many Americans of the time viewed their hard work as virtuous in a religious sense.

Overall, it was those self-sustaining, freedom-living, and freedom-loving colonists who played such an important role in formulating the idea of America, which would reach a pinnacle in the form of the American Revolution, its Constitution, and the Bill of Rights.

CHAPTER 5

The American Ideal

*The United States has always been to ourselves
and to the world primarily an idea.*

—**Gordon S. Wood**, *The Idea of America*

When the colonists declared their independence from Britain in 1776, there was no popularly elected republic or democracy in the world. Not one. At the time, the European continent was still in its Age of Absolutism, which occurred roughly between 1550 and 1800. With limited exceptions, that age featured the absolute rule of monarchs and their dynasties. Across the European continent, however, a philosophy was stirring which came to be known as the Enlightenment, an intellectual movement focused in significant part on individual liberty in contrast to the absolute power of kings during the Age of Absolutism.

That focus of the Enlightenment reached the American shores in earnest in the eighteenth century. The American Revolution, and the subsequent founding of America, became ideological by siding with that growing philosophy of liberty. The Revolution was also another example of the many times in history when, after gaining economic maturity, an emerging commercial/economic class then seeks corresponding political influence—sometimes by resorting to revolution.

So it was for America. With more than some abandon, and in the wake of *the shot heard 'round the world*, the colonists did the unimaginable. They went to war against the superpower that was Britain and set about changing the world's understanding of governance. Incredibly, and almost immediately, with bullets flying in the air, the rebel colonies began drafting state constitutions. Eight of the thirteen adopted a written constitution in 1776. Just over a decade later, the colonists would then adopt the US Constitution—and, with that, and rather profoundly, the state and federal constitutions written by the Founders would vest enormous and unprecedented power in the hands of "We the People."

As Gordon S. Wood wrote in his essential book, *The Idea of America*, those revolutionary Americans "expanded the idea of representation to all parts of their federal and state governments"[1]—something that, when combined with an independent judiciary, had never been tried in history.

That remains a fact of history, notwithstanding so much of the commentary that is prevalent at the time of the writing of these lessons of the American civilization. As with the other historical circumstances we are considering in these lessons, as Thomas Sowell counsels, we must always ask, "Compared to what?" In this case, compared to the other leaders and governments of the world—at the time, what did the Founders of America do by comparison? That answer is, while risking their very lives, the revolutionary Americans established governments about which the anti-Federalist and anonymous writer Brutus would write, "History furnishe[d] no example of a free republic, anything like the extent of the United States."[2]

FOUNDING PRINCIPLE: GOVERNMENT BY THE PEOPLE

Indeed, the Founders had declared, and placed into writing, several extraordinary principles. First, the Declaration of Independence had declared that the Americans had been "endowed by their Creator with certain unalienable Rights, that among these are Life, Liberty and the pursuit of Happiness." Second and correspondingly, the source of government power was the American people—not the divine rights of any rulers or the consequence of military might. Those governments that the colonists enacted did not confer rights on the people, as had grudgingly occurred under the monarchs of Europe in such limited degrees. Instead, their governments had the authority to act—but only in the ways conferred on them by the citizens of the Republic.

Those declarations were no small changes or advancements in history. While influential philosophers such as England's John Locke had discussed the rights of individuals, including a natural right to "life, health, liberty, or possessions,"[3] and advocated for the separation of powers, as did France's Montesquieu, it was quite another matter to even attempt to establish the first-ever government on those principles, over a massive territory (nearly 50 percent larger than England and Scotland combined) and especially in the wake and the remaining uncertainty of the Revolutionary War and the western frontier. Those founding principles, which proved to be a work in progress, and likely always will, represented sea-changes and enormous leaps forward in thought and practice that would influence the globe immediately and to this day.

Keep in mind that, at the time, there was no written constitution, let alone a time-tested constitution, that any of the American Founders could consult to enshrine their idealism in their state and federal governments. In the absence of any such working examples, and given the exigencies of the time, the question remains as to how the founding of the United States succeeded in creating a republic that has lasted more than 230 years—a period of time during which no less than five different republics have governed France.

The answer as to how the Americans succeeded must begin with the experience of the colonists. Unlike their Old World cousins, by comparison, the revolutionary Americans had considerable experience in establishing and running governments in addition to owning their own farms and businesses. They also had learned and measured leaders that rose to meet the serious challenges of the founding. Finally, the new Americans benefited greatly from the distance between them and any potential European adversaries. That distance allowed them the luxury of time to succeed, despite missteps, without the constant threat of foreign invasion.

Before we consider, at greater length, how they did it, let us start by first considering the basic form of this new republic. The US Constitution, adopted in 1789, created three largely independent branches of government. They included an executive branch (the office of the presidency), a legislative branch (a House of Representatives and a Senate with differing responsibilities), and a judiciary. Americans voted directly for their House of Representatives and, in time, directly for their senators. They also voted for their presidents—although electors, chosen under differing and evolving rules, would cast the formal votes for president on a state-by-state basis. At the federal level, judges would be appointed by those presidents chosen with popular input. In those ways, the American federal government was said to be a republic—that is, a representative government whereby voters elected people to represent them in the administration of government.

Prior to the American founding, there were two classical examples of governments that incorporated some forms of popular sentiment and that had "branches" of government. Both were known to the Founders, who were quite studied. They were the Roman Republic (509 BC to 27 BC) and the ancient Greek democracy (fifth to fourth century BC). The Roman Republic did not have a written constitution. Greece had the Constitution of the Athenians, which was written. However, that document was not discovered until 1879 and, thus, not available to the

American Founders and writers of the American Constitution*—though second-hand accounts were available.

The Founders knew that the Roman Republic, at its height, featured three "branches" of government—the Senate, the Consuls, and the Assembly. The real power of the Roman Republic resided with its Senate, which made the laws and controlled the expenditures of the Republic. The Senate members, three hundred in all, were chosen for life by the Consuls from the elite families of Rome. In other words, they were not popularly elected. To the contrary, they were an elite, and rather closed, class. The Consuls, often two at a time, were the "heads of state" for the Republic and directed the often-vaunted Roman army. The two Consuls were chosen, for one-year terms, from the ranks of the Senate. Thus, they too were elite.

The third "branch" of the Republic was that of the commoners, the Assembly and its subgroups. The Assembly was open to all adult male Roman citizens. However, the commoners were not afforded an official position with the Republic; they were not recognized as "Assemblymen." Further, there was no official building designated for the Assembly to conduct business. Instead, their power lay in their voting, usually in the open air of the Roman Forum. The Assembly decided which of the Roman senators would serve as Consul. The Assembly also could propose laws and even war, but their actions were subject to being overridden by that elitist Senate.

Thus, even though the commoners chose the Consuls from among the senators, most of the power of the Roman government resided with those

---

* History now knows of the Constitution of the Athenians. Aristotle, likely with the help of at least one of his students, referenced the written laws of the Greek states and that of Athens in particular. However, the actual text of that constitution was not discovered until 1879 and, thus, not available to the American Founders who wrote the American Constitution. Therefore, the Founders' understandings of the ancient Greek "democracy" would have been limited to descriptions of its workings, not an actual written constitution.

unelected elite Roman families. Further, while the practice, rights, and laws of the Republic evolved over time, there was no written "constitution" Roman citizens could rely on with certainty—nothing that could ensure what few rights were granted to them.

The same could be said for ancient Greek democracy. It too featured three branches, so to speak, of government. They included the *ekklesia* (the Assembly), the *boule*, (Council of Five Hundred), and the *dikasteria* (popular courts). The ekklesia was open to participation by any of the approximately 40,000 eligible Athenian males. It is generally believed that Athens had approximately 250,000 to 290,000 inhabitants, of which perhaps 100,000 to 150,000 were slaves and those eligible males. The remainder were women and ineligible males. Thus, only a very small percentage of Athenians participated in government either directly or by voting.

Laws originated with the Athenian Assembly, as did some foreign policy decisions and certain decisions about war—all by a simple majority vote. The five hundred boule members were chosen by lot, equally from each of Athens' ten "Tribes." The popular courts were manned by Athenian males older than thirty and they decided the cases brought by the general public. The boule handled the day-to-day administration of the state and, importantly, chose the matters to be considered by the ekklesia. Thus, the boule, who were not popularly elected, held enormous control over the government.

Of course, there were other "republics" in history. The Republic of Venice lasted for over a thousand years, but it was not a republic in the same manner as the United States. The so-called Venetian Republic evolved from the autocratic rule of a doge, whose powers were diminished over time and then shared with an evolving sets of branches of government. They included the Major Council of Venice, a Minor Council, the Quarantia, the Signoria, a *collegio*, and a Consiglio dei Pregadi (senate). None of those, however, were chosen by popular vote. The Republic of Florence had a similar history. Their "assembly" was a *signoria*, chosen by the *gonfaloniere*, who, in turn, had been elected to a term, as little as two months, by members of a certain class of Florentine guilds. In practice, only 10 percent of the population was eligible to serve in the government and corruption of the selection process was often a given. Popular elections to office did not occur, although occasionally the voice of the crowd, in the Piazza della Signoria, was polled for decisions large and small.

All in all, the Founders of the American governments were quite aware of the European governments that were republics, some more democratic than others in their popular input, and that utilized the separation of powers. Understandably, however, the Founders found defects in each of them and set their own path to creating the world's first popularly elected governments that were limited in power.

THE COLONISTS' EXPERIENCE IN SELF-GOVERNANCE

As we consider their efforts, we would do well to keep in mind that governments, as with individual elections, are often reactions to what happened before. Pendulum swings often occur from one party to the other in elections. By the same but larger token, the American government, under the Constitution, would be a far pendulum swing away from what had occurred before and how the colonists were ruled. The colonists had been subjected to the sometimes swift and arbitrary rule of the King of England. Britain had taxed Americans without representation and stationed troops, not only in Boston but within their homes. Perhaps worse yet, their speech was regularly suppressed and/or severely punished.

With that treatment in mind, the Founders set about forming rather decentralized governments with provisions designed to prevent or at least forestall the unrelenting historical dynamic of centralizing government power—and its corresponding loss of individual freedom. They did so after gaining an unusual level of experience in forming and administering governments.

We know that America was settled with the laws and edicts of England.

But unlike the subjects of the Old World, given the distance between those initial lawgivers and the colonies, by necessity, it was the settlers that administered those laws and the local governments. While there was "titled aristocracy" with "legal distinctions and privileges,"[4] which ran the bureaucracies and offices of English governments, in America that was not the case. In the majority of situations, it was settlers who performed those functions even if they did not make the rules or had been loyal to the Crown before the Revolution or the run-up to the Revolution. The Founders of the United States were among them.

The collective experience that generations of settlers gained from the 1500s, to the time of the Revolution, to the time of the adoption of the Constitution and beyond, proved invaluable in establishing and maintaining the post-Revolutionary local, state, and federal governments. Stated simply, generation after generation had been slowly but surely gaining experience founding and administering governments for centuries before some of them grabbed the reins of power in 1776.

In addition to that, by the time of the Revolution, Americans also had centuries of experience owning and running businesses. The farmlands, which were the backbone of the 1776 American economy, were almost exclusively owned by settlers. Those farmlands were assets they were not willing to, and had no reason to, destroy—even in the fury of a revolution. The same could be said of their commercial enterprises. Those Revolutionary Americans had produced wealth they wanted to keep, regardless of the outcome of the Revolution. It was that economic maturity, and the accompanied development of a commercial class, that led the Americans to seek greater political self-determination—as they had in the Italian city-states of the Renaissance and in many other places and times in history. That maturity would serve the colonists well in victory.

Once the Revolution was over and the colonists were afforded even greater freedom than they had before, their business experience and assets allowed them to sustain themselves as they had before their Declaration of Independence. Yes, America suffered a deep economic depression in the aftermath of the Revolution, brought on in significant part by the cost of the war and its associated debt and taxes, along with the English trade blockades. However, because a huge percentage of the 1776 economy was the self-sustaining farms of the settlers, the post-Revolutionary Americans were able to slowly recover and then prosper.

AMERICA'S REVOLUTIONARY SUCCESS VERSUS FAILURE IN EUROPE

By contrast, if we look at the European revolutions subsequent to the American Revolution, and the French and Russian revolutions in particular, we find they failed, in significant part for lack of such experience and the lack of a mature commercial class. The French Revolution started, in some respects, the year of the American Constitution and certainly occurred in the intellectual wake of the American Revolution. However, a missing attribute from the French experience was sufficient economic maturity and widespread ownership of assets and land among the agitated. There simply was no pervasive middle or commercial class. When thought turned to violence, the destruction of property occurred wantonly, in significant part, because those perpetrating the violence, regardless of their reasons, did not own the property they were destroying. Nor did they have much experience in governance. To the contrary, the reins of power and titles to property were largely confined to the upper classes, the nobility, and the Church.

The same historical analysis applies to the Russian Revolution. While it may have been that the regimes of the czars had run their historical course, leaving the economic maladies of the era on the deaf ears of Nicholas II, the vast majority of Russians lacked significant property ownership and/or enough political experience to hold steady the reins of power that were liberated from the czar in revolution.

In final analysis, both France and Russia attempted an all-too-brief step between absolutism and democracy. In absence of the experience that helped the American colonists to succeed, the revolutions of France and Russia failed. That left them subject to France's Jean-Jacques Rousseau's dark assessment that, with respect to those unaccustomed to self-governance, "if they attempt to shake off the yoke, they still more estrange themselves from freedom, as, by mistaking for it an unbridled license to which it is diametrically opposed, they nearly always manage, by their revolutions, to hand themselves over to seducers, who only make their chains heavier than before."[5] Indeed, both France and Russia suffered dictatorships not long after their revolutions.

Of course, we must not forget that the initial form of the federal government that was established by the colonists was not a lasting success. The Founders decentralized power so much under the Articles of Confederation, the forerunner to the US Constitution, that those Articles were likely doomed from the outset. They did not allow for the collection of taxes by the "federal" government; nor could that government speak in a unified voice on foreign policy.

Under that system, the powerful and separate state governments printed their own money, taxed as they saw fit, and engaged foreign governments. In time, a dangerous competition grew between the former colonies over trade, taxes, and otherwise. It became so intense that the likes of Alexander Hamilton believed there was a distinct risk of war among the states during that time.

THE FOUNDERS' GENIUS AND THE CONSTITUTION

Not surprisingly, the Founders' answer to the inefficiencies of the Articles of Confederation was in keeping with two laws of history: that dispersed power is inefficient; and that, over time, power tends to centralize—especially during a crisis of division or security. So, amid growing strife, the US

Constitution, as compared to those Articles of Confederation, centralized much greater power in the federal government. Its added powers included the power to tax and the sole right to mint coinage and conduct foreign policy, among many other items.

At the same time, however, the colonists and their Founders, now having become constitutionalists of liberty, would adopt a Bill of Rights. Within those rights would be specific countermeasures to the excesses of the English monarchy. Whereas the king could order the quartering of soldiers in the homes of the colonists, the Third Amendment provided that "no Soldier shall, in time of peace be quartered in any house, without the consent of the Owner, nor in time of war, but in a manner to be prescribed by law." The Fourth Amendment would require "probable cause" to investigate someone of a crime in reaction to the arbitrary use of power to do so under the English king. Of course, the freedom of speech and religion, along with the right to keep and bear arms, were born of the settlers' ideological counter-reaction to rule by a monarch as well. Even so, as the next chapter makes clear, the constitutional practice of choosing our elected officials—in essence, the democratization of the United States—was a work in progress.

It is also important to note how much the colonists' drive for independence benefited from their being so geographically remote. While it was true Britain was a superpower at the time of the Revolution, strategically it was a supply-line nightmare for the British to fight that war across an ocean. That difficulty played no small part in the eventual victory of the colonists. That same geographical advantage worked to the favor of Americans in the years that followed. Once the British army left, along with many of the English loyalists, the Americans could engage in trial and error in the transition from the Articles of Confederation to the Constitution with relative safety, with a few exceptions.

One of those exceptions was the War of 1812, which actually lasted into 1815. In that war with the British, the now United States once again benefited geographically at home and abroad. Closer to Britain, a war with France would limit England's ability to fight the War of 1812 in America. After the War of 1812, which featured the British burning the White House, the US Capitol, and other parts of Washington, DC, the European powers no longer viewed America as a nation given to invasion across the Atlantic.

One more thought regarding the Founders is in order. The luxuries of their experience and benefits of their locale do not tell the whole story of the success of the American experiment. In their book *The Lessons of History*, Will and Ariel Durant point out that

> what determines whether a challenge will or will not be met, the answer is that this depends upon the presence or absence of initiative and of creative individuals with clarity of mind and energy of will (which is almost a definition of genius), capable of effective responses to new situations (which is almost a definition of intelligence).[6]

The Founders of America possessed such genius and intelligence. Rarely has history been witness to such a collection of individuals of such far-reaching vision and virtuous character being assembled in one moment.

The history of Great Britain includes such great thinkers and monumental figures as John Locke, Adam Smith (Scottish), Francis Bacon, Thomas Hobbs, and David Hume. However, they lived in different eras. By contrast, the American Revolution of thought and action included Benjamin Franklin, James Madison, James Monroe, John Adams, John Hancock, Alexander Hamilton, Thomas Paine, Patrick Henry, Thomas Jefferson, and George Washington—as contemporaries living for the most part in close proximity in time and place.

Their number and character allowed them to rise to the occasion and found a country. All of them were essential to this history—but none compared to George Washington. Washington was larger than life. In stature and fame, no one measured up to Washington, which gave him a unique opportunity to realize his goals for the nation. Washington also had extraordinary character. His political selflessness combined with his natural and humble leadership not only defined Washington but also defined the Continental Army and inspired the nature of the presidency as outlined in the Constitution. Just as importantly, Washington was a visionary. He possessed an extraordinary and single-minded vision of a United States.

No one incident defines the break with history that was the successful Revolution than George Washington's decision to peacefully relinquish his military power after defeating the British. At the end of the Revolutionary War, many people in America and Europe thought Washington would retain the reins of power to become the leader of the new nation, or even king. When told by the American artist Benjamin West that Washington was going to resign, King George III of England said, "If he does that, he will be the greatest man in the world."[7]

It was that genius and character that elevated the revolutionary challenge to a constitutional reality.

In the years that followed the American Founding, a new standard for governance took hold. It was no mere coincidence that the Age of Absolutism would come to an end shortly after the American Revolution and the adoption of the US Constitution. To be sure, an Age of Liberty had begun.

CHAPTER 6

From Revolution to Revolution— America Comes of Age

The fulfillment of our manifest destiny [is] to overspread the continent allotted by Providence for the free development of our yearly multiplying millions.

—**John O'Sullivan,** *New York Democratic Review* (1845)

In the years between the American Revolution and the height of the Industrial Revolution, the United States of America would undergo many profound and rapid changes. A self-assured country in the throes of its Manifest Destiny, it seized and then mastered the American continent. Millions upon millions of opportunity seekers immigrated to America as part of its stunning population explosion and urbanization.

Economically, the United States would become the world's commercial superpower in a "triumph of capitalism."[1] As for the self-evident ideals set forth in the Declaration of Independence, the American Republic would, in fits and starts but continually, expand the very definition of participatory democracy. Of course, along the way there would be serious challenges for the new Republic to face. They included another war with Britain and then two wars that would result in the United States acquiring huge swaths of territory—a war with Spain and another with Mexico. The latter would prove to be the last full-scale war with a foreign adversary on the American continent. Most significantly, there would be a bloody civil war fought over slavery that would take the lives of some seven hundred thousand Americans—many of whom made the ultimate sacrifice to end slavery.

That was not all, however. There also would be three assassinations of presidents and a plot against at least one other. Despite all of those national traumas and others, the American civilization stepped forward into the twentieth century with great momentum.

GEOGRAPHICAL EXPANSION

If we start our survey of the years between 1776 and the early 1900s geographically, we find that, at the time of the Declaration of Independence, the thirteen colonies were confined to the area east of the Mississippi to the Atlantic seaboard, from the far northern corner of Maine, along the Great Lakes, and down to Georgia (see Figure 6.1).

It was an area one and a half times larger than England and Scotland combined, and so far from England that the colonists' eventual break with Great Britain was all but inevitable. Once the colonies declared their freedom, it was just as inevitable that they would look westward for expansion. Before that expansion started in earnest, however, the colonies would begin to settle their competing claims to the land that first comprised the colonies and, in doing so, formed the modern states we recognize today.

Chapter 6: From Revolution to Revolution—America Comes of Age 77

Figure 6.1. The original thirteen colonies of North America in 1774, at the time of the Declaration of Independence. (Courtesy of the Library of Congress)

After the adoption of the Constitution, new states beyond the original thirteen colonies would soon be added, beginning with Vermont in 1791. The ambitions for an American empire would begin in earnest with the Louisiana Purchase in 1803, which extended the United States more than halfway across the continent. The otherwise cautious Thomas Jefferson presided over the constitutionally disputed purchase, which literally doubled the size of the United States and its territories. The acquisition was pursuant to the Louisiana Purchase Treaty between France and the United States was signed on April 30, 1803. Jefferson's envoy to France, Robert Livingston, who was one of the Committee of Five that drafted the Declaration of Independence and who signed the Louisiana Purchase Treaty, declared at the time that "we have lived long, but this is the noblest work of our whole lives. . . . From this day the United States take their place among the powers of the first rank."[2]

In 1818, US territorial claims on the continent reached the West Coast with a treaty with England that created the Oregon Country—although that land was initially shared with Britain. In 1821, Florida was finally ceded by Spain to the United States, in part because of the successes of then-general Andrew Jackson in the First Seminole War. The Republic of Texas was added in 1845 and the United States took sole control over the Oregon Country in 1846. The next year, the United States purchased Alaska from Russia, which was the culmination of Russia's decision to abandon its interests in North America.

Then, in 1848, with the Treaty of Guadalupe Hidalgo, which ended the Mexican-American War, the United States took control of territories, including California, that made up the remainder of what we recognize as the continental United States. With that triumph, and in just over fifty years, the United States went from one and a half times as large as England and Scotland to nearly the size of continental Europe.

That expansion of the United States was the fulfillment of what became known as Manifest Destiny. Although that now controversial phrase did not come into being until the middle of the 1800s, part of its spirit was divined long before the Revolution. The young George Washington, while still under British rule, had surveyed the colonies as much as any prerevolutionary figure. He viewed the inland waterways for their commercial possibilities and was among the first to envision an expansive, united country. Importantly, he was joined in that vision by Benjamin Franklin. Both would, as we know, become essential figures in the founding of the United States.

Although it could be argued Thomas Jefferson compromised his principles in furtherance of that expansion, James Madison, known as the Father of the Constitution, saw its wisdom, according to the historian Anders Stephanson. Madison thought it was a "blessing" to the Republic because it would prevent "any single interest, faction, or region from dominating and so destroy the whole."[3] According to Stephanson, in his book *Manifest Destiny: American Expansionism and the Empire of Right*, "After the 1820s, Jacksonians would indeed take the logic one step further and make it dynamic: popular republics positively needed to expand to stay healthy."[4]

Later, the United States' iconic Supreme Court Justice, John Marshall, in his 1823 decision of *Johnson v. M'Intosh*, which reads more like a history book about American expansionism than a legal decision, granted that expansionism legal justification when he declared:

> Discovery gave title to the government by whose subjects, or by whose authority, it was made, against all other European governments, which title might be consummated by possession. . . . The history of America, from its discovery to the present day, proves, we think, the universal recognition of these principles.[5]

Then in December of 1823, when he was the fifth president of the United States, James Monroe, who also had signed the Louisiana Purchase Treaty, gave the transcontinental expansion immense military and strategic significance with his Monroe Doctrine. Under that doctrine, Monroe effectively declared the entire Western Hemisphere, not just the United States, off limits to any further European colonialism. He asserted that "we should consider any attempt on their part to extend their system to any portion of this hemisphere as dangerous to our peace and safety."[6] He did so without the military forces necessary to defend the massive continental area that was the United States and its territories at the time—let alone Central and South America. Regardless, his doctrine was an early and significant projection of American power on the world stage.

POPULATION AND ECONOMIC GROWTH

The population of the newly formed United States exploded in the same fashion as its borders. It took almost three hundred years for the United States to reach approximately 2.3 million people by the time of the

Revolution. Just twenty-four years later, in 1800, that population more than doubled to over 5.3 million people. By the mid-1800s, that number reached over 23 million, surpassing England, and then more than tripled to over 73 million by 1900, whereas England, a country older by more than a millennium, had only some 41 million. Of course, the great continental expanse simultaneously fulfilled America's ambitions for a great nation and proved to be an outlet, despite the deadly Indian Wars, for the millions of immigrants that were coming.

At the outset of the 1800s, immigrants came "mostly from countries like Great Britain, Ireland, Norway, the German states, and Prussia."[7] Then Chinese and Japanese immigration surged in the middle of the century before European immigration once again dominated the late 1800s. Between 1890 and 1900 alone, "there was a large acceleration in immigration, with an influx of nearly nine million people."[8]

Despite that massive land mass that had become the United States, the enormous population growth was part of the transformation of America from a rural, agriculturally based civilization to an industrialized economy with massive urban centers. In 1800, New York City, with its 60,000 residents, was the most populated city in America, in significant part because it had been the US capital under the Articles of Confederation, and then under the Constitution, between 1785 and 1790. London's population, by contrast, was 1 million in 1800. By 1900, however, nearly 3.5 million people lived in New York City, which by then had absorbed Brooklyn. Incredibly, that meant in a country of nearly 3.8 million square miles, nearly 1 in every 22 Americans lived in New York City alone. The 1920s census showed for the first time in American history that "over 50 percent of the US population was defined as urban."[9] With that, in just over one hundred years, the American civilization had transformed the very nature of its society.

Economically speaking, America underwent enormous changes as well. In 1776, the seminal economist Adam Smith published his *Wealth of Nations*. Within it, Smith declared:

> There are no colonies of which the progress has been more rapid than that of the English in North America . . . plenty of good land, and liberty to manage their own affairs their own way, seem to be the two great causes of the prosperity of all new colonies.[10]

According to the economic historian Edwin J. Perkins, "in comparison with the economies of its more regulated European counterparts, colonial North America was a much closer approximation of the open, free market society advocated by Adam Smith."[11] With that foundation, along with abundant energy and people, according to the economic historians Gary M. Walton and James F. Shepherd, the American economy rose to incredible heights, creating "standards of living undreamed of by the signers of the Declaration of Independence."[12]

American economic growth took an important step forward with its first factory, which was built in 1790 by Samuel Slater, known to history as the "Father of the American Industrial Revolution." His Rhode Island cotton-spinning mill was enhanced by the power of water. Eli Whitney invented the cotton gin just two years later. Combined, they helped propel the textile industry for decades. Of course, that meant slavery's role in the early American economy would increase as well. The transcontinental railroad, commercially and strategically, connected the American coasts as part of a dramatic increase of railroad construction after the Civil War. "By the 1870s, machines were knitting stockings and stitching shirts and dresses, cutting and stitching leather for shoes, and producing nails by the millions."[13] Those "machines changed the way people worked. Skilled craftspeople of earlier days had the satisfaction of seeing a product through from beginning to end. When they saw a knife, or barrel, or shirt or dress, they had a sense of accomplishment. Machines, on the other hand, tended to subdivide production down into many small repetitive tasks with workers often doing only a single task."[14] Most of that industrial growth was concentrated in the Northeast, which "facilitated the development of transportation systems such as railroads and canals, which encouraged commerce and trade."[15]

Of course, it was also the era of the "great capitalists,"[16] such as J. P. Morgan, Andrew Carnegie, and, the richest of them all, John D. Rockefeller. In the words of historian H. W. Brands, in his essential read *American Colossus: The Triumph of Capitalism*:

> Carnegie dominated steel, the industry on which modern America was, almost literally, built, and Rockefeller controlled oil, which lit, lubricated, and was beginning to power American life. . . . Morgan commanded money, the philosopher's stone of modern capitalism. . . . [Together], Morgan and his fellow capitalists . . . lifted the standard of living of ordinary people to a plane associated . . . with aristocracy.[17]

In doing so, those capitalists, and the labor on which they relied, and some would say exploited, propelled America to economic superpower status. In 1870, Great Britain, where the Industrial Revolution first took root in the 1830s, laid claim to 32 percent of the world's industrial production. By the mid-1880s, however, the United States surpassed it to become the world's leading industrial economy. By the turn of the century, America had doubled the output of Great Britain. Output, however, was not the most historically significant impact of the Industrial Revolution.

CULTURAL SHIFTS AND THEIR CONSEQUENCES

Prior to the Civil War, more Americans worked in agriculture than in manufacturing. Between 1800 and 1860, farming in America continued to prosper. The number of farm laborers grew consistently during the prewar period.[18] After the Civil War, however, the labor market shifted. Throughout the 1870s, the number of Americans employed in farming and industry was roughly the same. By 1920, however, the number of nonagricultural workers, mostly concentrated in cities, was more than twice the number of agricultural workers.

With that shift also came what has always proven to be one of the most fundamental and profound change civilizations endure. The economic unit for much of America shifted away from the family on the farm to the individual in urban settings. Over the next hundred years and beyond, those individuals, unmoored from the structure and reverence of the family farm, in a cluster of changing mores, would begin to live on their own, often away from their families. They would seek economic and educational opportunities and delay marriage in the process. When they did marry, children who were once economic necessities on the farm became economic burdens in the cities—and so, today, there are studies about the costs of "raising" a child where once those children provided the labor that supported the early American families and their farms.

Adding to that, as wealth rose and contraception and then abortion became more common, and then socially acceptable, those dynamics combined to cause birth rates to enter a predictable decline—a decline long associated with commercial societies. In turn, the decline of the family structure would begin. Meanwhile, the wiles and allures of the city eventually would lead to the loosening of morals and the weakening of the ethic of the countryside that was the very foundation of the American civilization.

Of course, those changes did not affect the whole of the country and certainly not right away. Throughout history, those dynamics have affected the coasts and commercial centers of civilizations far more than rural areas and resulted in a growing contrast compared to the more conservative way of life in those rural settings. So those in and around ancient Athens tended to be socially and political more "liberal," in the modern sense of the word, than the conservatives of the Greek countryside. The same could be said of the inhabitants of Rome as compared to the patient farmers in the many valleys and small towns of Italy. Today, the United States expresses the same dynamic in the context of the politically Blue cities and coastal states compared to the more rural "flyover" Red states and counties.

Returning to our consideration of the 1800s, there were major political changes that accompanied the changing demographics as well. The Founders, by their work, were well aware that their Revolution had let loose an idea—perhaps irresistibly so. John Adams, in 1815, wrote the following to his Revolutionary counterpart, Thomas Jefferson, after both had been president and reconciled the bitter differences that arose during their competitive pursuit and then exercise of presidential power: "What do We mean by the Revolution? The War? That was no part of the Revolution. It was only an effect and consequence of it. The Revolution was in the Minds of the People, and this was affected, from 1760 to 1775."[19]

Continuing with that thought process, if the American Revolution was a war, it had been won in 1783. If it was an idea "in the Minds of the People," as John Adams had diagnosed, then it was a war in perpetual progress. In other words, the system of government the Founders established was not a finished work. After all, *the history of mankind is a continuum, not a destination. Thus, even though* the Founders "democratized" government in ways *untried and even unfathomed by those who went before it, their work was not a finished product any more than the foundation of the house is the only work necessary to create a home that could endure centuries of weather.*

FOUNDING PRINCIPLE: BALANCE OF POWER

When considering that work in progress, it is also important to remember that the Founders' achievements were not pursued without hesitations. According to the historian Sean Wilentz, in his book *The Rise of American Democracy*, among a number of the Founders, "philosophically, the assumption prevailed that democracy, although an essential feature of any well-ordered government, *was also dangerous and ought to be kept strictly within bounds.*"[20] That thought process is in keeping with Will Durant's admonition that for freedom to be stable, there must be a significant degree of order lest freedom be consumed by uncontrolled license.

There were American Founders who extended their stability concerns to a disbelief that ordinary Americans were fit to govern, including John Adams and Alexander Hamilton. John Adams belied such concerns when he wrote to John Sullivan, who had been a major general in the Continental Army and governor of New Hampshire. On May 26, 1776, Adams predicted that "new claims will arise; women will demand a vote; lads from twelve to twenty-one will think their rights not enough attended to; and every man who has not a farthing will demand an equal voice with any other, in all acts of state."[21]

Thomas Jefferson did not agree with John Adams or Alexander Hamilton in those regards. Jefferson had watched power gather in the nation's capital at the expense of the states and rural Americans. He decried what he called "monocrats"—those, like Alexander Hamilton, whose views tended more toward a monarchy than the democratization of government. Jefferson wanted truly limited government and believed that those rural Americans, who were not trusted by Adams and Hamilton, were the most important bulwark against those who would pursue and then use power in the federal government. Jefferson believed, in true Enlightenment fashion, that "the will of an educated . . . majority could and should prevail"[22] and that "all men in political associations are free and equal."[23] In Jefferson's mind, the phrase, "all men are created equal" was an undeniable purpose that had only one logical destination—actual equality under the law and in practice. In Jefferson's first inaugural address, he told a divided country that "though the will of the majority is in all cases to prevail, that will, to be rightful, must be reasonable; that the minority possess their equal rights, which equal laws must protect, and to violate would be oppression."[24]

Jefferson's and Adams's opposing views were on display in two presidential elections. Adams prevailed in the first, the 1796 election, becoming the second president of the United States. Jefferson prevailed in the second match. In defeating Adams and becoming the third president, Jefferson pursued what became known to history as "Jeffersonian Democracy." According to historian Sean Wilentz, "the Jeffersonian ascendancy opened up" the American political system. "Against Federalism's immense condescension and determine obstructionism, Jefferson and his party vindicated the political equality of the mass of American citizens."[25] Because of this, "popular participation in politics grew . . . to levels unimaginable in the 1790s"—literally doubling in some states.[26] Importantly, Jefferson's impact would be lasting. According to historian John Meacham, in his work *Thomas Jefferson: The Art of Power*:

> Thomas Jefferson was the most successful political figure of the first half century of the American Republic. For thirty-six of the forty years between 1800 and 1840, either Jefferson or a self-described adherent of his served as president of the United States.[27]

One of those adherents who became president was Andrew Jackson. His legacy included "Jacksonian Democracy." From Jefferson to Jackson, the selection of the electors, those who actually voted for the presidents in the Electoral College, would be democratized by changing how those electors were selected, from the votes of state legislators to "the ballots of ordinary voters."[28] In other words, the popular vote within individual states would determine the electors.

Andrew Jackson took great advantage of that change and cast himself as the guardian of rights against the elites. Like Jefferson, Jackson championed those ordinary voters. He railed against the establishment of his day in his First Annual Message to Congress by stating, "Corruption in some and in others a perversion of correct feelings and principles divert government from its legitimate ends and make it an engine for the support of the few at the expense of the many."[29] Voter participation would surge under Jackson as it did under Jefferson, so much so that the historian William MacDonald would opine that Jackson "made middle class democracy what it had never been before in the United States, a working scheme of government."[30] Of course, that had never been seen in history either.

Beyond that, in the wake of the Civil War, which is discussed in the next chapter, the legal right to vote would be extended to those who were formerly slaves. Black men and women, through the Emancipation Proclamation and a series of constitutional amendments and civil rights laws, would gain their freedom and make other substantial and meaningful gains, including their election to Congress.

★ ★ ★

In addition to that political expansion, the most significant part of the story of the United States, from the Revolution to the Industrial Revolution, was the building of the foundation for the spreading of the national economy and wealth away from the centers of political power in the East. As discussed at greater length in chapters 11 and 13, *there can be no sustainable democracy where economic and political power are controlled by the same elites.* We shall find that dynamic is rising in America today as large special interests work with government elites not only to determine policy but also to grab the spoils of government. As for the 1800s, the democratization of wealth that began in that era played an essential role in the furtherance of the democratization of the American political system.

In the years following the Industrial Revolution in America, the dynamic to which Adam Smith had alluded—an economy increasingly based on individual initiative—would go hand in glove with a system of limited government and afford the greatest freedom in history to date—with self-sufficiency begetting an ever-greater desire for self-determination.

CHAPTER 7

America at War with Itself

*Democracy is a process, not a static condition.
It is becoming, rather than being. It can easily be lost,
but never is fully won. Its essence is eternal struggle.*

—Attributed to William H. Hastie

The 1800s were the United States' most trying and bloody century—and, of all the trials endured by the new Republic, the Civil War took the largest toll. Of course, at issue was slavery. With the election of Abraham Lincoln in 1860, and the resultant secession of Southern states, slavery moved to the very center of American political life and then to the many battlefields of the Civil War. In no uncertain terms, the Civil War became a battle for the soul of America and an epic struggle over its core purpose to democratize.

The number of Civil War deaths, from its battles or related illnesses, would far outpace any war in America's history. By some estimates, over 700,000 Americans perished, an amount equal to approximately 2.5 percent of America's total population at the time. That percentage, if applied to America's 2024 population, would equate to the death of well over eight million Americans. By comparison, the number of deaths on the battlefield in the Mexican-American War, which preceded the Civil War by just over a decade, numbered only 1,733.

Slavery, as we know, had been known to the world at large for thousands of years before 1860 and was not then, or now, confined to a single race. European-style slavery was introduced to America in the early 1600s. Consistent with the prevailing views of the vast majority of the world at the time, "for most of the eighteenth century, slavery had been condoned throughout the American colonies."[1] In keeping with America's limited central government principles, prior to the Civil War, the "legalization of slavery had been a matter left entirely to the individual states to decide for themselves."[2] Not surprisingly, given slavery's comparatively limited practice in the North, when compared to the South, it was the Northern states/colonies that took the lead in abolishing slavery in the late 1700s, starting with Vermont in 1777. Given those dynamics, "some slaves remained in seven of the eleven [Northern] free states as late as 1820, though they were numerically significant in only two of them."[3]

That difference in the prevalence of slavery was due, in significant part, to the fact that large-scale plantation farming was never the basis of the Northern economy. As we have seen, the farms of the Northern colonies, now states, had always been more likely to be self-sustaining family farms than what would become the huge agribusinesses of the Southern and the Mid-Atlantic colonies. By 1860, the Northern states and their growing cities and ports were on their way to becoming commercialized economies. Indeed, as the Civil War approached, "more than 90 percent of the nation's manufacturing was in the North."[4] Consistent with that, "Northern prosperity was being built, to an important and ever larger degree, on the idea of "free labor."⁵ At the time, that literally meant "free" men working for a wage as opposed to slaves or indentured servants working for a "master." That "free labor" naturally gravitated toward the Northern domestic manufacturing, which the US governments sought to "protect" over the years from foreign imports. Their protectionist policies imposed tariffs (taxes) on products manufactured abroad in an effort to reduce demand for those foreign products in favor of the comparable domestic products being manufactured in the North.

Politically, as stated by William B. Hesseltine, in his book *The Tragic Conflict: The Civil War and Reconstruction*:

> The North, increasingly driven by emancipationists, thought of the Constitution as a document which, when applied in its spirit, would eventually ensure that all people in America, whatever their color, black or white, whatever their status, slave or free, would be equal before the law.⁶

Abraham Lincoln, before he gave his life to that belief, had declared, "In due time the weights should be lifted from the shoulders of all men, and . . . all should have an equal chance."⁷ Most of the South, of course, did not see it that way. By 1860, according to historian Russell McClintock, the "Deep South . . . had been a true slave society . . . for twice as long as it had belonged to the union of states."⁸ According to Bruce Levine, in his book *The Fall of the House of Dixie*:

> Slaveholding was not simply an economic necessity. It was not only the source of their wealth and physical comfort. It was not merely one possible enterprise, one possible investment, among many. It was, instead, the unique basis of the particular outlook, assumptions, norms, habits, and relationships to which masters as a

social class had become deeply and reflexively attached. It defined their privileges and shaped their culture, their religion, and even their personalities.[9]

Although, as historian Paul Johnson concluded, "slavery was not the only issue between the North and South,"[10] it certainly was the driving force for the secession of Southern states after the election of Lincoln. Eventually, the battle to end slavery became the reason Americans fought with other Americans in a completely unprecedented fashion and in ways not even remotely seen since. In plain terms, no other civilization would endure such a horror in the battle to end slavery.

THE CONTRADICTION OF SLAVERY IN AMERICA

Together, slavery in America and the fighting of the Civil War raise serious questions about the nature of the American civilization, its purposes and beliefs. If America was founded on religious grounds, along with the pursuit of freedom and individual opportunity, and if it was to be a place where all men had inalienable and equal rights, what then should be said about slavery in America? Moreover, what can be said of our Founders, some of whom owned slaves, and who signed a Constitution years after the signing of the Declaration of Independence, but who did not constitutionally end slavery? Also, why did it take eight decades and a bloody war to advance the democratization of rights in America, one of its basic founding purposes, to its millions of Black slaves and those Blacks who were free before the Civil War?

The answers, of course, are unsatisfactory to many and, for some, always will be unsatisfactory. We must note that no civilization is without serious fault. In American history, whether it was President Jackson's treatment of American Indians, President Andrew Johnson's resistance to civil rights,

Franklin Delano Roosevelt's internment camps during World War II, or numerous other actions of the American people and its elected officials, serious questions about the virtues of America can be raised.

As for slavery, it is no small scar on the soul of time. When considering the questions posed earlier, it is of course rather easy to sit in judgment of the actions of those who have come before us. It is just as easy to assume that we, individually and collectively, would have been wiser, more capable, and even more brave than our forebears. How pleasant a world it would be if such self-declared daring represented reality. In truth, however, *rarely do we judge our own youthful actions with that same level of assuredness, let alone indignation, as we do the actions of others. For better or worse, it is human nature to be nostalgic about our own prior acts and to be more judgmental about the acts of others.* Knowing that, we should endeavor to understand our shared past and apply such lessons of history that may shed light on the circumstances.

As we do, first it must be stated that slavery was not the only history of those of African descent in America. Throughout the early centuries, there were free Blacks in America, the majority of whom lived in urban settings,[11] although, to be certain, the percentage in any one colony was not high. The Black historian and founder of the Association for the Study of African American Life and History Carter G. Woodson placed the percentage of those Blacks who were free in America in 1830 at 13.7. Prior to that, in Maryland, the 1755 census found 4 percent of Blacks to be free—a number presumed to be similar throughout the South.[12] It was said that a majority of them were young "mulattoes, the children of white women."[13] According to Ira Berlin, in his work *Slaves without Masters: The Free Negro in the Antebellum South*, for a time, some Blacks "enjoyed the full fruit of the rich new land. They earned money, accumulated property, and occasionally held minor offices."[14] Some were also allowed to vote. Georgia, for a time, offered "free mullattoes all the rights of 'persons born of British parents,' except voting and sitting in the General Assembly."[15]

It is also important to note that, even amid slavery, America provided important firsts in world history. In 1641, the Colonial Legislature of Maryland elected the first person of African descent, Mathias de Sousa, to public office. Even before the adoption of the Constitution, Wentworth Cheswell, of African descent, was elected Constable of Newmarket, New Hampshire, in 1768. He served in that role until 1817.* Further, the 1783 Massachusetts Constitution "gave equal rights and privileges to all (male) citizens of the state."[16] Of course, there was also an American history of brave Black abolitionists, including Frederick Douglass, William Wells Brown, Leonard Grimes, Frances Ellen Watkins Harper, and, of course, Harriet Tubman, among many others. In addition to them, in 1827 the *Freedom Journal* was published in New York, and was the first of dozens of newspapers that would become known as the "Black Press."

Those, however, were the exceptions to the plight of those of African descent in America. Up to the Civil War, the vast majority of Blacks in America were slaves who endured varying degrees of hardship, abuse, and even death. Even those who were free were subject to suffering and discrimination.

Second, we know that throughout all of history, and in every civilization and in every stage of those civilizations, the economic well-being of some has benefited immensely from the toil of those less fortunate. Throughout history, some have referred to that process as "exploitation" or "oppression," especially in the early stages of a capitalist/industrialized society, in which the stratification of society, before economic maturity lifts the standards of

---

* According to the UK Parliament, Great Britain did not elect a Black representative until 1987. See UK Parliament, "The First Asian and Black Parliamentarians," accessed March 18, 2024, https://heritagecollections.parliament.uk/exhibits/pioneers/. However, others dispute that date: "In 1772 James Townsend became the Lord Mayor of London. Townsend's mother was mixed race and his grandmother was a Black South African." See Black Presence in Britain, "Black British Politicians," accessed March 18, 2024, https://blackpresence.co.uk/black-british-politicians/; see also Wolfram Latsch, "A Black Lord Mayor of London in the Eighteenth Century?" *Notes and Queries*, December 2016, p. 615.

living for the masses, can be most glaring. The less fortunate more often than not did benefit from their work, especially in an economy like that of the United States, as Adam Smith described. That is also true when compared to the generational poverty of others around the globe. Nevertheless, that was not always the case. Of those times and places when they did not, slavery represented the harshest and worst of those circumstances.

Third, slavery was anything but new when the European practices arrived in America—although it became a greater enterprise in the colonies than it had been in most other places. Thousands of years before the Americas were discovered, the ancient world mostly accepted slavery.[17] As Professor Roger Anstey notes in his preface to the *History of Slavery*, Aristotle believed that "from the hour of their birth, some are marked out for subjection, others for rule."[18] Hammurabi, the Babylonian king (1792 to 1750 BC), in his written Code, acknowledged the existence of slavery, as did the Apostle Paul, in his Epistle to Philemon. Further, Professor James Walvin notes that the "Spaniards and Portuguese had legal traditions, derived from Roman law, which made special provisions for slaves."[19]

Beyond that, the Greeks of ancient Athens, as we have seen, permitted democracy among a select few whose number was far outweighed by the number of slaves that maintained their economy. Rome for centuries imported slaves from the peoples they vanquished—slaves who often displaced workers of the lower Roman classes. The etymology of the word "slave" is from a time when Slavic people were enslaved as early as the 900s. Slaves were prevalent during the Viking Age with as much as 10 percent of those living under the Vikings being enslaved. The Mongol Empire (1206–1368), likely the largest land empire in history, regularly enslaved people who were among their vanquished, as did the Songhai Empire in North Africa in the 1400 and 1500s. Further, "as early as 1300, Europeans were using Black and Russian slaves to raise sugar on Italian plantations. During the 1400s, decades before Columbus's 'discovery' of the New World, Europeans exploited African labor on slave plantations built on sugar producing islands off the coast of West Africa."[20] However disturbing, it remains a fact of history that the economies of those times and places were dependent on slaves.

It is also true, and much underreported, that slavery was not limited to those of African descent. In his book *Slaves and Slavery: The British Colonial Experience*, Professor James Walvin writes, "Many modern readers will simply assume that to speak of slavery is to speak of black slavery. Yet it was only really in the Americas that being black came to be associated with slavery."[21] Consistent with that, in addition to the example of Russian slaves above, when the Muslims ruled the Iberian Peninsula (modern-day Spain and Portugal), they enslaved white Christians. United States Senator Charles Sumner, in 1847, famously spoke of "white slavery, or the slavery of Christians, throughout the Barbary States."[22] As Tom Pocock wrote in his book, *The Royal Navy's War against White Slavery*, "When The Napoleonic wars ended [in 1815] . . . the enslavement of Europeans by North African states—semi autonomous regencies of the Ottoman Empire—continued with Algiers as its driving force."[23] That practice was not a transient practice. To the contrary,

> Slavery never disappeared from medieval Europe. While slavery declined in northwestern Europe, it persisted in Sicily, southern Italy, Russia, southern France, Spain, and North Africa. Most of these slaves were "white," coming from areas in Eastern Europe or near the Black Sea.[24]

Consistent with that, American historian Thomas Sowell notes that the number of white slaves in North Africa exceeded the number of black slaves in the American colonies.

We have already noted the existence of white servitude in America, a dynamic written about at length in David W. Galenson's book *White Servitude in Colonial America: An Economic Analysis*. Don Jordan and Michael Walsh, in their book *White Cargo: The Forgotten History of Britain's*

White Slaves in America, chronicled how that servitude often rose to the level of slavery. Importantly, they also point out:

> Black slavery emerged out of white servitude and was based upon it. As the African American writer Lerone Bennet Jr has observed: "when someone removes the cataracts of whiteness from our eyes, and when we look with unclouded vision on the bloody shadows of the American pass, we will recognize for the first time that the Afro American, who was so often second in freedom, was also second in slavery."[25]

It must also be noted that slavery was also practiced by American Indians. For example, the Choctaw and Chickasaw tribes bought, sold, and owned Africans as slaves, as Barbara Krauthamer points out in her work *Black Slaves, Indian Masters: Slavery, Emancipation, and Citizenship in the Native American South*.[26] Further, as noted in the book *The Indian Wars*, published by National Geographic:

> The extent to which Europeans used slaves as an oppressed labor force was new to most tribes, but some quickly adopted the European practice. The Cherokee, for instance, integrated slavery wholesale. . . . Even more commonly, many tribes, especially on the Atlantic coast and Southeast, started to raid their neighbors and sell captives to their European allies.[27]

It is also true that Blacks in America owned slaves in "each of the thirteen original states," if only to a minor degree.[28] Carter G. Woodson famously published a book, in 1930, called *Free Negro Owners of Slaves in the United States in 1830*. In it, Woodson estimated that 3,776 freed former slaves owned 12,907 slaves.[29] Anecdotally, after the Civil War, in

1876, the *Raleigh News* ran a story of a white mother and her three children "let out at auction to the lowest bidder," a "negro."[30] Since Woodson's pronouncement, the extent of such Black slave ownership has been subject to revaluation. However, it remains that "there were instances . . . in which free blacks had a real economic interest in the institution of slavery and held slaves in order to improve their own economic status."[31]

The nature of slavery, however, changed with the growing Americas by an order of magnitude.[32] In the article "Atlantic Worlds: Enslavement and Resistance," it is noted that

> slavery existed in Africa before Europeans arrived. However, their demand for slave labour was so great that traders and their agents searched far inland, devastating the region. Powerful African leaders fuelled the practice by exchanging enslaved people for goods such as alcohol, beads and cloth. Britain became the world's leading slave-trading country. Transatlantic slavery was especially lucrative because ships could sail with full holds on every stage of their voyage, making large profits for merchants in London, Bristol and Liverpool. Around 12 million Africans were enslaved in the course of the transatlantic slave trade.[33]

Finally, the role of Africans in the slave trade must be noted. In a vast majority of cases, Europeans did not go into the African mainland to capture slaves. To the contrary,

> most slaves sold to Europeans had not been slaves in Africa. They were free people who were captured in war or were victims of banditry or were enslaved as punishment for certain crimes or as repayment for a debt. In most cases, rulers or merchants were not selling their own subjects, but people they regarded as alien.[34]

In other words, and again, the history of slavery is not simply a matter of racism—even for the slavery that was prevalent in early America.

Thus, if we consider the entire history of slavery in all places and time, it is safe to conclude that slavery, however egregious, brutal, and wrong, was a widespread and accepted practice in antiquity and into the 1800s, so much so that Thomas Sowell wrote that "nowhere in the world was slavery a controversial issue prior to the 18th century."[35] It is also true that slavery has known no racial boundaries, either as to who is willing to enslave, who was willing to trade slaves, or as to who has been subject to being enslaved. Those are the dynamics that existed in the years leading up to the founding of the United States.

THE CONSTITUTION AND THE JUDGMENT OF HISTORY

How then should we look at slavery's prevalence for so many years in America, even after the adoption of the Constitution? Some readers may choose to accept the French philosopher Voltaire's view that history is "a collection of the crimes, follies and misfortunes" and end their inquiry there.[36] Using that perspective, a great deal of those that have gone before us, indeed almost all of history, can be condemned wholesale—especially on the issue of slavery.

By the same token, they may also condemn the Founding Fathers for not outlawing slavery with the adoption of the Constitution. However, I don't believe that history supports such a judgment, even for those who owned slaves, for numerous reasons beyond its historical prevalence.

First, we must understand that the adoption of the Constitution was no assured matter even without consideration of slavery. Although the Articles of Confederation referred to the former colonies as "The United States of America," the thirteen former colonies and now separate states had a very fractious existence under that original founding charter. Issues like taxation, tariffs, trade, border disputes, debt, disruption of contract rights, paper money, debtor relief, and more vexed those newly minted nation states. So divided and fractious were the times, including the taking up of arms between some colonies, that Founders like Alexander Hamilton openly worried that there would be war among the states. That fear and the intensifying divisions were no small motivating factors for the Founders who desired "a more perfect union."

Once the Constitution was drafted to replace the Articles of Confederation, added to those existing disagreements was a bitter fight over the consolidation of power in a national government at the expense of the states. No less than Patrick Henry, of "Give me liberty, or give me death" fame and an essential figure in the intellectual nature of the Revolution, parted company with the other Founders over that issue—and bitterly so. He believed the proposed Constitution was a betrayal of the Revolutionary purposes he helped ignite.

It is largely unknown to Americans today that, joining Patrick Henry was Rhode Island, whose leaders and citizens were so suspicious of that consolidation of power that they sent no delegates to the Constitutional Convention that produced the Constitution. Indeed, no representative of Rhode Island signed the Constitution, and delegates from other colonies refused to sign it because it violated the rights of states. So certain were the Founders that the Constitution they drafted would not be ratified by all the states, that they artificially limited its ratification requirements for its adoption to just nine of the thirteen states. Even then, the fate of the newly drafted Constitution was in such doubt, and the times marked by such division, that George Washington, during the difficult and fractious fight to adopt the Constitution, wrote that "should the States reject this excellent Constitution, the probability is . . . the next will be drawn in blood."[37] Not persuaded, the Rhode Island legislature rejected ratifying the Constitution eleven times in less than three years before capitulating in response to the US Senate passing an economic boycott of Rhode Island.

Beyond that internal division, there was the issue of external security.

Today, we see a country that prospered after its Revolution in relative peace. At the time, however, there was no assurance that the frontiers of the new nation in the 1780s and 1790s were secure. The Revolution had been officially concluded with the Treaty of Paris just four years before the Constitution was written. At the time, the Founders could not be certain that this experiment they devised would not be subject to European invasion again. As time would tell, England would wage war on the United States not long after the adoption of the Constitution. Before that, President George Washington worked to keep the United States out of conflict between France and England. John Adams's presidency became embroiled in the Quasi War with the First French Republic. President Jefferson had to navigate economic warfare between England and France, and then James Madison faced the War of 1812 with England, which lasted nearly three years.

Viewed in the context of those many intense disputes and uncertainties, can it really be argued that, at that time, a seriously divided set of states could have constitutionally ended the age-old issue of slavery as well? To answer that question, we must add a simple but important consideration to this discussion. We have seen how the Northern states were not only less reliant on slavery but were beginning to abolish it even before the Constitution was adopted. The South, however, was of no such mindset in the 1770s and 1780s. Most significantly, just before the Revolution, Southerners were substantially better off than the Northerners and those in the Middle States. Quoting the economic historians Gary Walton and James Shepherd again, we find the following:

> Physical wealth per free person varied sharply among the regions. By far the richest was the South, where average wealth holdings per free person were more than double those in New England and in the middle colonies. . . . [D]ifferences between regions are also of the order of two to one per free person in the categories of livestock,

producer durables, farm tools and household equipment, and inventories. Even the value of land holdings per free person in the South was more than twice those in New England or the middle colonies.[38]

That continued into the early 1800s. Between 1830 and 1860, without even considering tobacco exports, the South's cotton industry alone accounted "for about half the value of all the United States' exports."[39]

Given that stark economic reality, and the lack of the commercialization in the South in the late 1700s, there is no reason to believe that the Southern states would have voluntarily agreed to end the practice of slavery—the practice that literally sustained their economy and lifestyle for hundreds of years—in connection with signing the new Constitution. Indeed, it took a horrific war and the destruction of their cities and economy eight decades later to bring that about—and even then, in the years after the Civil War, many in the South fiercely resisted the rights of African Americans.

It is worth noting that, in that same century, in the context of his desired reunification of Germany, the German statesman Otto von Bismarck famously said that "politics is the art of the possible, the attainable—the art of the next best." The adoption of the Constitution can be seen in that light. Indeed, even under all of those circumstances we have noted, the Founders still attempted the broadest democratization of rights in world history to date.

They did so even though the Founders were deeply conflicted—George Washington supported a plan for gradual abolition along with John Adams. Washington owned slaves; Adams never did. Nevertheless, the Founders as a group unleashed the aspirational and radical idea that *all men are created equal*, which was a necessary precursor or foundation on which abolition could succeed and Lincoln could base his philosophy.

If the Founders had not pursued *the possible*, but instead pursued the abolishing of slavery with the extended negotiation of the Constitution, it is more likely, in my judgment and that of others, that there would have been no such coming together of a nation. The United States, certainly as we know it, would not have come into existence. What then would have occurred?

It is certainly possible, if not likely, that we could have followed the dangerous path that Alexander Hamilton and Washington saw coming—warring conflict between the states and not necessarily just between the North and South. It is also likely that the people of that time could have gravitated toward establishing a separate country of Southern states where slavery could have lasted, if not increased, for an unknown length of time. Keep in mind, there was no Northern army of 1789 that could have subdued the South. While it was true, in the decade before, the Americans successfully outlasted the English forces and their oceanic supply lines, that Revolution left the former colonies heavily in debt, in a depression, and, ironically, more taxed than they had been under the British. In fact, in the years before the signing of the Constitution, the "United States" was in default to France for its Revolutionary War loans, which debt was refinanced "primarily through Dutch bankers."[40]

Under those circumstances, the notion that the poorer North could have subdued the richer South, legally or by force, is not reflective of the reality of the time. It would take decades of wealth accumulation by an increasingly industrialized North to overtake the South economically, politically, and militarily. None of that means slavery was ever right. It does, however, provide some context of how and why it existed.

THE LEGACY OF SLAVERY

We should also consider two more points as we look back on our Founders. First, as Thomas Sowell points out, more people were enslaved in the world in 2023 than were seized in four centuries from Africa.[41] In 2022, the UN Office of the High Commissioner for Human Rights' damning August 2022 report on Xinjiang concluded that the abuses were so severe and widespread that they "may constitute international crimes, in particular crimes against humanity."[42] Nevertheless, in 2023, the United States under President Biden, who promised the most "progressive" White House in history, refused to take a principled stand against China's use of "forced" labor—over 200 years after the adoption of the Constitution and over 150 years after the Civil War.[43] Any judgment of the Founders should be made in light of those truths.

Given the above, it is historically unreasonable to demand that millenniums of slavery could have been resolved in 1789 with the adoption of the Constitution. Therefore, it is unreasonable to condemn the Founders for not doing so. Again, how easy is it to sit in judgment of the past for those who maintain otherwise?

While that non-resolution had serious consequences, including hardening the practice by decades, the glass-half-full of historical analysis recognizes the advances that were made by the Founders—advances that had never been made in history anywhere else, including those many places where slavery existed. *With the Founder's advances, in the growing conscience of the Americans led by emancipationists, the practice of slavery was doomed in America.* As time would tell, it was a history not suited for a nation that aspired to such enlightened heights under its Declaration of Independence.

To be sure, the world knows that during the Civil War, President Lincoln used an executive order to free Southern slaves who were emancipated by Union army forces or who risked their lives to cross the combatant lines. After the North vanquished the South in the Civil War, because of its now superior population, military and industrial capacity, and growing wealth, it sought to remake the South according to Northern principles in what became known as Reconstruction. As part of that process, the Thirteenth Amendment was adopted, which outlawed slavery and involuntary servitude.

In response to continued Southern Democrat resistance to the further democratization of rights, the seminal Fourteenth Amendment was adopted. It provided the following:

Chapter 7: America at War with Itself

> No State shall make or enforce any law which shall abridge the privileges or immunities of citizens of the United States; nor shall any State deprive any person of life, liberty, or property, without due process of law; nor deny to any person within its jurisdiction the equal protection of the laws.

To this day, the Fourteenth Amendment provides the most important legal rationale for equality under the law for all in the United States. Returning to the Reconstruction era, the Fifteenth Amendment would be adopted with particular clarity on the issue of the right of Blacks to vote. It read as follows:

> The right of citizens of the United States to vote shall not be denied or abridged by the United States or by any State on account of race, color, or previous condition of servitude.

As those additions to the Constitution came into being, controversially,[†] so too did Black participation in electoral politics. On January 20, 1870, the Mississippi state legislature appointed Hiram Revels, a Black man, to a seat in the US Senate that had been vacant ever since Mississippi seceded from the Union nearly a decade earlier.[44] Later that year, three Black Republicans won congressional seats in South Carolina. Others would follow and, with those elections, begin a process that has continued to this day. Although there would be many setbacks along the way, including further brutality and racism, more than most other countries at the time

---

[†] The manner in which the North imposed laws on the South has been the subject of much discussion. For more on the subject, see Bruce Ackerman, *We the People*, vol. 2, *Transformations* (Cambridge, MA: Harvard University Press, 1998).

lived an ideal to create a society where all would "not be judged by the color of their skin but by the content of their character," as Martin Luther King would say in the 1960s.[45]

For now, let us conclude this part of our discussion by stating that the Thirteenth, Fourteenth, and Fifteenth Amendments, and the related civil rights laws adopted during the Reconstruction era, represented historical advances in the written law. They constituted more American building blocks in the democratizations of rights that were not seen anywhere else in the world at that time. Although they did not represent the end of the story by any means, they represented important next steps in the realization of the basic purposes of the American civilization. Rather than claim, in a vacuum of moral superiority, that those advances should have occurred in 1789, we should understand history for the truth of what it was, not the fiction we would want it to be. If—and only if—we do so, we can learn not only how to understand the past but also how to approach the future and understand that democratization is a process with no end.

Finally, there must be mention of another legacy of slavery in America. There is little doubt that that legacy includes racism. That is not to say that racism is exclusive to American history. It is plainly not. However, because of the manner in which slavery developed in the United States, including by segregation during and after slavery, that manner likely amplified racist views about Blacks among some, including claims of racial inferiority. One hundred years after the start of the Civil War, additional civil rights laws were passed in the 1960s, which certainly is an indication of the continued prevalence of the issue.

There are differing views of the extent of that prevalence today. Certainly, this book cannot possibly cover the breadth of the causes and nature of that issue. However, two observations, in my view, are important at this juncture. While spending an extended period of time in Singapore, I was struck by the multiplicity of races, from around the globe, there in the 1980s—in rather close proximity on that small island. In following Singapore in the decades since, it appears manifest that an abundance of economic activity and opportunity played a significant role in easing the assimilation of those that have called Singapore their home throughout its history, much like it did for so many Americans and immigrants in the late 1800s.

While I am not positing that vibrant economic activity alone will solve all matters of any continuing racism, it is quite evident that a stagnant American economy has a history of worsening division in America, of which racism is a part. Given the poor history that large, centralized governments have through the ages of fostering economic opportunity or of lifting a particular race, Americans would be wise not to further burden the American economy, which is already growing at a historically low rate. Lower economic growth never benefits assimilation. To the contrary, it pits the haves and have-nots of history against each other politically and contributes to class division and even the segregation of people, which will never be an answer to racism.

Rather, Americans would be wiser to realize government is not the answer to every problem and to not forget the societal benefits that self-sufficiency and opportunity has played in history and that, overall, the differences between groups of peoples lie in the differences of their opportunity and experience, not in their DNA.

CHAPTER 8

America as a Superpower

There is no escaping our obligations.
—**John F. Kennedy,** address to Congress, March 22, 1961

AMERICA'S GOLDEN AGE

The American civilization reached unprecedented heights in the 1900s in what may well be considered its Golden Age by future historians. American entrepreneurs and their employees took advantage of favorable government policies, abundant labor and natural resources, as well as technological advances, and made America the world's economic superpower. As the enormous wealth their genius and sweat produced by the late 1800s reached heights previously unseen, and as that wealth became more widely dispersed as the 1900s unfolded, the standards of living of Americans steadily rose.

A broad middle class emerged, and then, in the second half of the twentieth century, the nation reached what we may term "economic security." The relatively stable US economy produced a consistent flow of jobs, savings, and consumer goods. Starting some twenty years after the Great Depression, the level of prosperity of Americans rose to the point that it permitted Americans at large to begin to look beyond their day-to-day personal welfare to the long-term social issues facing the nation at large. Indeed, at the outset of the 1900s, Americans spent just 20 percent of their income on nonnecessities. By the end of the century, however, that percentage had risen to over 50 percent.[1] No other country of such size can boast such a claim.

Capitalizing on that economic and social sea change, American politicians would then enlarge American governments in the name of "public welfare" or "social justice" to unrecognizable proportions. In this way, what began with the New Deal of the 1930s, in response to the economic hardships of the Great Depression, would culminate in the pursuit of a redistributive welfare state, facilitated by the accumulation of great wealth.

America would also transform itself on the world stage during the 1900s. Following the examples of great economic powers of the past, such as Ancient Greece (eighth to sixth centuries BC), England (late 1500s and 1600s) and Spain (1500s), after gaining sufficient economic strength, the United States would look to assert itself in international affairs. To do so, America had shed its isolationist traditions that delayed its emergence on the international scene. When it did, America decisively entered World War I, World War II, and then the Korean War. Even before then, the United States began to acquire territories, sometimes thousands of miles away. Later, in the second half of the 1900s when America became the world's preeminent military superpower, in addition to being its economic superpower, the United States extended its military protection to millions of people in countries around the globe.

Importantly, during this period, the United States also would maintain and expand its core founding purposes of democratization and expanding opportunity. In 1920, the Constitution was amended with great consensus so as to grant women the right to vote. America also cemented its status as the world's destination for economic opportunity for investments and immigrants. That standing was immortalized when France bestowed the gift of the Statute of Liberty on the United States in 1885. Culturally, America exported its ethos and styles around the globe as well. All of those things combined to make America the world's most dominant civilization of the 1900s.

DEMOCRATIZATION AND WOMEN'S SUFFRAGE IN AMERICA

At the outset of the twentieth century, the United States continued its democratization of the right for citizens to legally participate in government. In 1920, the Nineteenth Amendment to the Constitution was adopted, which granted women the right to vote. It reads "The right of citizens of the United States to vote shall not be denied or abridged by the United States or by any State on account of sex." While the United States led the world in 1789 with granting broad rights under its Constitution, and with the Thirteenth, Fourteenth, and Fifteenth Amendments in the wake of the Civil War, all of which expanded democratization in unprecedented ways, the United States granting the right to vote for women in America was amid a greater worldwide movement.

As we have seen in part, and throughout history, the status of women has had a direct relation to the socio-economic dynamics of any given age. For most of history, the patriarchal family system grounded in agrarian societies held sway. Under that system, the roles of men and women were quite static and women's legal rights quite limited. Several historical dynamics, however, would change the role of women in society over the millennia. Most prominently, as civilizations urbanize, commercialize, and industrialize, and as wealth rises, the individual replaces the family as the main economic unit. The patriarchal system correspondingly wanes, and the roles of women in society expand economically and then legally.

For instance, the Italian cities of the economically vibrant Renaissance era provided more and different job opportunities for women than the toil of the countryside in the centuries before.[2] For example, in Venice in the 1500s, rising commercialism and wealth attracted many women immigrants in search of work outside of their family roles.[3] According to Venetian government records, Renaissance women worked as "glass bottles makers, alcohol distillers, glass factory owners, nurses, singers, herbalists" and more.[4]

Prior to the Renaissance, aristocratic societies also saw women excel, including politically—although not in great numbers. We can note the example of Fulvia (Rome, 83 BC–40 BC), who was of a noble family and driving force in the Roman civil war known as the Perusine War in 41 BC. In addition to that, Fulvia was a considerable force behind the careers of her "remarkable . . . progression of husbands," the Roman politicians Publius Clodius Pulcher, Gaius Scribonius Curio, and Mark Antony.[5] So prominent did she become that her visage appeared on a Roman coin,[6] the first non-mythological woman's to do so.[7] By contrast, the American Susan B. Anthony coin, a tribute to her suffragette leadership, did not appear until 1979.

Returning to the Renaissance, a period which focused on the individual more than the divine, we find that women also achieved great prominence, including Verona's Isotta Nogarola, likely the first prominent female humanist.[8] Perhaps none should be considered more prominent, however, than Catherine de' Medici. She was of the famed commercial Florentine family whose patriarchs, Cosimo de' Medici and later Lorenzo de' Medici, were the greatest patrons of Renaissance art and whose family bank financed much of the Renaissance. For political purposes and at just fourteen years old, Catherine de' Medici was married off to the future King of France, Henry of the House of Valois, the Duke of Orléans and the second son of Francis I of France. She would become mother to no less than three kings of

France, Francis II, Charles IX, and Henry III. Given their youth, however, Catherine effectively ruled France on and off for decades and, in the process, in addition to her political role and force, brought Italian culture and its cooking to France. She remains one of the more important, and underrated, figures in European history. The same could be said for the inspirational and brave Queen Elizabeth I of England, Joan of Arc of France, Caterina Sforza of Milan, and the d'Este sisters Isabella of Mantua and Beatrice of Milan. Beyond such notables, with the rise of education, commerce, and wealth, "an unparalleled number of women became writers during the Renaissance era."[9] It was also an era that "embraced women artists [and] also enabled their names and reputations to survive,"[10] a dynamic that simply could not occur in the Middle Ages.

As for the right to vote, to obtain that, women had to overcome the prejudices of history. That included arguments as to whether they were fit for such rights. An 1855 publication in London, written by Mrs. Ashton Dilke, noted that arguments were made that "because women are the weaker, therefore they are not to be considered capable of performing the duties of citizenship" and that "women are intellectually inferior to men" and that women would be "less womanly" if they participated in politics.[11] Similar arguments were made in the United States and many other countries as well. It would be the early 1900s before such arguments would finally be overcome.

Globally, there were sporadic instances of women obtaining the right to vote in the late 1700s, including briefly in Corsica off the Italian coast, in Sweden, and in the colony of Massachusetts. In the 1800s, suffrage became a worldwide movement from the Pitcairn Islands of the South Pacific, which allowed women to vote in 1838, to the Grand Duchy of Tuscany (inclusive of Florence) in 1849, which was the first European nation to do so. Along with other such advances around the globe, in the 1890s, the British colonies of New Zealand[12] and South Australia granted women the right to vote. South Australia went a step further by granting women the right to run for its parliament in that same decade.

In the United States, the role of women changed dramatically in the 1900s. At the outset of the twentieth century, the percentage of women in the nonfarm workforce was approximately 10 percent, which is not surprising given the agrarian nature of the economy. As the US economy expanded, commercialized, industrialized, and urbanized—creating historically unprecedented wealth along the way—by the end of the 1900s, women represented over 45 percent of the workforce.[13] With respect to education, in the early 1900s, women received only 19 percent of bachelor's degrees. By the end of the century, they garnered over half of those degrees.[14] During that same period of time, not surprisingly, the average family size in America fell from just under 5 people to 2.5 people[15] as more and more women, and men, delayed or forewent marriage in pursuit of education and careers.

Amid that societal change, the suffrage movement's first national legislative success came with the introduction of a constitutional suffrage amendment in 1878. Although that amendment failed, another was introduced in May of 1919. After Senate ratification in June of that year, remarkably, just fifteen months later, thirty-six states had ratified what we know as the Nineteenth Amendment. By then, the early 1900s had seen women gain the right to vote in Germany, Russia, Finland, Norway, and England, among other places. On the other hand, it would not be until 1945 that French women would cast their first general election ballots. Returning to the United States, one measure of the democratization of voting finds that, for the last forty years, women have voted at a higher percentage than men and in greater overall numbers.

ECONOMIC AND MILITARY GROWTH RISES IN AMERICA

If we turn to look at America's economic fortunes, Robert Gordon, in his book *The Rise and Fall of American Growth*, described the period of economic growth in America between 1870 and 1970 as a "special epoch" of economic growth. According to Gordon, that was a moniker that applied only to the United States because it was "the nation which has carved out the technological frontier for all developed nations since the Civil War."[16] It was also true that America, until the late 1900s, generally had favorable government policies for fostering economic growth. A prominent proponent of such policies, President Calvin Coolidge famously stated that "the chief business of the American people is business. They are profoundly concerned with producing, buying, selling, investing, and prospering in the world."[17]

For most of the 1900s, American governments supported that mantra by limiting regulations and tax schemes. By doing so, they would allow the American economic engine to thrive, including turning the trade deficits of the 1800s into trade surpluses for most of the 1900s. As the twentieth century came to a close, so dominant was the United States economically that "with just five percent of the world's population, the United States was accounting for 25 percent of the world's economic output, outproducing its closest rival Japan by nearly double the amount."[18] Of that economic output, by the end of the 1900s, over 10 percent of America's economic output would be in the form of exports[19] that reached the shores and borders of every country in the world.

Historically, advancing economic powers have generally led civilizations to extend themselves militarily and internationally. Internal economic prowess almost uniformly precedes a civilization's desire to shape external affairs—and so it would be for the United States. As part of that sustained economic growth of the 1900s, which was spurred on by technological advances, America's total agricultural production soared despite agricultural employment falling from 41 percent of the US economy overall in 1900 to just 4 percent in 1970.[20] The United States would use that agricultural proficiency, part of which would garner California's San Joaquin Valley the description of being one of the "bread baskets of the world," to address world hunger.

Writing in 1968, Will and Ariel Durant described the "recent spectacle of Canada and the United States exporting millions of bushels of wheat while avoiding famine and pestilence at home."[21] Count among mankind's greatest achievements the ability of one part of the world to create such surpluses that it could allay some of the economic challenges of poorer countries thousands of miles away.

Militarily, America kept a distinct and deep isolationist nature for itself well into the 1900s. During his farewell address to the nation, President George Washington cautioned future leaders that "it is our true policy to steer clear of permanent alliance with any portion of the foreign world."[22] Before then, despite the requests of the likes of Jefferson and Hamilton, Washington kept his young country neutral and therefore out of the French revolutionary wars—wars principally with England but which also engulfed Austria, Prussia, and Russia. He did so knowing that such an involvement could divide his fledgling country perhaps irretrievably between England or France or could invite retaliation to American interests. As we have seen, President Monroe warned off European powers from the American continent with his Monroe Doctrine. It is true that Jefferson famously and controversially sent American forces to deal with the piracy of North Africa's Barbary Coast to preserve America's economic interests and to stop the enslavement of Americans by North Africans. There would be two such short-lived Barbary Wars. Beyond those incursions, however, American foreign policy remained remarkably limited in its projection during the 1800s. Overall, the protection of the oceans and quiet nature of America's neighbors to the north and south permitted the United States to remain isolationist without significant negative consequences.

It did, however, include the further expansion of US territories, including the purchase of Alaska in 1867 and then Hawaii in 1900—both of which eventually became American states. The United States' international ambitions at the turn of the century also included the acquisition of several other territories, including the Philippines (1898—later relinquished), Guam (1899), Puerto Rico (1899), American Samoa (1900), and then, in 1917, what would become the US Virgin Islands. Each of those territories would develop elected legislatures in keeping with the values of American governance.

Just after that last acquisition, however, and despite President Woodrow Wilson's 1916 campaign to keep America out of the "Great War," which would become known to history as World War I, Wilson presided over the United States' entry into a European war. He did so even though that war did not directly threaten American shores. Wilson did so over the fierce objections of American isolationists, who firmly believed the United States had no business fighting in European wars. Despite that opposition, the American entry into the war helped turn the tide of World War I, likely decisively so. Consistent with America's foundational purposes, President Wilson used these words when asking Congress to declare war on Germany:

> The world must be made safe for democracy. Its peace must be planted upon the tested foundations of political liberty. We have no selfish ends to serve. We desire no conquest, no dominion. We see no indemnities for ourselves, no material compensation for the sacrifices we shall freely make.[23]

The United States' entry into World War I was a major leap forward in America's evolving role on the world stage. Keep in mind that "on April 6, 1917, when the United States declared war against Germany, the nation had a standing army of [just] 127,500 officers and soldiers."[24] Just eighteen months later, however, by war's end, an incredible 4.5 percent of the American population had joined the US military and/or served in that European war. "Four million men had served in the United States Army, with an additional 800,000 in other military service branches."[25] Of those, nearly 117,000 Americans would lose their lives.

At the end of the war, Wilson continued to march away from George Washington's restriction on entanglements by becoming the first American president to visit Europe while in office. After World War I, as a sign of a civilization still within its organic phase of unified purposes, when the "boys" came home they were greeted as returning heroes who had performed noble deeds. They had, indeed, defended democracy.

Even so, after World War I, America demobilized its forces rather than claim conquered lands. In that regard, Congress passed the National Defense Act of 1920, which allowed for a postwar force of 280,000. That "legislation was significant in that it marked the first time after a war that Congress debated at length the peacetime role and organization of the Army."[26] Nevertheless, from the height of World War I, American forces were reduced from 4.8 million to 280,000.

Even as America demilitarized, Wilson advocated a more interventionist foreign policy for the United States. Importantly, at the end of World War I, the entanglement known as the League of Nations came into being. It was the first international organization of its kind. Although the United States did not join the League because of its remaining isolationist resistance at home, the decision of its participants not to provide the League with a military arm carried with it the implication that the United States would not be able to detach itself from international conflicts for long. When the League failed at its basic purposes—to prevent wars—and World War II ensued, America once again entered a European war.

The United States would also once again use its economic and military powers to make the difference—this time in the defeat of the Axis powers of German, Japan, and Italy. In the lead-up to World War II, however, isolationists, including the internationally known transatlantic pilot Charles Lindbergh, relentlessly fought the US entrance into the growing war. President Franklin Delano Roosevelt, however, saw Hitler's advances for the "gathering storm" they proved to be and alternately cajoled or relied on public opinion to move America closer to saving its European friends. Events then overtook public opinion and even the isolationists could not stand in the way of US involvement after Japanese forces bombed Pearl Harbor. That was the casus belli some say Roosevelt wanted to enter the War.

World War II would be more challenging even though the case for it became increasing more obvious. After Hitler's Germany had subjugated almost all of Europe and part of Russia, the United States responded dramatically to the task at hand. Prior to America's entrance in the war, the American military had grown to over 334,000 personnel in the twenty years between wars. By 1945, in aid of America's effort to turn back the brutal fascism of Germany, Japan, and Italy, America's troops number would reach a high of over twelve million, well over eight percent of the American population.[27]

Much more so than any prior American war, the United States' efforts in World War II were not limited to the military. After the Japanese bombed America, World War II proved to be a unifying national event. Indeed, it was supported by American industry and its citizens in unprecedented fashion. Citizens were known for their "Scrap for Victory" drives that saw Americans saving metal, paper, rubber, and rags for the military effort (see Figure 8.1).

Figure 8.1. "Save Scrap for Victory" poster, circa 1941–1943. (Courtesy of the Library of Congress)

American factories were converted to military use. Overall, "American industry provided almost two-thirds of all the Allied military equipment produced during the war: 297,000 aircraft, 193,000 artillery pieces, 86,000 tanks and two million army trucks. In four years, American industrial production, already the world's largest, doubled in size."[28] Even America's burgeoning film industry supported the war effort with a series of patriotic or pro-war films made by the government and the private sector, utilizing legendary directors such as Frank Capra and John Huston. One such film was *Casablanca*, which was released in 1943. Meanwhile, American icons like Clarke Gable, Elvis, Jimmy Stewart, Ted Williams, Joe DiMaggio, and Yogi Berra would be lionized for their military service.

Once again, but to a greater degree than after the end of World War I, Americans celebrated the end of World War II. "New York was the site of the largest V-E Day celebration, by far, within the United States. Crowds gathered in Times Square, and thousands marched down Fifth Avenue, with confetti raining down on them."[29]

After the war, the United States would again draw down its forces. This time, however, the number would drop to 1.5 million.[30] Perhaps learning from the deficiencies of the League of Nations, the prevailing combatants created the United Nations. This time, the United States would take a central role. Nevertheless, and not long after, America would again decisively enter a foreign war—this time in Korea. Importantly, with respect to those three major, foreign wars, each of those wars could easily be cast as the forces of freedom triumphing over the dictatorial forces. Thus, the United States' participation was in keeping with its basic purposes of democratization.

In the wake of those wars, America's international stature grew exponentially. The use of nuclear bombs to end the Japanese theater of the war was beyond an unprecedented show of force. After World War II, President Truman, who had authorized the use of nuclear weapons, declared to Americans that the United States had to "maintain the military bases necessary for the complete protection of our interests and of world peace."[31] With that, the United States would expand its international presence well beyond the United Nations. As of the writing of this book, the United States had more than 750 military installations/bases in 80 foreign countries, including 174 in Germany and 113 in Japan.

America did more than extend its military power after the war. It also championed what became known as the Marshall Plan. The devastation that was left in the wake of World War II in Europe left it unstable. In an effort to keep it from falling into the hands of future dictators, the Marshall Plan "sought to stimulate European production, promote adoption of policies leading to stable economies, and take measures to increase trade among European countries and between Europe and the rest of the world."[32] Although in the years after World War II, the rise of a communist Soviet Union would divide the world between Western and Eastern Europe and lead to creation of the North Atlantic Treaty Organization (NATO) to combat that rise, there is little doubt the Marshall Plan provided an enormous hand up to the European countries who lost so very much in the war. America's leadership in NATO cemented its status as the leader of the Free World. After the Korean War, the United States would continue to expand not only its military presence in the world but also the foreign aid it started in earnest with the Marshall Plan. President John Kennedy summed up America's efforts in that regard when he proclaimed:

> There is no escaping our obligations: our moral obligations as a wise leader and good neighbor in the interdependent community of free nations—our economic obligations as the wealthiest people in a world of largely poor people, as a nation no longer dependent on the loans from abroad that once helped us develop our own economy—and our political obligations as the single largest counter to the adversaries of freedom.[33]

THE RISE OF THE ARTS

Finally, we should briefly consider the metamorphosis of the arts in America as well. As I state at the outset of the book, for most civilizations the arts flourish after wealth, rarely before. In the words of Will Durant:

> Civilization is social order promoting cultural creation. Four elements constitute it: economic provision, political organization, moral tradition, and the pursuit of knowledge and the arts. It begins where chaos and insecurity end. For when fear is overcome, curiosity and constructiveness are free, and man passes by natural impulse towards the understanding and embellishment of life.[34]

The America of the 1900s had certainly completed the economic, political, and moral stages of which Durant wrote. America's curiosity and constructiveness had been set free. As it approached the twenty-first century, the embellishments of life, if not the art of life, moved to the center of the culture. Starting just after the turn of the century, the medium of Hollywood captivated a nation and then the world. Roosevelt's New Deal instituted federal spending on the arts. Three decades later, President Lyndon Johnson established the National Endowment for the Arts and the National Endowment for the Humanities in the 1960s. Meanwhile, consumer spending on entertainment rose from an average of 1.6 percent of annual expenditures at the start of the century to 5.3 percent by century's end.[35] Similarly, it is estimated that over 3.5 percent of America's economy as a whole, in 2000, related to the arts and culture.[36] In other words, gathering wealth fostered the arts nationwide, as it had in other places and times, such as in Renaissance Italy.

The impact of the arts in 1900s America was hardly just a matter of numbers. In addition to America becoming economically and militarily dominant in the 1900s, "America's biggest export [was] no longer the fruit of its fields or the output of its factories, but the mass-produced products of its popular culture—movies, TV programs, music, books and computer software."[37] More than mere consumer consumption abroad, however, *The Cambridge History of America and the World* posited that "because the United States has arguably been the biggest producer of consumer goods in the global marketplace since the early twentieth century, the global distribution and consumption of these products was frequently equated with 'Americanization.'"[38]

In other words, during the 1900s, the American civilization was not only becoming ubiquitous but also shaping world culture. From McDonald's to Coca-Cola to American Express and Federal Express, from our military bases to our foreign aid, the twentieth century was witness to the American century. As we shall find, however, even as its influence abroad was cresting, the doubts about which Saint-Simon and Goethe warned had already begun to alter the trajectory of the American civilization.

CHAPTER 9

America in Doubt

*In organic periods men are busy building;
in critical periods they are busy destroying.*

—**Claude Henri de Rouvroy, comte de Saint-Simon,**
quoted in Durant, *The Lessons of History*

At the outset of the book, we discussed the views of great historical philosophers with respect to the rise of civilizations and their decline. They wrote of corresponding periods of belief and unbelief. Thomas Carlyle wrote of "vernal growth" and "winter dissolution."[1] He also wrote of periods during which faith could "remove mountains," and then, when it's in decline, "heroic Action is paralyzed" as "divinity [is] withdrawn."[2] Saint-Simon blithely stated that "in *organic* periods men are busy building; in *critical* periods they are busy destroying."[3] Further, he believed that in a civilization's decline, "all community of thought, all communal action, all coordination have ceased, and the society is only an agglomeration of separate individuals in conflict with one another."[4]

So far, we have surveyed America's rise, concentrating on the dominant dynamics and cultural consensus of its rise. In chapters 2 through 8, even allowing for the Civil War and its underlying and unresolved issues, the American civilization's confident upward trajectory for most of its first four hundred years was on display. America was busy building and by almost every measure it grew—in geographic size, population, culturally, and economically. Once founded, the United States pursued its foundational purposes of democratization and opportunity, although unevenly at times. It pursued those purposes almost relentlessly and with great success. No place in history assimilated so many millions of immigrants and provided as much opportunity to that diverse set of peoples for so long. Amid that diversity, in a very real sense, opportunity was America's cultural DNA and it flourished across a continent of limited governments and largely unlimited personal freedoms.

As we know, however, there is never just one story for any one life, much less a civilization. No group of people monolithically agree, let alone centuries of minds across thousands of miles and landscapes. So, from its inception, not all of America, let alone its indigenous populations and slaves, accepted that America's rise was laudable. The point of the historical philosophers is that in a civilization's initial, organic, unifying growth phase, by and large, a people act in concert and within a small range of beliefs. Yes, there is dissent—especially in a civilization that makes use of elected governments. *What marks the rise of any one civilization, however, is the great level of consensus for its founding principles and purposes. Conversely, what likely marks a decline is a substantial growth in the level of dissent and doubt about those founding principles and purposes.* The American civilization is witness to that growing dissent and doubt at the writing of this book.

Indeed, an increasing number of Americans doubt the validity of America's Founding purposes. Others question whether America has lived up to those ideals for everyone, and still others doubt whether America ever was, or still is, exceptional. The Founders and their actions, once immortalized in monuments that define the nation's capital and our cities, are now subject to withering criticism, if not removal. Those dynamics are so prevalent that, as Saint-Simon would have it, it may be hard to argue otherwise than to say that America is firmly within a critical period.

We shall find, with the benefit of hindsight, that America's organic growth phase, at least its first such phase, likely peaked in the 1950s. The 1960s, by contrast, likely represents the fulcrum on which our civilization pivoted, and when America's current critical phase began in earnest. As we consider that, we must understand that this critical period of doubt in which America finds itself today did not manifest itself all at once. To the contrary, a variety of factors have been at work, and for a considerable period of time, to bring America to this moment. Indeed, even amid America's vernal growth, if not because of it, the seeds of doubt were becoming evident.

Finally, one caution: The purpose of this chapter is not to decide the issue of whether the doubts that exist today among so many Americans are right or wrong. The purpose of this chapter is to demonstrate that America has reached this point in its historical continuum—much like Rome and Greece did as part of their critical phases. We should then, hopefully, draw lessons from those comparisons.

In the process, we must note that the Greek democracy outlined earlier and that of the Roman Republic were both lost as those civilizations descended into class warfare and violence. Disenfranchised citizens, and the politicians who catered to them, more than questioned whether those government systems benefited the well-to-do at the expense of commoners. The ends of both of those experiments in democracy were marked with deadly class violence over that issue.

We also must recall that we noted at the outset that excessive internal strife at the outset of a civilization could result in a civilization not progressing or coalescing at all. The history of Italy is one such example. It is also true that excessive internal strife can mark the decline of a civilization, as in ancient Greece and Rome. It was amid the internal strife of class-violence that the self-confidence of the once vast Roman and Greek civilizations, which in their times ruled the Mediterranean, was lost. Cynicism had set in in both times and places.

On that point, the great Roman historian Livy, who lived and wrote during the final days of the Roman Republic, wrote:

> I invite the reader's attention to . . . the process of our moral decline, to watch, first, the sinking of the foundations of morality as the old teaching was allowed to lapse, then the rapidly increasing disintegration, then the final collapse of the whole edifice, and the dark dawning of our modern day when we can neither endure our vices nor face the remedies needed to cure them.[5]

More broadly, Sallust said of the ancient Romans:

> The division of the Roman state into warring factions, with all its attendant vices, had originated some years before, as a result of peace and of that material prosperity which men regard as the greatest blessing. Down to the destruction of Carthage the people and the Senate shared the government peaceably and with restraint, and the citizens did not compete for glory or power; fear of its enemies preserved the good morals of the state. But when the people were relieved of this fear, the favourite vices of prosperity—license and pride—appeared as natural consequence. Thus the peace and quiet, which they had longed for in times of adversity proved, when they obtained it, to be even more grievous and bitter than adversity.[6]

Centuries before them, the great Athenian orator Isocrates bemoaned the state of affairs in his once great country when he wrote, "When I was a boy, wealth was regarded as a thing so secure as well as admirable that almost everyone affected to own more property than he actually possessed. . . . Now, on the other hand, a man has to be ready to defend himself against being rich as if it were the worst of crimes."[7]

In the end, while so many fought among themselves in Greece, its borders and democracy fell to the conqueror Philip II of Macedon. As for the Romans and their Republic, they endured what historians have termed "the crisis of the Roman Republic." At the end of that crisis, republican values gave way to the imperial powers of the Caesars.

AMERICA'S SEEDS OF DOUBT

As we contemplate the origins and nature of America's current critical phase, let us briefly consider the issue of slavery again. There were, of course, those who believed slavery was very wrong at our Founding. Revolutionary John Adams, who never owned slaves, described slavery as a "foul contagion in the human character" and as "an evil of colossal magnitude." Adams, who would become the United States' first vice president and second president, said that the American Revolution would never be complete until all slaves were free.[8] In addition to Adams, not long after America declared its independence, throughout the northern colonies, there were legal and legislative efforts to end slavery. As was noted earlier, Vermont outlawed slavery in 1777 and provided voting rights to African American males. The Northern states followed and one by one outlawed the practice before the Civil War. We also noted, however, that the South was twice as rich as the North, and no union would have been possible in 1789 if it was contingent on ending slavery at that time. If it had been tried, excessive internal division likely would have resulted in two countries rather than one.

Importantly, for most of America throughout the 1800s, the existence of slavery did not result in a sizeable percentage of Americans calling into question the very founding of America and its purposes. To many at the time, like Adams, it represented an uncompleted challenge. The same can be said of the 130-plus years it took to provide women with the same voting rights as men. Although the nature of those dynamics is glaring in retrospect, the evolutions of those events took place largely within the social norms of their day—something that is lost on the critics of today.

Further, once progress had been achieved on those issues, that progress was most often seen, *at the time*, as progress for the nation as a whole and in keeping with the foundational purposes—especially when objectively compared with the rest of the world. In a phrase, progress on those issues created a "more perfect union," and as John Adams said, completed an important aspect of the American Revolution. In short, by and large, most Americans saw their country as a work in progress, warts and all.

The same could *not* be said of the fallout from the Great Depression and the growing doubts about capitalism that had been developing in America. As we explore this subject, we must always keep the following in mind. Throughout all of history, the early stages of the commercialization and urbanization of a society upend living patterns, social norms, and families. They have also produced great economic disparities among the affected populace. For example, in his book *The Ugly Renaissance: Sex, Greed, Violence and Depravity in an Age of Beauty*, Alexander Lee writes that "if the Renaissance was an age of cultural angels, it was also a period of worldly demons."[9] Of Florence, the center and financier of the Italian Renaissance, and among the wealthiest cities of its time, Lee writes, perhaps dramatically so:

> Regardless of its wealth, Florence continually struggled to overcome the unpleasant effects of its thriving mercantile trade. The ostentatious displays of wealth indulged by the city's merchants were frequently the object of opprobrium,

not least from the Dominican Friar Girolamo Savonarola, whose attacks on the rich concentrated on their luxurious palaces, extravagant clothing, and lavish private chapels. It all struck a discordant note with the standards of living experienced by the overwhelming majority of ordinary Florentines. As mercantile fortunes rose, the wages of the unskilled fell. Poverty was always around the corner. Begging was rife, and crime was endemic.[10]

In England, the early stages of industrialization brought with it the movements of hundreds of thousands of would-be workers from surrounding areas to work in textile processing factories and associated commercial activities. Between the 1440s and 1800, the percentage of those living in cities of greater than 10,000 people jumped from 3 percent to 20 percent.[11] Since industrialization happened first in England, such mass-movements within a country were unprecedented. No town-turned-city had the experience of planning for such rapid and large movements, let alone a history of housing and feeding so many. When businesses failed or worse, when they set off downturns as often happened in nascent capitalism, the plight of the overcrowded and meagerly paid was made only worse.

The American experience included those same dynamics, *only more so*. Similar to England, the initial movements of people from the countryside to the city resulted in the great deal of dislocation as people lived and looked for jobs in unfamiliar environments and in great proximity. Beyond that though, the great economic freedom afforded the American people during that period, who we have seen were not shackled by class distinctions or government edicts, unleashed an enormous flourish of economic activity. In addition to that, those two societal changes occurred at the same time as the beginning of America's industrialization revolution—in contrast to England, which underwent a more drawn-out commercialization to the industrialization process. Those three dynamics, rapid urbanization, rapid economic growth and industrialization, occurring together in America created enormous societal changes, great wealth, and also very large disparities among Americans—disparities in wealth that simply did not exist when the American economy was based on farming. Remember, *in history, the inhabitants of the countryside always have been more "equal" in circumstances than those of the city.*

History is well aware of the enormous wealth made by the Americans Cornelius Vanderbilt in shipping and railroads, John D. Rockefeller in oil, Andrew Carnegie in steel, and J. P. Morgan in banking, among others. It was said that Vanderbilt's assets were worth as much as 5 percent of all of the money and demand deposits in America at his death in 1877.[12] Rockefeller's 1913 wealth alone is estimated by some to be equal to a staggering three percent of the entire US economy at the time.[13] When the wealth of Carnegie and Morgan was added to Rockefeller's, never in American history had so much wealth been so concentrated in such few hands—nor has it occurred since. By contrast, the wealth of the richest American in 2022, Elon Musk, represented only a quarter of one percent of the US economy, and so much of his wealth was concentrated not in hard assets but in stock.

In contrast to Rockefeller and the other titans of American capitalism, the average income of an American in 1913 was likely just $750 per year. Along with that, the stark conditions of factory workers in the newly urbanized economy were startling and often dangerous, just as they had been in England and every industrializing economy since. In America, those conditions became the subject of the writings of so-called Muckrakers such as Upton Sinclair in his novel *The Jungle*. They chronicled the hardships and conditions of Americans, perhaps to an excess, at least in the mind of Theodore Roosevelt, who was no supporter of American industrialists, among others.

It would take decades for the maturing American economy to disperse its growing wealth. As it did, the economic base of America broadened, and the enormous, and largely unprecedented, middle class of the United States emerged. That dispersement process was accelerated by the lack of entrenched classes. Given America's unique beginning, nowhere else in history had seen or has seen so many succeed without the benefit of class distinction or inherited wealth. Keep in mind that Vanderbilt came from a poor family and began working at eleven years old. Rockefeller was born to a "vagabond" of a father who was rarely at home and sold elixirs to the unwary. Over one hundred years later, the grandson of Jewish emigrants from Austria, Germany, and Poland, Facebook's Mark Zuckerberg, a college dropout, would become one of America's richest billionaires. Meanwhile, nearly 80 percent of America's current millionaires are self-made—they did not receive any inheritance.

THE EARLY POLITICS OF AMERICAN DOUBT

Before the American middle class emerged in the 1900s, during the late 1800s, the power and wealth that had amassed among the few became the controversy of the 1896 election in the person of Williams Jennings Bryan. He was the Democratic nominee for president that year as well as the nominee of the Populist Party. As he undertook the first-ever tour of the country as a presidential candidate, featuring his sharp class-based oratory, Bryan became known as the Great Commoner. Unlike the advent of the Socialist Labor Party (1876) and the Populist Party's efforts before him, William Jennings Bryan's popularity represented a direct and real threat to the monied interests he'd decried—so they stopped them. Rockefeller, Carnegie, and J. P. Morgan cast aside their individual competitive desires to be America's richest person for the joint sake of stopping Bryan. They did so by spending an unheard of $250,000 in a successful campaign against Bryan and in favor William McKinley, who was considered friendly to American business interests.

Despite losing the election, William Jennings Bryan set the stage for the class-based politics that last to this day in America. In his legendary 1896 "Cross of Gold" convention speech, Bryan bellowed:

> There are two ideas of government. There are those who believe that if you just legislate to make the well-to-do prosperous, that their prosperity will leak through on those below. The Democratic idea has been that if you legislate to make the masses prosperous their prosperity will find its way up and through every class that rests upon it.[14]

It was the most direct and largest class-based campaign in American history up to that time. Over 110 years later, Barack Obama and Joe Biden would still speak of a "bottom-up" economy. They based their policies, as has virtually every Democrat since Franklin Delano Roosevelt, on the very same themes as William Jennings Bryan. Bryan's candidacy was truly a sensation for its time and has never been forgotten. Most pertinent to the purposes of this book, as had occurred in ancient Greece and Rome in the critical periods that heralded their decline, Bryan's class-based theme, and those who agreed with him, had planted, if not cultivated, seeds of doubt about the virtue or heroic nature of the American experience.

ECONOMICS, WAR, AND DOUBT

A quarter century after Bryan's oratory, several significant events added to the changing views of America's economic standing. First, in the 1920s, the American economy would take off like rarely before. Those Roaring Twenties, as they came to be known, were an economic boom that was initiated, in significant part, by the lowering of federal income tax rates from a high of 77 percent to 25 percent. Not long before that, in 1916, the federal income tax came into being with a top rate of just 7 percent. In less than two years, it had been raised to 77 percent and a recession predictably followed. Once incentives were restored, however, the boom of the 1920s ensued, along with the first great splurge of American consumerism. Not all Americans, however, viewed that amassing of wealth and overt consumerism with approval. There were those who disdained that unbridled pursuit of economics and, in their view, its undignified showiness. They included numerous intellectuals and artists such Ernest Hemingway, who was part of an expatriate movement that grew out of the doubts about the America in the 1920s.

Then, the stock market crash of 1929 appeared to bring America and its laissez-faire economics to its knees. Although America's economy stabilized months later, the response of the politicians was distinctly unlike those that had gone before. Unbridled capitalism was no longer universally favored. To the contrary, capitalists and their unchecked "greed" were labeled a danger. As we shall see in the next chapter, the doubts of the efficacy of freedom would engender a complete change in America's view of government—a changed view which lasts to this day and fostered a government that does not resemble the limited government of the Founders in nearly any respect.

America at war in the twentieth century would also raise major doubts about its foundational purposes. The wars Americans fought in the first half of the 1900s featured clear rights and wrongs, authoritarians with bad intentions (Hitler), and democracy at risk. Americans could and did unite under those circumstances. The Vietnam War, however, provided no such societal clarity.

As the first US war to unfold on American televisions sets, Americans saw young men die in a faraway place for reasons that left many unconvinced that there was a purpose to American participation in the Vietnam War. That war would eventually bring down a powerful president in Lyndon Johnson in the wake of protests on university campuses around the country. Returning soldiers received few heroes' welcomes like in years past and American media, from news outlets to movies, would turn on the war effort. Along the way, America's Vietnam War efforts were often portrayed as unjust if not worse. The damage would be lasting. Tellingly, no American war since has enjoyed the widespread and historically sustained support of the American people like that of World

War I, World War II, and the Korean War.* To the contrary, *between the end of the Korean War and the Vietnam War, America had crossed the bridge between assurance and doubt.*

MEDIA, TECHNOLOGY, AND DOUBT

All of this brings us now to mass media and its enumerable mediums. Will Durant once mused of a time when the news of the village barely interrupted our lives—and so it was at our Founding when mere pamphlets and small local newspapers of limited reach were customary. Eventually, newspapers became a thriving industry in the 1800s with daily, weekly, and monthly newspapers. There were "commercial papers focused on the world of business and commerce"[15] and political papers. Initially, few such "newspapers" were known throughout the colonies, and the same could be said of writers save for the likes of Benjamin Franklin, Thomas Paine, and Samuel Adams as the Revolution approached.

Contrary to the assumptions of most people, up to the early 1900s, the vast majority of the publications that focused on politics were highly politicized.[16] Indeed, those papers sometimes rose to the level of being "organs of the party" to which they were allied and often were given printing contracts by the political party or candidate that they supported. That period in American history is referred to as the party press era.

Prior to the Revolution, Samuel Adams and James Otis sensationalized the actions of the British in Boston, and Thomas Paine turned many colonists against King George and not always with objectivity. In the run-up to the Civil War, most towns of any significant size had newspapers on both sides of the rhetorical battle. In the South, "Firebreathers" was the name

---

* For a period of time, the first Iraq War garnered very high approval ratings. However, over time that approval was lost.

given to the vitriolic supporters of Southern secession and those who fueled the coming war, while Republican newspapers often preached otherwise.

Nevertheless, the rural nature of American life and the narrow reach of the newspaper medium limited the speed of the effects newspapers had on the American culture for its first hundred years and more.

Today, of course, thanks to the Industrial Revolution, and then the Technological Revolution, the news mediums and their reporting have become ubiquitous. We literally carry news outlets in our hands in the form of smartphones. Despite a respite in the first half of the 1900s from intensely partisan news outlets, the 1960s, and especially during the Vietnam War, saw news outlets return to the historical norm of partisan reporting. In the years since then, the whispers of the village have been replaced by the bullhorn of the "national" news. What happens today in Florida also happens immediately in the homes of Californians and every other state in the form of instantly published reports. As the news media have grown, and as the competition for viewers, if not adherents, has increased, reporting regularly sensationalizes for effect and no subject seems immune from media's reach. As a result, the modern media, again with the aid of technology, has quickened the pace of societal change.

In not unprecedented fashion, they most often push the American culture ever further away from the cultural norms and values of its past. Keep in mind that throughout much of history, those within the media and the arts, who most often lived in urbanized areas, have been more socially liberated than society as a whole. The inhabitants of Athens, its politicians, and its artists were more liberated than those who lived in the Greek countryside. The same could be said of the city of Rome compared to its colonies, and that is true in the America of the twenty-first century.

With respect to artists, from the plays of Euripides in ancient Greece to Shakespeare of the late 1500s, from poets such as Horace from the end of the Roman Republic to the storyteller Chaucer in the late 1300s, they all wrote of lives far more daring than the lives of those who tilled the land or nurtured a family. They have often been critics of the culture as well. It is the laborer, the manager, and the financier that construct the economy, whose profits, in turn, fund the artists who often later demean, if not debase, the stoic culture that gave birth to them.

America today is not different in that regard except in speed and scale. Today, the internet gives license to millions to seek attention with ever more shocking, if not indecent, language and art. Where once television extolled the traditional values of *Father Knows Best* in the 1950s and into the 1970s with *Little House on the Prairie*, as the twentieth century came to a close, television and movies, on balance, became advocates for social change and their brand of social justice. They came to favor network shows such as *Modern Family*, which featured a same-sex family, and cable television, which offered *The L Word*, exploring what some have termed "queer sexuality." Not always and everywhere, but with an ever-greater frequency and explicitness, the modern media has pushed a social agenda unlike the lives of most Americans, and a deep contrast to the 1950s, let alone the 1650s. In the process, the critical views of which the great historical philosophers wrote have gained greater currency.

AMERICAN EDUCATION AND DOUBT

As we continue to survey America's growing critical period, we must also consider the sea change in American education and what that dynamic says about the American civilization today. As noted earlier, American education began in the home with the Bible, and where available, it was originally associated with religious institutions. By the time of the colonization of America, Europe had had great universities for centuries. The University of Bologna was founded in 1088—long before the American continent became the subject of European competition. When they arrived in America, the Europeans almost immediately set about establishing such universities in the new colonies. Harvard, for instance, was founded in 1636 by the Puritans.

Harvard's mission statement, given in 1642, was clearly evangelical:

> "Everyone shall consider as the main end of his life and studies, to know God and Jesus Christ, which is eternal life. John 17:3." The Harvard motto, from 1650, emphasized its core Christian commitment: "In Christi Gloriam" ("For the glory of Christ").[17]

The same could be said of the founding of Yale by Connecticut Congregationalists in 1701, Princeton by Presbyterians in 1746, and many, many others. In those early times, Harvard and the like were funded by members of their founding churches. Over time, however, the American education system would move away from its religious moorings and become funded by government. With that, but not all at once, the focus of education would eventually change. The explosion in publicly funded and then publicly administered education would occur in the 1900s. Where once schools were dedicated to the glory of Christ, prayer in the school would be eliminated and God, contrary to the views of the Founders, would be forced from the public square by due process of law. Meanwhile, the *New York Times* would write of the "mainstreaming of Marxism in colleges" in 1989,[18] a process that was accelerated by the doubt that the 1920s and the Great Depression spread.

Along the way, the three "Rs" of education—reading, writing, and arithmetic—once the focus of the American education, would become deemphasized. The teaching of American history waned as "civics" gave way to "social studies"—a dynamic that accelerated in the 1960s. In the process, the proficiency of students nationwide has suffered and fallen noticeably behind international competitors like China, whose students frequent American universities. In America, at the time of the writing of this book, there is considerable turmoil over public education, as falling test scores and a lack of proficiency in those three Rs troubles parents from the inner cities to suburbia and beyond. Calls for charter schools continue to gain ground. Meanwhile, even America's once religious universities present views on the existence of God, the validity of freedom of speech, capitalism, limited government, socialism and Marxism that are unrecognizable from America's earlier days.

CANCEL CULTURE AND DOUBT

As we close this chapter, we must also consider the rhetoric and actions of those in the media, politicians, and others, in the vernacular of the day, who seek to "cancel" the American Founders and other aspects of American history and culture. Their actions are also evidence of an America in doubt.

Previously, I noted that monuments to the Founders define Washington, DC. The very name "Washington, DC" was in reverence to the father of the United States, George Washington. Now, however, there is a concerted effort to erase or at least change the legacy of the Founders and many other aspects of American history.

For instance, a statue of Thomas Jefferson was removed from City Hall in New York. The Virginia Department of Education considered a proposal "to remove references to George Washington as the 'father of our country' in state schools, underscoring the need to 'tell our history accurately.'"[19] They also wanted to strike "the reference to James Madison as the 'father of our Constitution.'"[20] In San Francisco, there was a proposal to paint over a school mural of George Washington. Meanwhile, "the homes of Jefferson and Madison, Monticello and Montpelier, respectively, are going 'woke' and being turned against their legacies."[21]

Similarly, the 1619 Project, created in 2019, seeks to redefine all of American history on a narrative that would abandon the traditional view of America's founding "by placing the consequences of slavery and the contributions of Black Americans at the very center of the United States' national narrative."[22] In doing so, the founders of the project almost explicitly seek to teach American students, using highly disputed claims, that America is not exceptional. To the contrary, they believe America to lack virtue—a position quite in keeping with the decline of a civilization.

Consistent with that, one of the most visible aspects of the American Left, known as the "Squad," four congresswomen by the names of Reps. Ilhan Omar of Minnesota, Alexandria Ocasio-Cortez of New York, Rashida Tlaib of Michigan, and Ayanna Pressley of Massachusetts, lent their endorsements to a Democratic candidate in Wisconsin who wrote that the "'founders' intent' has been used as the basis of oppression for too long. We should be making decisions based on the future, not the raw ideals of a colonial, slave holding, sexist past."[23] Perhaps there can be no more direct contrarian view of America's past than to assert that it is wholly illegitimate because of the manner in which the Europeans came to these shores.

Similarly, we can also note that, since the 1960s, the America flag has become the object of controversy, insults and even burning. The Supreme Court declared that flag burning is protected free speech activity even after Congress voted criminal penalties for such actions—a vote that touched off a fresh round of flag burning. Meanwhile, in American schools the recitation of the Pledge of Allegiance to the American flag has diminished, and even places where the flying of the American flag has become the subject of disputes.

Finally, we would be remiss not to mention the fate of "nationalism" in America. In its historical meaning, the word connotes "a sense of national consciousness . . . exalting one nation above all others and placing primary emphasis on promotion of its culture and interests as opposed to those of other nations," as stated in Webster's dictionary.[24] Simply stated, no civilization has been founded or succeeded without nationalism. Without a common purpose and identity, there is no unity.

Today, however, a slice of modern America, especially in the media, believes that nationalism is a sin. Perhaps they felt freed to say so when they heard President Obama state that "I believe in American exceptionalism, just as I suspect that the Brits believe in British exceptionalism, and the Greeks believe in Greek exceptionalism." In other words, America was no more exceptional than any other civilization. Of course, that is a far cry from the words of prior American presidents, such as Abraham Lincoln, who truly believed that "in giving freedom to the slave, we assure freedom to the free—honorable alike in what we give, and what we preserve. We shall nobly save, or meanly lose, the last best hope of earth."[25]

★ ★ ★

We have now considered many aspects of America's prolonged period of growth. America was busy building, as Saint-Simon would say, for over four hundred years. Along the way, millions of immigrants were assimilated into America's culture of opportunity. America became the world's most wealthy, productive, and dominant civilization. It provided the widest sustained democratization of a nation in history. Its products and culture landed in every port and city in the world. Civic pride and nationalistic fervor were real. That was America's organic phase of purpose, faith, and growth.

Now we have seen how America has firmly entered a critical phase. Nationalism is decried. Exceptionalism is questioned. Skepticism abounds and no longer is there a strong consensus about America's present or past. Many curse America's motives and actions in coming to be. In the chapters ahead, we shall delve deeper into those differences on such topics as religion, government, and culture. For now, we likely should agree that, *at the beginning of a civilization, a people will do anything to survive. Toward the end, they apologize for doing it.*

CHAPTER 10

America, Capitalism, and Socialism

Democracy and socialism have nothing in common but one word, equality. But notice the difference: while democracy seeks equality in liberty, socialism seeks equality in restraint and servitude.

—**Alexis de Tocqueville,** speech to France's Constituent Assembly, September 12, 1848

As we have seen, the America of today is quite unlike the America of its founding. Once a civilization of sustenance farmers, very small towns, and quite limited governments, it has become an industrial and technological society dominated by cities, mass media, and governments that comprise nearly half the economy. Despite starting centuries behind England, the United States roared past England to become the world's largest economy in 1871 and has been the world's largest economy ever since.¹ Even before then, in 1830, Americans' per capita income was already the highest in the world.²

AMERICAN GROWTH AND INNOVATION

At the turn of the twenty-first century, with just 6 percent of the world's population, America produced an incredible 30 percent of worldwide goods and services. As for their standard of living, Americans topped the list of the OECD's measurement of actual individual consumption,* which measures total individual consumption of goods and services. We have already noted that more than half of Americans' purchases are for nonessential items. Remarkably, the *bottom* 10 percent of Americans have an OECD Better Life Index rating equal to or better than the *top* 10 percent of those in Italy, Israel, Russia, Portugal, Brazil, Turkey, and Mexico.³

For centuries, the American economy benefited from limited government, a relatively low tax system, sparse regulations, the rule of law, and an abundance of labor and natural resources. We can add to that the US patent law system, which was instituted on the first day of the First Congress and which encouraged and protected innovation. Taking advantage of all of that, American entrepreneurs and their genius for inventions changed life on earth while lifting the standard of living of everyone regardless of their country or continent.

Among the many American important inventions were Samuel Morse's telegraph of 1832, which became Alexander Graham Bell's telephone of

---

* According to the OECD, "Actual individual consumption is measured by the total value of household final consumption expenditure, NPISH final consumption expenditure and government expenditure on individual consumption goods and services." OECD, "Concepts and Classifications," OECD.Stat, accessed April 23, 2024, https://stats.oecd.org/OECDStat_Metadata/ShowMetadata.ashx?Dataset=NAAG_2015_NOV15&Lang=en&Coords=[INDICATOR].[P41CPC].

1876, both of which forever changed and accelerated communication. In 1859, the American oil rig unleashed oil production, which has fueled the world ever since. Thomas Edison's commercially viable light bulb began to light the world in the 1880s and extended the day deep into the night in a manner safer and cheaper than oil. The American Wright brothers took to the air with their 1903 Wright Flyer and, far beyond transporting people around the globe, the trade routes of the world began to take a straight line of efficiency. Henry Ford's 1913 moving assembly line transformed not only the automobile industry but all of manufacturing, which vastly lowered prices for consumer products. Then, in 1947, the invention of the transistor, the foundation of all that is considered to be "tech," spawned an entire industry that is nearly one-tenth of the American economy today, including the digital computer and the internet—also of American derivation.

Those represent just the beginning of what Americans, of all backgrounds, have invented that have brought hitherto unknown luxuries to all of the world in the last 150 years. We should also note such other American inventions as the sewing machine, the lawn mower, the ironing board, the vacuum cleaner, the dishwasher, the air conditioner, moving pictures, the guitar, the microwave oven, GPS, commercial plastics, the revolver and repeating rifle, structural steel bridges, gas-powered cars, rockets, frozen foods, nylon, atomic reaction, lasers, optic fiber, bar codes, anesthesia, vaccines, pacemakers, the artificial heart, and so much more. Those many inventions transformed and eased the lives of countless millions across the globe—in addition to raising the world's standard of living.

As the 2020s got underway, nearly 40 percent of Americans worked at least partially from home. On the average day, 96 percent of Americans over the age of fifteen engage in "some sort of leisure and sport activity, such as watching TV, socializing, or exercising."[4] In addition to standard appliances, 83 percent of American households have a microwave, over 85 percent of Americans have a smartphone, with 97 percent owning a cell phone.[5] With those luxuries, the Americans of today live with a level of ease not seen by anyone in centuries past.

Indeed, chapter 6 quotes historian H. W. Brand, who wrote that American capitalism of the 1800s and early 1900s "lifted the standard of living of ordinary people to a plane associated . . . with aristocracy."[6] American capitalism fostered the unprecedently large American middle class, which included "a clear majority of American adults."[7] We cited the statistics that at the outset of the 1900s, Americans spent just 20 percent of their income on nonnecessities. By the end of the century, however, that percentage had risen to over 50 percent.[8] Despite that historical success, discontent with capitalism and an affinity for socialism is occurring in America, as it has in other times and places.

AMERICANS' CHANGING VIEWS TOWARD CAPITALISM AND SOCIALISM

Given such accomplishments and levels of personal consumption, why is American capitalism losing favorability in the twenty-first century, especially among the young? Also, why are so many promoting socialism and planned economies, despite the records of socialist countries throughout history and the current examples of Cuba, Venezuela, and Russia?

There are several answers to those questions. In significant part, it is a genuine desire by some, as have others in the past, to address real and perceived inequities, which become apparent as wealth rises in any given civilization. For still others, it is a result of a lack of historical understanding compounded by what is taught and not taught in American schools. For still others, it is from their desire to dictate the lives of others. Finally, it is also a function of the number of Americans receiving government benefits or spoils.

As we address this issue, let us note some examples of the level of favorability among Americans of socialism and capitalism in the twenty-first century. First, it is worth noting that the socialist part of America was founded in 1912—after the industrialization of America. The appeal of the socialist often finds a more receptive audience, not during the self-responsibility of a civilization's agrarian phase, but, instead, as disparity in income appears during its commercial phase.

At the height of the riches of Rockefeller, Morgan, and Carnegie, the Socialist Party garnered over 901,000 votes in the 1912 election—the year Woodrow Wilson became president. In 1920, its presidential candidate received over 913,000 votes when Warren G. Harding became president, which equated to one-tenth of the votes that the Democratic nominee James Cox received. Those were the highwater marks for the Socialist Party. However, combined with newly formed communist parties in America, there is little doubt that in the post-industrialization era, before the America middle class fully emerged, a sizeable number of Americans were sympathetic to the socialist/communist message.

Decades later, although the Socialist and Communist parties have all but disappeared on the national stage, sympathies for socialist views have gained ground. In the years before the publication of this book, according to Pew Research, in 2019 as many as 42 percent of Americans viewed socialism in at least a somewhat positive light. The positive views of capitalism, on the other hand, while still over 50 percent, were declining.[†] Predictably, American Democrats (60 percent) viewed socialism more favorably than Republicans (14 percent).[9]

America's youth have an even more favorable view of socialism. A 2019 survey found that more than 64 percent of those born between 1997 and 2012 were "somewhat/extremely likely to vote for a socialist candidate" and 70 percent of those born between 1981–1996 had that opinion.[10]

---

† In 2022, 36 percent of US adults said they view socialism somewhat (30 percent) or very (6 percent) positively, and while a majority of the public (57 percent) continued to view capitalism favorably, that is eight percentage points lower than in 2019 (65 percent). See Pew Research Center, "Modest Declines in Positive Views of 'Socialism' and 'Capitalism' in U.S.," September 19, 2022, https://www.pewresearch.org/politics/2022/09/19/modest-declines-in-positive-views-of-socialism-and-capitalism-in-u-s/.

Similarly, a 2023 survey found that 37 percent of college/university students believed that world decline was being caused by "not enough government rules, regulations, and abilities to redistribute resources," as opposed to 27 percent who believed it was caused by "not enough economic and political freedom." In that same survey, 53 percent of college/university students believed that US decline over the last fifty years has been caused by "not enough government programs to make sure resources are used wisely."[11]

Finally, given those numbers and socialism's historical record, the question arises as to what perspective Americans and its students, have been provided about socialism, America and the world at large. Have they considered such questions as: What was the world like before capitalism? What benefits did America derive from capitalism? Is the standard of living in America better or worse than elsewhere? Are the rights of US citizens greater than elsewhere? What is socialism historical record?

Without answering those comparative questions, many in America have come to believe that their civilization's past was "bad," if not worse, and that other places were better. It also has led to demands that the past be corrected legally and monetarily at the expense of future generations.

Based on available statistics, it would appear that American students have not been provided with a sufficient historical perspective about actual American history. Recall that in American history, schooling usually started with the family and then moved to religious institutions before it became a private luxury for some. As the American government grew, schooling became financed by taxation and, eventually, government became the primary provider of schooling. Along the way, government institutions and government funded institutions adopted different ethos than the private sector entities they supplanted.

That has become most evident in American public schooling today, in which the teaching of American civics and history have diminished.[12] "As of 2018, fourteen states did not require high school students to complete any type of civics or government course. Twenty-eight states require[d] a single semester, and only eight states require[d] high school students to take a yearlong course in civics or government."[13]

Not surprisingly, therefore, a report by the National Assessment of Educational Progress, indicated that just "18 percent of American high school kids were proficient in US history."[14] According to a 2016 survey by the Annenberg Public Policy Center, only a quarter of Americans are able to name the three branches of government.[15] Further, a 2017 poll found that 37 percent could not "name any of the rights guaranteed under the First Amendment."[16] American education woes do not stop there. In 2023, in 40 percent of Baltimore City high schools where the state exam was given, no student was proficient in math.[17] Nationwide, in 2009, only 26 percent of twelfth grade students were proficient in math.[18]

Returning to views on capitalism and socialism, it has also become evident that school systems are more populated with those philosophically inclined to support government over the private sector. For instance, faculty at American colleges and universities have increased their leftward lean with a 2016–2017 finding that "60 percent of the faculty identified as either far left or liberal compared to just 12 percent being conservative or far right."[19] With regard to political donations, one study found that "federal Democratic candidates and groups received 96 percent of total donations from Ivy League professors in the 2022 midterm elections."[20] That number hit 99 percent for USC in 2023.[21] Even in America's political swing states in 2020, "Democrats raised 95 percent of all the funds collected from faculty members in America's most politically competitive states."[22]

Apparently, even primary schools are not immune to political bias either. For instance, in 2023, one school administration, the Colorado Education Association, "the state affiliate of the . . . National Education Association," passed a resolution stating that it "believes that capitalism requires exploitation of children, public schools, land, labor, and/or resources."[23] Given the above, we should not be surprised at students' changing views on capitalism and socialism. However, there is much more to the changing views on socialism and capitalism than what is occurring in American schools. Stated simply, America as a whole seems unaware of the history of poverty, capitalism, and socialism.

A SHORT HISTORY OF THE PERVASIVE POVERTY OF MAN

Any serious debate regarding capitalism and socialism in history must start by acknowledging that, throughout the vast majority of history, the lot of almost all human beings was one of persistent and often desperate poverty. That is the plain, harsh truth of history. Indeed, a remarkably tiny percentage of humans lived in the luxury of their time during the thousands upon thousands of years before the 1900s.

According to Professor Steven M. Beaudoin, in his work *Poverty in World History*, in the premodern world (before Christ), "chronic hunger and undernourishment . . . was the most common form of poverty." He adds that, "given the limitations on agricultural surpluses, the vast majority of the world's population could easily slide" into what he termed "conjunctural poverty," poverty brought on by circumstances.[24]

> They had the physical means to support themselves in optimal conditions . . . but rarely produced enough to withstand variations in their precarious living conditions. In good years the meager surplus they produced help provide for the destitute and structural poor, and the elite, those who might join the conjunctural poor if the crisis was severe and long in duration. The history of poverty is to be found, then, not just among the destitute and infirm, but also among the multitudes whose lives weaved back and forth across the line separating hunger and subsistence.[25]

As we moved into the centuries after Christ, many lived in socio-economic systems, ruled by monarchs or despots, that provided little freedom and even less transferable wealth. As much as 70 percent of Roman subjects, at the height of the Empire, rose barely above Professor Steven M. Beaudoin's description.[26] Moving on to medieval Europe, Professor Dorsey Armstrong notes that, in and around the year 1000, 90 to 95 percent of Europe's inhabitants were dependent on "subsistence farming."[27] What that meant, according to Professor Armstrong, was that

> the margin between bounty and starvation was painfully razor thin. If one year of frost came late or the rains were unexpectedly heavy or the summer was too cool or too hot, then the crops failed and people didn't eat. Archaeologists examining skeletons from this period see clear evidence of malnutrition by today's standards and evidence also of back-breaking labor.[28]

As for the political/economic structure of society, prior to the 1700s, most people lived in a system where those in political power—the king, nobles, gentry, and churches—also owned the greatest accumulations of land, which was the wealth of that age and of almost of all other times and places before it. Your service to them was often required and just as often you would be tied indefinitely to their land to produce for yourself and them. In exchange, you putatively received protection from the roaming bandits and foreign armies of the age unless, of course, you were pressed into service by them and risked, if not lost, your life. Those circumstances were not confined to the West. Egypt, India, China and most everywhere in the world experienced some form of that political/economic structure.

It is also important to understand that, at their height, those systems jealously kept economic and political power among a very few. Land meant wealth and power and that was usually redistributed among the rich and powerful—most often through death, either by the passing of a monarch or a lord, the conquest of war or sometimes through marriage. Even then, the masses were excluded from getting their overworked hands on the title to meaningful lands. Under those circumstances, social mobility was quite rare and, not surprisingly, almost all of the poor remained relatively poor—generation after generation after generation.

CAPITALISM MADE DEMOCRACY POSSIBLE

True democracy was not possible under those socioeconomic conditions, which conditions prevailed for thousands of years. *Democracy, defined here as the ability of the masses to effectively participate in and choose their government and its policies, cannot take hold where those in control of the economy also are in charge of the government.* Thus, whether under the communism of the twentieth-century Soviets, or the socialist emperor Diocletian's Rome of 300 AD, who nationalized industries, or under the self-declared gods of Egypt's ruling Ptolemies, who relied on slaves and a highly regulated economy, *when those in charge of the government also own and rule the economy, they hoard both the economic and the political wealth of the age.* Political and economic inequality under such systems is replete and often with pervasive and persistent poverty for the great masses who have no effective political voice.

The emergence of commercialization and freer markets changed that near historical constant and made democracy possible. That dynamic started on the margins of those controlled economies. Here and there, individuals scratched out a living with private property, as opposed to lands of others, selling food surpluses or low-cost goods. In fits and starts, they clawed away economic self-determination for themselves and others, often making their way to cities in the process. When they became successful enough, they turned farms into agricultural enterprises and the selling of goods in carts into retail stores. Occasionally, that dynamic occurred with great bursts when the Medicis of Florence, the Rothschilds of Paris, or the Morgans of New York financed markets with untold millions. Even with their push, however, it was largely the victory of countless and far less well-off individuals who allowed free enterprise to take hold. Over time, commercial and middle classes appeared—in a limited degree in the Florence of the 1400s, to a greater degree in the England of the 1800s and in the greatest degree in the America of the 1900s.

It is a fact of history, however, that *until those free markets of capitalism emerged, the lifting of the poor into a dynamic middle class had never occurred.* With commercialization, movable goods and services, along with money, became the new wealth. With that change, the merchant, the inventor, and the artist could become as rich as the landowner. In the process, the inhabitants of the globe today, to a large degree, live with luxuries never imagined by the rich of just one hundred years ago, including access to advanced healthcare, safe water, consumer products, and more.

With that, and just as importantly, *the advent of commercialization not only produced untold commercial goods and luxuries but also allowed, for the first time in history, for the meaningful separation of economic power from political power.* That statement cannot be overstated and is worth a second read.

In time, the economic maturity of a commercial class and a middle class begets desires among them for a political say—nowhere more importantly than in America where its presidents were not kings. That unfolding dynamic not only empowers people to speak before their town councils but also allows political titans such as Abraham Lincoln to emerge from poverty. Plainly stated, there are no Lincolns among state-owned political economies.

In that way and sundry others, a true, balanced democracy is born of markets that are more free than the centralized economies of monarchs, dictators, and socialists. That freedom to choose and to exercise self-determination—the political and economic expressions of free will—are ennobling. That right not to be oppressed is a dignity made possible only by economic freedom. *We must not forget that it was the success of Northern capitalism and its commercial prowess that empowered the North to end slavery among plantations of the South.*

In America, as the 1900s progressed, economic power became dispersed among millions—largely away from the centers of government. Even the powers of government were initially diffuse in America among the state and local governments of the fifty states—many of which were hundreds if not thousands of miles from Washington, DC. That dispersement of power was essential to the success of the American Republic. However, as we shall see, in the last fifty years, the combination of the centralization of power and the growing alliance of government and special interests is simultaneously diminishing the effective democracy and ending the freedoms that were the foundations of early America.

CONDITIONS UNDER AMERICAN CAPITALISM

History is quite clear on one subject: The human experience is imperfect. There have been countless tragedies, man-made and otherwise, and there will continue to be such tragedies because the human experience cannot be made perfect. Improved yes, perfected no. So, at this stage, let us consider two of the main complaints made by critics of capitalism throughout history and today in America: the working conditions under capitalism and the issue of "inequality." As we do, we will again ask, "Compared to what?"

As for working conditions, there is little doubt that, throughout history, *regardless of the locale*, early commercialization, and especially early industrialization, produces difficult, dirty and sometimes rather dangerous working conditions. Previously, we noted how those conditions in America were highlighted by the Muckraker journalists. It is also true that working hours, in the early development of a commercial economy, tend be quite long and arduous. Those conditions, along with disparity in pay, have given rise to labor unions throughout history, which have fought for and obtained improved conditions and pay—especially at the outset of commercialization and industrialization.

As for the long hours of early capitalism, we also know that the hours families spent working on the farm were no less as long than those of early capitalism. Entire families worked dawn to dusk. Even today, family farmers still work very long hours—in many cases significantly longer than the work week of nonagricultural jobs. Indeed, "in January 2024, the average working week for all employees on private nonfarm payrolls in the United States was at 34.1 hours."[29] Note the reference to "nonfarm payrolls," which is an acknowledgment that life on the farm remains arduous and long. One need only visit a family farm to find how little has changed over the centuries, with regard to how hard those families work, including children. Meanwhile, jobs go unfilled in the American economy. At the start of 2024, there were some "9.5 million job openings in the U.S., but only 6.5 million unemployed workers."[30]

Now let us consider child labor. We previously noted that child labor was once prevalent, but not unique, to America. Children also worked from dawn to dusk and we cannot forget that, when America was a farm economy, young children were "bound" out to apprentices before becoming teenagers—sometimes as young as eight years old. After industrialization, children worked in the often-harrowing factories of early capitalism—around the globe. In American, "In 1890, more than 18 percent of children ages 10 to 15 were employed."[31]

As commercialization advanced in America, and societal wealth rose, child labor was restricted. In 1938, child labor was regulated in America—although not on the family farm. The Northern Hemisphere of the 1900s world did largely the same. As a matter of historical fact, no such restrictions were prevalent in the early agrarian phases of civilizations. The same could be said of the poorer countries of the world today.

According to World Vision, "nearly 1 in 10 children worked in child labor in 2020."[32] In Africa, conditions are worse than that. According to the International Labour Organization, "The 2016 Global Estimates of Child Labour indicate that one-fifth of all African children are involved in child labour, a proportion more than twice as high as in any other region.

Nine per cent of African children are in hazardous work, again highest of all the world's regions."[33] Of course, commercialization in Africa has not matured as it has in other regions of the world and the African countries are much poorer than their Northern counterparts.

In the final analysis, it can fairly be said that, as civilizations transition from an agricultural economy to early capitalism to mature capitalism, that transition occurs from very difficult conditions on the farm to the different and often difficult commercial, manufacturing, and urban conditions of early capitalism. History is more aware of the latter difficulties for several reasons. First, the lights of concentrated cities are more glaring on work conditions than the conditions of dispersed farmlands. Second, as we have seen, income disparity is greater in commercial societies, where innovations and opportunities multiply endlessly. The America of 1700 saw much less income disparity than that of 1900 and today. Third, invariably, in the commercial and industrial phase of a civilization, the means of communication and the forms of media multiply and, often, highlight the conditions of the city to a much greater extent than the conditions of any farm. History also knows, however, that if capitalism is permitted to run its course long enough, greater wealth and improved conditions have occurred throughout history—as we shall see in the coming pages.

AMERICA'S RESPONSE TO DISPARITY

Disparity in outcomes is a constant of history, politically and economically. There has never been a place on earth where equality of outcome for all has existed. Of course, there have been many attempts in history to reach such an outcome. Even the American pilgrims engaged in a collectivist experiment. It failed, however, because, in the words of the head of the colony, Governor Bradford, it "was found to breed confusion and discontent and retard much employment that would have been to their benefit and comfort."[34]

That dynamic has been repeated over and over in history. In modern-day Venezuela, the imposition of socialist central planning has seen that country go from being the fourth wealthiest country in the world in the 1950s to "poorer than it was prior to the 1920s."³⁵ In 2021, the BBC published an article titled "Venezuela Crisis: Three in Four in Extreme Poverty." That articles notes that "according to the report, the National Survey of Living Conditions (Encovi), extreme poverty rose to 76.6 percent, from 67.7 percent last year. . . . Since 2014, the country has suffered from shortages of basic supplies and hyperinflation."³⁶ Nearby in Cuba, according to Human Rights Watch, decades after socialism took hold there, "the government continues to repress and punish virtually all forms of dissent and public criticism, as Cubans endure a dire economic crisis affecting their rights."³⁷

Meanwhile, in Russia, the number of Vladimir Putin critics who died violently or in suspicious ways, according to a *Washington Post* article, reached double digits between 2003 and 2015.³⁸ In 2024, that number rose to twenty. Of course, that pales in comparison to the socialist/communist death tolls of Hitler and his National Socialist Party (17 million or more people, not including war deaths). The death toll from Stalin's Russia varies between 6 million to 20 million. However, "both Hitler and Stalin were outdone by Mao Zedong. From 1958 to 1962, his Great Leap Forward policy led to the deaths of up to 45 million people."³⁹

History, however, is not always so bleak. As we further consider the issue of income and wealth disparity, we know that wherever and whenever commercial societies have been free to produce great riches throughout the ages, such as in Athens, Florence, Rome, London, and New York, *the inequality of abilities in people has led to an inequality in income and wealth.* When those differences become significant, almost universally throughout time, cries emerge to address such disparities along with the plight of the poor in the cities. Keep in mind that the American civilization had no federally funded welfare programs in its first four centuries. In America, as elsewhere in history, toward the beginning of a civilization, those cries are usually met by the charity of individuals and churches. As economies and their governments correspondingly grow in complexity, along with their cities, governments take an ever-larger role—sometimes going so far as to regulate and then crowd out private charity.

America today, of course, has been in the throes of that latter dynamic for over a century, which explains why government is now the largest industry in America. Also, with well over half of the American population *voting for or receiving* some money from their governments—from jobs, to government contracts, to education, to healthcare, to social security, to Medicare, and countless other benefits in between—for so long a period of time, we cannot be surprised that so many Americans' views of government have changed over the centuries. So much so that it cannot be surprising that socialism's favorability grows with the growth in government and capitalism's favorability correspondingly declines.

THE GROWTH IN THE US GOVERNMENT AND ITS CONSEQUENCES

So, how much have American governments changed in the last fifty years? Figure 10.1 is a chart of the spending of all of the American governments, local, state, and federal, since 1900. The explosion in spending is unmistakable.

Obviously, the American governments of today are dramatically different than those of the early days of the American civilization. In number, size, and reach, the United States' governments of today are nearly ubiquitous where once, by the Founders' design, they were limited. Those governments, their spending and the costs of their regulations, comprise nearly half of the US economy. With that spending comes a corresponding increase in government power.

Despite the designs and efforts of the Founders for limited government, several basic laws of history have been at work to thwart their design. First, *always and everywhere, power tends to centralize over time—especially*

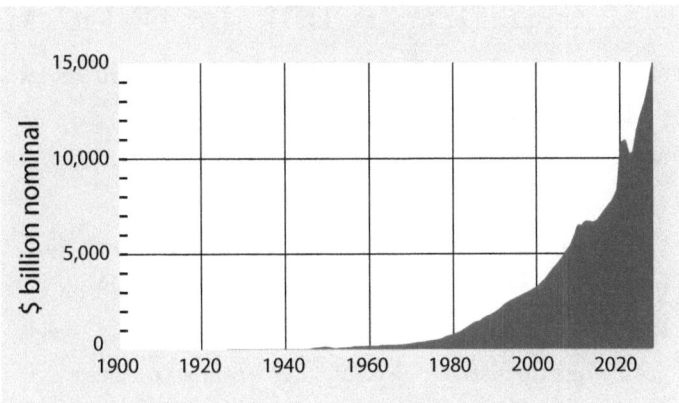

Figure 10.1. US government spending, 1900–2028. (Data source: Christopher Chantrill, "Government Spending Chart," US Government Spending, accessed April 16, 2024, https://usgovernmentspending.com/spending_chart_1900_2028USb_25s2li011mcny_F0t.)

in the hands of politicians. Second, as civilizations commercialize, if not industrialize, and as wealth rises and society complicates, the cries for government to regulate commerce and address the "wrongs" of society proliferate. *Limited government has always been more plausible in the simplicity and self-responsibility of the countryside than in the complexity of large cities.*

Third, those cries are loudest during crises, which tend to accelerate the growth of governments and the centralization of power. Finally, over time, the citizens of free governments often lose sight of the private sources of income and wealth in favor of government "benefits" that come at the cost of higher taxation, which too often they believe is at someone else's expense. Once that latter process starts, ambitious politicians seek to buy votes with ever more government spoils. With those historical dynamics in mind, let us now look at some of the seminal moments in American history along the path from limited government to what can be described as a growing tendency toward socialism in America today.

THE RISE OF THE US FEDERAL GOVERNMENT

If we look back at the start of the American civilization, again, we are struck by Harlow Giles Unger's description, in his book *Lion of Liberty: Patrick Henry and the Call to a New Nation*:

> Settlers isolated in the hamlets and woods of New England had lived free of almost all government authority for more than 150 years . . . cooperating with each other, collectively governing themselves, electing their militia commanders and church pastors and turning to assemblies of elders to mediate occasional disputes. . . . Like Patrick Henry, they had lived in freedom, without government intrusion in their lives and saw little need for it.[40]

Soon, however, powerful Americans saw a need for more government. As you read what follows, keep in mind these words of the early American statesman Daniel Webster: "Good intentions will always be pleaded for any assumption of power."[41] The same could be said for the "need for public safety" or the "welfare of the people at large" or other similar claims about the public or common good.

After the colonists declared their independence, they hurriedly created individual state governments—most by the end of 1776, while the Revolution was underway. With the end of that successful Revolutionary War, a weak federal government, as we discussed, was then created under the Articles of Confederation. It was so weak that the federal government had no power to tax. Between the states and the federal government, far more power resided in the states.

That balance of governments changed in response to crises throughout American history. Previously, we noted how Alexander Hamilton feared war between certain colonies. George Washington believed the new Constitution was needed or the next would be "drawn in blood." The reasons for such division included a growing national economy that sought increased trade across state lines and abroad. That dynamic created intense competition between states, including over tax dollars from tariffs—there was no income tax at the time. Conflicting state laws and currencies also hampered commerce. Meanwhile, state court systems were favoring debtors over creditors in those difficult economic times and state governments were printing money, which only further complicated the stability of trade. *The Founders' response to the crisis was to centralize more power in the federal government at the expense of the state governments*—a dynamic that would infuriate Patrick Henry and many more. In the 240 years since, that dynamic of centralizing power combined with the growing complexity of society and crises (even or especially those created by government) would result in ever larger governments time and again.

The added complexity of commerce and banking provided another example in American history. In successive fashion, and in an attempt to bring stability to the early American banking systems and facilitate growing trade, Congress chartered the private Bank of the United States for twenty years (1791 to 1811) and then the Second Bank of the United States (1816 to 1836), despite Jefferson's unconstitutionality argument. Nevertheless, when many banks failed in the Panic of 1819, causing severe economic conditions, the people of that period did not expect their governments to provide them direct assistance to replace the money they lost to failed banks.

Of course, we now know that most of America at that time lived and worked in the countryside and provided for themselves. Thus, there was no great government response at the time to those bank failures, and James Monroe, in 1820, despite those economic troubles, became one of only two US presidents in American history to win reelection unopposed—George Washington being the other. That lack of a federal response to a significant crisis would be among the last.

In 1862, amid the Civil War, President Lincoln signed the first federal income tax into law—a law that later would be declared unconstitutional by the Supreme Court. However, it served its purpose during a crisis. After the Civil War, in unprecedented and likely unconstitutional fashion, it was the federal government that forcibly shaped and created the new state governments of the South, while the Union Army was encamped throughout the South.

Thereafter, the repeated bank crises of the second half of the 1800s centralized even more powers in the federal government. According to the Federal Reserve:

> Between 1863 and 1913, eight banking panics occurred in the money center of Manhattan. The panics in 1884, 1890, 1899, 1901, and 1908 were confined to New York and nearby cities and states. The panics in 1873, 1893, and 1907 spread throughout the nation. Regional panics also struck the midwestern states of Illinois, Minnesota, and Wisconsin in 1896; the mid-Atlantic states of Pennsylvania and Maryland in 1903; and Chicago in 1905.[42]

One result of those numerous banking crises was the creation of the Federal Reserve in 1913. Today, that institution exerts enormous control over America's money supply and interest rates—despite being nowhere in the Constitution. Then came another major crisis and a seminal change in America and its governments.

The political response to glare of the market crash at the end of the 1920s, in a newly urbanized America with a growing media, was like no other. Most American politicians, many so-called intellectuals, and others laid blame for the stock market crash and subsequent economic problems on the evils of capitalism and the greed of its capitalists. Never mind that American politicians, on both sides of the aisle, instituted economic policies that strangled the 1930 economic recovery. They did so with the Smoot-Hawley Tariff Act, which greatly diminished international trade, and the raising of income tax rates to a high of 63 percent,[43] which greatly reduced economic incentives for American entrepreneurs. Not to be outdone, the newly minted Federal Reserve, which was created to deal with bank instability, presided over bank runs and the unprecedented shrinking of the amount of money in circulation by a stunning 30 percent.[44] All combined, the response of government deeply harmed the American economy and sent it into the Great Depression.

As the economy deteriorated, President Herbert Hoover, the Republican who signed the Smoot-Hawley Tariff Act, pushed an unprecedented 25 percent spending increase from $3 billion a year to $4 billion.[45] Despite campaigning against Hoover's "socialist" spending, Franklin Delano Roosevelt became president amid a weakening economy. FDR, as Roosevelt was known, would then proceed to change the very nature of the US federal government and the Constitution. FDR proposed a New Deal for America composed of many new spending programs and centralized government industrial policies.

For a time, the founding principles of American law stood in his way. The Supreme Court initially ruled FDR's New Deal programs were unconstitutional—in keeping with America's constitutional origins of a limited government of enumerated powers. In response, FDR attacked the Supreme Court justices in dramatic fashion. He declared that Americans "cannot seriously be alarmed when they cry 'unconstitutional' at every effort to better the condition of our people." To the contrary, he asserted that "we will no longer be permitted to sacrifice each generation in turn while the law catches up with life."[46] *The law to which he was referring was the US Constitution.*

Faced with such legal barriers, FDR proceeded to bully the Supreme Court. His legislative "court-packing scheme," as it became known, to add more favorable justices to the Supreme Court, was unprecedented in American history. Although it never became law, because politicians and significant portions of the American population recoiled from the idea, FDR's threat worked. A change in view on the Court and a retirement changed the legal outcome of the constitutionality of FDR's programs. With that, where once the strict enumerated powers of the federal government were honored, the now modified judicial view of government powers under the Constitution allowed for an enormous expansion of spending and New Deal programs. FDR's rationale for such government expansion was straightforward and revolutionary. In one of his famed "fireside" radio chats, he declared:

> In 1933 you and I knew that we must never let our economic system get completely out of joint again—that we could not afford to take the risk of another great depression. We also became convinced that the only way to avoid a repetition of those dark days was to have a government with power to prevent and to cure the abuses and the inequalities which had thrown that system out of joint.[47]

The magnitude of that change and its effect on American history cannot be underestimated. Forever after and in growing numbers, Americans would come to believe, quite unlike their forebearers, that it was the role of government to right societal and economic wrongs.

The New Deal of the 1930s would become the Great Society of the 1960s and the government bailout spending of the COVID pandemic in 2020. Step-by-step, crisis-by-crisis, America would arrive at the point that the spending at all levels—local, state, and national—would rise to nearly half of the entire US economy in the 2020s. By contrast, under President Jefferson, government was somewhere between 2 and 3 percent of the economy. Not surprisingly, where once the American national debt was capable of being retired under President Jackson on January 1, 1835, by 2024, the American national debt had reached well over $35 trillion and was increasing rapidly with no prospects of ever being reduced let alone repaid. That is America today.

WEALTH (IN)EQUALITY AND SOCIALIST TENDENCIES

Now that we have seen how we arrived at this moment in time, we should answer a few more questions about the American experience. Is there income and wealth inequality in America? Is that bad? Does it matter that the American governments are so large and trending toward socialism? What will those current socialist tendencies mean for America?

As we consider those questions, recall that *inequality* only became a national issue after commercialization and industrialization were underway in America. In the 1896 campaign, it was championed by William Jennings Bryan in his fight against the barons of capitalism. FDR spoke of inequalities to justify his New Deal and, today, virtually every politician on the Left and many on the Right speaks of it as they offer new government taxes, spending, or programs to combat it.

It is true there are differences, sometimes great, in income and wealth in the United States. In recognizing that, we cannot forget that the only *equality in history has been limited to poverty for the masses in economies prior to commercialization or in economies owned or dictated by monarchs or other authoritarian governments.* Income equality, without the hope of a material increase, was the hallmark of the thousands of years before the 1800s—except for a tiny percentage of people among the ruling elite.

Once a civilization makes its way to the city, on the other hand, in a relatively free economy, income differences begin to arise as entrepreneurs exploit their newfound freedoms and find their niches. As they do, we must appreciate that *income inequality is essential to a growing economy and job production.* To open a restaurant, its owner must have had a greater income than its dishwasher. The factory that produces consumer goods at a lower cost relies on savings that turn into investments; no savings can amass, and no investments can be made, without income inequality.

We have seen the great riches of the likes of Rockefeller, Carnegie, and Morgan. Today, we hear names such as Jeff Bezos, Elon Musk, Bill Gates,

Mark Zuckerberg, and Warren Buffet. There have been the very rich in every age. America is no different in that regard. On the other hand, the American barons were largely self-made, the rich of Europe often benefited from their class.

What of the rest of Americans? Do those rich Americans really own most of America's wealth? According to the US government, recently the top 1 percent is said to be sixteen times richer than the bottom 50 percent.[48] However, that should not be the end of the discussion, because the top 1 percent is not a static group, and neither is the bottom 50 percent. Beyond that, US government statistics on income and wealth, like that statistic, quite often are misleading.

With regard to mobility, a study by economists Andrew Rettenmaier and Donald Deere demonstrated that, toward the end of the 1900s, with regard to income, of those workers in the lowest 20 percent, 32 percent moved up to the next-highest twentieth percentile within a year, and 1 percent of them moved into the highest twentieth percentile. Over a fifteen-year period, two-thirds had moved to the next-highest group.[49] Continuing on that theme, according to a government study, 70 percent of the population will have experienced at least one year within the top twentieth percentile of income.[50]

On the other end of the scale, there is downward mobility. Of those in the top twentieth percentile, in one year, 25 percent of them fell to the next-lower twentieth percentile, and 2 percent of them fell into the lowest twentieth percentile. Fifteen years later, 61 percent had dropped from the top percentile. Further, with regard to wealth, as pointed out by Robert Arnott and colleagues in their 2015 study, "The Myth of Dynastic Wealth," only thirty-four of the original *Forbes* four hundred richest people from the 1982 list are on the list today.[51] Indeed, Mark Zuckerberg of Facebook wasn't even born when that list debuted.

It is also plain and logical that many of those who populate the lower 50 percent are the young, who have shortened work tenures and therefore lower income and wealth. Thus, in 2005, for example, "the median income of households aged 45 to 54 was 2½ times greater than that of households aged 15 to 24."[52]

Further, once other factors are considered, so-called inequality and income and wealth can be seen in a different light. For instance, "the high-income group works around 700 percent more . . . than the low-income group."[53] Beyond that, the manner in which people actually live and the wealth they have is affected by the fact that the income differences reported by the US government are based on *pretax income*. A large majority of Americans receive government benefits. Further, government-reported income differences don't take into account family size. When those factors are considered, rather than "the official census measure of 16.7 times as much," the top quintile of households "receive 4 times as much."[54] In short, there is income and wealth inequality in America as there have been in all other places and times. Overall, Americans still enjoy the highest personal consumption rate in the world and have the broadest middle class in the world. However, that doesn't mean that will last forever.

FEDERAL GOVERNMENT GROWTH LIMITS ECONOMIC GROWTH

If America benefited economically from its initially limited governments, it should be obvious that the growth in American governments is having a negative effect on economic growth. We have seen that government spending has risen dramatically since the 1970s. Prior to that time, going back to the 1950s, America's average annual economic growth averaged 4 percent a year. If we go back further, during the Gilded Age—the last twenty-five years of the 1800s, when government was below 10 percent of the economy—the US population surged and the economy grew, by some accounts, as much as 400 percent.[55]

In the time that the American governments exploded in size and scope over the last forty-plus years, including the costs of regulations that now exceed 10 percent of the economy, economic growth has fallen to 2 percent per year.[56] That dynamic is not unique to the United States. In Europe and its Eurozone, considered a model by some government proponents in America, the governments' percentage of the economy (spending and the costs of regulations) is even higher than in America. Government spending and the costs of regulations there can reach well over 50 percent of an economy, and, not surprisingly, Eurozone growth overall has been slowed to 0 percent over the last two decades.[57]

That dynamic of lower economic growth following sustained increases in government taxes and regulations is in keeping with one of the most basic economic laws of history, the Law of Demand, which takes into account that the more something costs, the less of it you tend to get—overall economies included. That lack of growth comes at a very high price. For instance, since 1995, government spending in Spain has averaged over 40 percent of the Spanish economy—reaching a high of 49.5 percent in 2012. Not surprisingly, full year GDP growth in Spain averaged just 1.92 percent from 1996 until 2022.[58] During that same period, that sustained lack of growth resulted in a Spanish youth unemployment rate that exceeded 40 percent in 2012[59] and then hit a high of 55.7 percent in 2013.[60] That nearly fixed economic pie, therefore, meant that youth could not find jobs and start to move up the economic ladder—for an entire generation, prompting references to that generation as the "lost generation."

Similarly, if America continues on its current path of the spectacular growth rate in government spending over the last fifty years and ever higher costs of regulations, it is safe to assume that America's economic growth rate will continue to decline and Americans' standards of living will be lower than they otherwise could be because lower rates of economic growth directly correlate to overall income. Further, it could well be assumed America will be a semi-socialist state, if not an actual socialist state in the years to come.

It is also very important to note that the reduced economic growth rates of socialist and semi-socialist states such as in Europe today present a very distinct challenge to the American civilization not seen in European countries. Recall we started by noting that America is quite unlike any civilization in history. America is a culture that was forged by an ethic, not a common genetic background. America's early immigrants, from all over the world, immigrated to seek opportunity. While America was growing, with relative calm, it assimilated those millions of immigrants along with its high internal population growth as the American economic pie expanded.

As American economic growth has slowed, that will no longer be the case; the number of Americans becoming dependent on government is rising. As for immigrants, according to a report on the 2014 census, 63 percent of non-citizens are accessing welfare programs, and that figure grows to 70 percent for immigrants here ten years or more.[61] That was before the great American immigration crisis of 2022 to 2024. In short, reliance on government, once disdained, is now becoming an American "cultural" norm—even for immigrants, which is a far cry from America's Founding.

Also, and not coincidentally, class warfare is on the rise as politicians and their constituents fight over diminishing economic returns. That dynamic was part of the decline of democracy in ancient Greece and the end of the Roman Republic. Of ancient Greece, Will Durant wrote that the "poor schemed to despoil the rich by legislation and revolution [and] the rich organized for protection against the poor."[62] So bitter were the times that the great Greek Isocrates, orator and teacher, wrote, "The rich have become so unsocial that those who own property had rather throw their possessions into the sea than lend aid to the needy, while those in poorer circumstances would less gladly find a treasure than seize the possessions of the rich."[63]

Certainly, America hears strains of that today. What followed in the bitter class warfare of the time included not only government efforts at redistribution and a distrust of "democracy as empowered envy" but also murderous class violence that left ancient Greece and its allied states badly divided—so divided in fact, that with their energy sapped, they all but ignored the outside world until they were conquered by Philip of Macedon in 338 BC. America's preoccupation with internal division today is coming at the cost of foreign policy errors.

A not dissimilar dynamic occurred in Rome as well. The populist Tiberius Gracchus became Tribune in 133 BC. In succession, Tiberius Gracchus and his younger brother Gaius Gracchus fanned the flames of class warfare as they proposed the redistribution of land from rich to poor and corn subsidies. Tiberius took on the political establishment of Rome, including its legendary Senate not only by announcing a run for a second term as Tribune, which was unlawful, but also by bypassing the Senate and taking his reforms directly the Popular Assembly. Such populism was not taken lightly and seen as a direct threat to the political status quo—so much so that Tiberius and three hundred of his followers were murdered by a mob. His brother Gaius befell a similar fate. The political violence did not subside thereafter and amid such violence, the Republic fell.

The American civilization is especially vulnerable to the dangers of class warfare. Most countries can fall back on their shared DNA and cultural heritage in difficult times. Their shared cultural DNA binds them through thick and thin. America does not have that attribute. *If the United States becomes a society of a nearly fixed economic pie, with its inhabitants dependent on government, it would no longer be a culture forged together by the pursuit of opportunity. If that cultural glue is lost, the signs of which we have seen since 2010 in the form of dissent between recent immigrants and the older populations, America's melting pot could well become a place of different cultures fighting each other politically instead of enriching themselves economically.* Thus, in a very real sense, and unlike in any other place in history, the question of welfare state socialism, which uniformly produces low economic growth rates, in America is not just one of economic fortunes. There is a distinct risk that it could pull the American civilization apart.

THREATS TO THE REPUBLIC FROM GOVERNMENT CENTRALIZATION

Beyond the dangers of class warfare, there is the basic threat to the American Republic in the form of the centralization of power in Washington, DC, and in the state houses. Combined with the regulatory state, nearly every aspect of American life is affected by a government program or edict. With every such dictate, American freedoms are correspondingly reduced. The response to COVID provided a dramatic example of that when government-induced shutdowns transformed American lives and resulted in millions receiving government benefits. Before then, in increasing fashion, the United States governments' impact on education, housing, transportation, energy, health care, retirement, and commerce was becoming ubiquitous.

While those governments may not own the salt mines as they did under the socialism of the Roman emperor Diocletian, the complexity of regulations of the countless government agencies from Washington, DC, to Honolulu, and everywhere in between, literally dictate much of American economic life. When you combine that with government spending that will exceed half the US economy, it may be that new socialism of the twenty-first century, or "modern socialism," as the one-time presidential candidate Steve Forbes describes it, is life by government regulation and taxation.[64]

The danger of such modern socialism goes beyond the economic. The ever-closer relationship between big government and big business in America is a direct threat to a functioning Republic. Recall that the separation of economic power from political power was essential for the emergence of democracy from authoritarianism. Today in the United States, that separation diminishes with each passing day. The largest businesses of our day influence government policy far more than any normal citizen possibly can. The contracts advocated by and between large businesses and our government dictate public policy, as demonstrated by military contracts and health care contracts. Consider the huge contracts that were obtained by businesses during the COVID pandemic. Those contracts and the policies behind them were advocated and implemented by a close relationship between huge pharmaceutical companies and their allied politicians. Overall, *the more money big special interests obtain from government, the less voice average citizens have in their government.*

If we look at the COVID era again, the cooperation and/or push for censorship between government and big business, such as Twitter and Facebook, in reducing free expression was unprecedented—but should not be unexpected.[65] According to a report in the *Economic Times*, "Both . . . Joe Biden [related to anti-vaxxer accounts] and former Donald Trump administrations [related to panic buying] pressured Twitter and other tech giants like Google, Facebook and Microsoft to disseminate Covid information."[66]

The same can be said of the so-called intelligence services of America spying on Americans in the name of national security or weighing in on presidential elections.[67] It is the nature of man and organizations to protect what they have. In this case, businesses and politicians derive great power and money from government. Keep in mind that nine of the richest twenty counties in America surround Washington, DC. It is not surprising that they seek to protect themselves from anyone, anywhere, who seeks to disrupt their power.

As we saw earlier, the end of the Roman Republic was, in part, an example of that dynamic. Returning to the Republic of Venice, in response to a plot of dissenters, a Council of Ten was created complete with "secret funds, a system of anonymous informers, police powers, and broad jurisdictional mandate over matters of state security."[68] Beyond that, around the city, *bocches di leone* (mouths of the lion) were strategically placed. Citizens of Venice, among other things, were "encouraged" to denounce or report on others who were being disloyal to the regime. In the United States, Rockefeller, Morgan, and Carnegie sought to protect the establishment they helped create from the threat William Jennings Bryan posed in 1896. During the Obama administration, the White House director of new media, Macon Phillips, posted a note on the White House website: "If you get an email or see something on the web about health insurance reform that seems fishy, send it to flag@whitehouse.gov."[69] A great deal of objections to Donald Trump by the Washington, DC, establishment fall under that category as well.

As we look even deeper, it has always been true, as Durant states, that internal freedom varies inversely to external threats. The centralization of power within the Homeland Security Department after 9/11 was a direct response to external threats. In Lincoln's time, the freedom of the Southern states was dramatically curtailed in response to the Civil War. The US Constitution came about, in part, because of security threats.

Today, the power and reach of technology makes easier what the Third Amendment once outlawed: the stationing of a government agent, or a soldier, in the homes of citizens. Today, the US government can literally reach into your phone to determine the nature of your views and limit your ability to express them.

Given that democracies and republics are born of dissent, we must conclude that *history has shown time and again that the limiting of dissent is a signpost along the road to the demise of a free society.* No one should believe that American civilization is immune from that law of history or any other such lesson.

Finally, given the record of socialism in history, why do politicians and intellectuals continue to pursue that end? We have discussed that reason at length—a lack of historical understanding. We can conclude this chapter by noting that, throughout all of history, there have been those driven to obtain power over others. In the words of Daniel Webster in 1837, "There are men, in all ages, who mean to exercise power usefully; but who mean to exercise it. They mean to govern well; but they mean to govern. They promise to be kind masters; but they mean to be masters."[70]

That too is a lesson of history.

I

CHAPTER 11

America's Modern Morality, Religion, and Culture

At the beginning of a civilization, a people will do anything to survive. At the end, they will apologize for doing it.

—Thomas Del Beccaro

At a 2016 Boston University seminar, this definition of culture emerged: "Culture can be defined as all the ways of life including arts, beliefs and institutions of a population that are passed down from generation to generation. Culture has been called 'the way of life for an entire society.'"[1]

So far, we have surveyed much of America's way of life over the centuries. We have noted how America and its economy originally started with farms and that the family was the central economic unit. Today, 83 percent of Americans live in urban areas, and that percentage is expected to rise in the coming years.[2] With that change, individuals, men and women, became the chief economic units of the family—replacing the family unit that was so central to farming. That dynamic has contributed to a delay in marriages along with gathering wealth and expanding education. Adding to that, the increasing use of contraception and expanding abortion rates have caused America's reproductive rates to fall dramatically. American wealth remains atop other countries, and its standard of living remains among the highest, especially when government transfers are considered. However, economic growth has slowed steadily from the late 1800s to today. We also know that the progress of science continues unabated in this era, leading to breakthroughs in health care and the easing the burdens of everyday life. That progress also has spread doubt among society about religious beliefs.

Taken altogether, it becomes readily apparent, even to the casual reader, just how dramatically, if not drastically, the American civilization has changed over time. It may be comforting to know, or concerning, depending on your viewpoint, that the culture of the American civilization has evolved much like other dominant, educated, and rich civilizations of the past. In this chapter, we consider additional broad questions of history and culture and how they relate to the United States.

STOICISM VERSUS EPICUREANISM

As we do, recall that we used Will Durant's statement that "nations are born stoic" to understand the nature of civilizations as they form and then begin to progress. We can now consider his full admonition, by considering his belief that "nations are born stoic and die epicurean."[3] Epicureanism, like Stoicism, was an ancient Greek philosophy. The two had rival adherents. Recall that Stoicism focused on its believers living a virtuous life. Virtue, according to Stoicism, was "sufficient for happiness"[4] if not the highest good. There was also a character trait of enduring hardship without complaining. By contrast, Epicurus "regarded the unacknowledged fear of death and punishment as the primary cause of anxiety among human beings, and anxiety in turn as the source of extreme and irrational desires. The elimination of the fears and corresponding desires would leave people free to pursue the pleasures, both physical and mental."[5] Ultimately rather than virtue, Epicurus taught that "pleasure is the principle and end to a happy life."[6]

With that understanding, Durant's statement that "nations are born stoic and die epicurean" can come into better focus. At the beginning of most of the civilizations that history has known to date, there is not great wealth. Science and education are in their nascent stages. Perseverance, values, and strong character are necessary components to the birth and progress of those civilizations. Once wealth begins to accumulate and science and education progress, however, societies and their culture change.

If we look back in history at those mature civilizations that achieved great wealth, with a significant degree of commercialism, urbanization, and greater degrees of education, we tend to find societies with many people that lean toward the views of Epicurus more than the strictures of Stoicism. Plainly stated, at the outset, civilizations are built through hard work. They often triumph over adversity and even war. Later in time, with wealth, people tend to work less and luxuriate more. Pacifism becomes a rising sentiment and we find a loosening of the morals, traditions, and then the laws that once were the guardrails of that civilization.

As we consider these additional topics, we must always remember that history is the exceptional recorded.[7] The vibrant lives of the city tend to attract more attention than the steady work of the countryside. By the same token, in the media of any one age, the extraordinary individual often garners more attention than the everyday family. So, while historians may generalize about a society, myself included, the lives of the unnoticed, of the traditional, are often underreported and likely undervalued. Even so, there is no mistaking certain trends of which me must take note.

* * *

We can begin by considering the progression of the Venetian Republic from the Middle Ages to the late 1500s. Throughout the early and middle part that period, the purpose of the Venetian civilization, almost to the person, was that of commercial success. It was a very structured and stable society, inclusive of a class system, wherein most citizens served its purpose to one degree or another. With that singular and disciplined focus, Venice built perhaps the richest and most successful commercial empire of its time. Given its location, on the western shores of the Italian peninsula, Venice also developed a similarly disciplined military prowess not only to protect its trade routes throughout the eastern Mediterranean but also to protect Western Christendom from the ambitions of the Turks. By the mid- to late 1500s, however, a thousand years of wealth gathering and the exhaustion of wars had changed the values of Venetians to the point that its Carnival, which started as a brief celebration for a military victory, would last six months at a time, inclusive of the toleration of prostitution. At the same time, investments for the future had turned instead to conspicuous consumption for the time at hand—thereby providing an example of the progression from Stoicism to Epicureanism.[8]

Turning to the mature and prosperous ancient Greek civilization, with an eye on Sparta in particular, we find that where it was once known for its discipline, "towards the close of the fourth century the state became corrupt and disordered [and] their liberty degenerated into licence," according to Archibald Dobbs in his book *Philosophy and Popular Morals in Ancient Greece*.[9] Of other areas in Greece, Dobbs writes that it was "a time of weariness and moral reaction, such as came upon Rome in the years of opulence which followed the tumultuous activity of the Punic Wars."[10] Similarly, Durant concluded that the "Athenians of the 5th century are not exemplars of morality; the progress of the intellect had loosened many of them from their ethical traditions, and has turned them into almost unmoral individuals."[11]

If we move on in time and place to Rome, after visiting what was indeed an "opulent" Rome compared to his native Germany, Martin Luther, who was not without his biases, concluded of Rome that "if there is a hell, then Rome is built upon it." Edward Gibbon, in his masterpiece, *History of the Decline and Fall of the Roman Empire*, placed emphasis on Rome's moral decline. He also wrote of the "decay" of Constantinople of the Byzantine empire amid its opulence. Durant believed Rome to be more stoic in Fabius's time (circa 233 BC) than Nero's epicureanism (54–68 AD). As for the Renaissance, Durant concluded that "Germany and England in the fourteenth and fifteenth centuries," as the Italian Renaissance was reaching its height, "were too poor to rival Italy in immorality."[12]

The rise to the height of power in Florence of the ascetic Dominican friar, Girolamo Savonarola (1494), was achieved by castigating the sins of Florentines amid their wealth and "vanities" and confirms that view. Savonarola was born in Ferrara, another well-to-do Renaissance city-state of Italy. According to Jacob Burckhardt, in his work *The Civilisation of the Renaissance in Italy*:

> At the time when Savonarola was powerful in Florence, and the movement which he began spread far and wide among the population of central Italy . . . [o]n Easter Day, the 3rd of April [1496], a proclamation on morals and religion was published, forbidding blasphemy, prohibited games, sodomy, concubinage, the letting of houses to prostitutes or panders, and the opening of all shops on feast-days, excepting those of the bakers and greengrocers.[13]

From those quotes and others like them, we can conclude that the riches of the Renaissance, as with Greece and Rome before it, gave license among some to an easing of the morals and traditions that the poverty of the Middle Ages jealously guarded.

If we delve a little farther, and consider the sexual liberations of those ages, "a notable feature of ancient Greek society was . . . the relative degree of tolerance for homosexual relationships."[14] The same could be said of Renaissance Italy. In both cases, historians note that "respectable young ladies were fairly strictly confined to the home,"[15] in an effort to preserve their chastity, which, in those times, was an essential asset for marriages arranged by their families. As a result, men of those classes experimented with their sexuality in their youth within the cultural norms of their affluent class. Again, as with other aspects of recorded history, we must understand that what was significant in the minds of the clergy or the historian are not necessarily reflective of society as a whole. Even so, there seems little doubt that sexual experimentation and/or expression becomes more prevalent in the wealthier and perhaps latter stages of civilizations than in their early stages—if the history as recorded is any measure.

If we focus on religion, we have already noted several times that wealth, science, and education have a strong, negative influence on reverence. In the early stages of a civilization, its inhabitants are more religious. As the pleasures of this earth become more accessible, however, the concern of the afterlife tends to diminish. If we consider that dynamic with respect to Rome, according to Cyril Bailey, in his work *The Religion of Ancient Rome*:

> The Rome we know, in the epochs when we can fairly judge of character and morality, was not the Rome in which the 'Religion of Numa'* had grown up and remained unquestioned: it had been overlaid with foreign cults and foreign ideas, had been used by priests and magistrates as a political instrument, and discounted among the educated through the influence of philosophy.[16]

---

*   Numa Pompilius, according to Rome lore, was the second King of Rome after Romulus and is credited with establishing the initial religion of Rome.

In other words, reverence gave way to license and religion became a tool of the powerful. At the same time, philosophers spread doubt among the higher classes, a luxury that usually did not infect the lives of the poor. Beyond that, during the Renaissance, one measure of the changing views of mankind toward religion was the subject matter of art. Where once the paintings and sculptures of the medieval period were uniformly of religious themes, that changed dramatically during and after the Renaissance and the Humanist movement, which explored the human body and slowly but surely changed the subject matter of art—such that the promise of heaven and work of saints gave way to reality and toil of humans on earth.

AMERICA'S PLACE ALONG THE CONTINUUM

So, where is the American civilization along the societal continuum between Stoicism and Epicureanism?

We have seen the nature and character of early centuries of the American civilization. The early settlers required great bravery and fortitude. They had to fend for themselves on the frontier and from the very real danger of Indians. They fought wars over territory. The harsh winters had to be mastered and feeding themselves took long hours of work. During those early centuries, few became rich. Most lived to survive. Not surprisingly, that life required and sustained a stern moral code supported by the family structure. At the center of so many of their lives were their religious beliefs that symbiotically supported or were supported by a patriarchal system and an economy rooted in the land.

It does not take long to conclude that America of yesterday hardly represents the America of today. Like ancient Greece and Rome, and the Italy of the Renaissance, America has become quite wealthy. Like in those other places, science has progressed, and schooling has become more widespread.

Further, it is likely that the pace of societal change has quickened well beyond anything experienced before. Part of that latter dynamic is because of the ubiquitous nature of mass media. The changes absorbed by those prior civilizations took decades, if not centuries, to take hold because the pace of life was slower and news made its way slowly across the land. Today, technology allows for the saturation of society with a deluge of information, skepticism, and criticism of societal norms—*instantly*. What happens on America's East Coast happens in the living rooms of its West Coast and in the hands of mobile device users everywhere—and nearly all at once. As a result, to an incredible degree of significance, the pace of societal change has quickened significantly.

The effects are manifest in the American culture.

America's Changing Work Habits

If we start with the work ethic of Americans, as measured by hours worked, we find that for most Americans, America has become the land of the forty-hour or less work week. At the start of 2024, that number lessened to 34.1 hours. Yes, there are many entrepreneurs that defy such weekly averages but, as a whole, the modern America of wealth is a place where people work substantially less than the America at its founding. Indeed, after the COVID pandemic, it was a struggle for employers to get employees to return to the office. Such is the level of luxury in the America of the 2020s.

When America started, people worked to feed their family no matter how long it took—regardless of the conditions. It is estimated that in the 1800s "many Americans worked seventy hours or more per week."[17] By 1900, that estimate had fallen to somewhere between 55 and 60 hours per week.[18] After the Great Depression, the Fair Labor Standards Act of 1940 reduced that number by government fiat to forty hours per week. As a historical matter, however, it must be understood that the reduced number was a reflection of the wealth of the American civilization at the time. While it is true that the rise of labor unions played a significant role in ameliorating the worst of early industrialization's work conditions, no one would believe that such a law would have existed in 1720 America—just as no one would have told their employer in 1720 that they were only willing to work from home.

To the contrary, throughout history, as wealth is produced and accumulates, it becomes more possible for work conditions to improve. It is also true that as government regulations multiply, they can reach a point where they reduce output to such a degree that they limit increases in wealth and, therefore, limit standards of living. In other words, and usually in the latter years, government becomes an impediment to the improvement of lives. The America of today has reached that point in many respects amid economic growth of just 2 percent on average and reduced labor participation.[19] Even with reduced hours and growth, the America of the early twenty-first century still produces enormous and untold wealth when compared to the rest of the world.

US governments have further influenced work hour metrics by providing so much government assistance that it has had the effect of reducing many Americans' desire to work. As then-president Barack Obama acknowledged, "As somebody who worked in low-income neighborhoods, I've seen it where people weren't encouraged to work, weren't encouraged to upgrade their skills, were just getting a check, and over time their motivation started to diminish."[20] From the time that America started and into the twentieth century, a period of over four hundred years, there was virtually no government assistance and certainly no federal welfare assistance. In those times, a strong work ethic was a matter of survival as it had been in other places and times. That has changed. So much so that, during the COVID pandemic, while the government issued edicts shutting down huge portions of the American economy, government literally paid Americans not to work. The government assistance programs of America's 1960s Great Society and beyond have had the effect President Obama described.

Those programs also have had a significant effect on society as a whole.

Recall that we have discussed the dynamic of the transition from a rural economy to an urban one and how commercial society has a negative effect on the family. Once such effect is that the divorce rate of America as an urban society is higher than when America began as a rural society. The welfare programs that have paid unwed mothers for each child they have also influence the marriage and divorce rates. For instance, among the African American community, that dynamic has played a significant role in the increase of children born out of wedlock from 24 percent in the 1960 to 72 percent in 2010.[21] The societal effect of that dynamic has proven incalculable and its meteoric rise in such a short period cannot be explained simply by the long-term historical dynamics we have noted. To the contrary, the effect of government programs has been significant as well.

Education in Modern America

If we turn to education, in most America schools, once the domain of religious organizations, prayer is no longer welcomed. As stated in the last chapter, the teaching of civics and basics of American history dissipates with each passing day. In 2023, 673 university professors signed a letter opposing courses on America's founding, and its Constitution.[22] In the four decades before this book was published, at the expense of teaching history, schools at almost every level have focused on social studies turned social justice. Meanwhile, student proficiencies with respect to math and science have stagnated. Since World War II, government "public" schools have dominated the education market. However, despite an inflation adjusted 143 percent increase in spending since 1970, student proficiency has stagnated.[23] The government response to COVID was particularly damaging. During the pandemic alone, "math scores for eighth graders fell in nearly every state. A meager 26 percent of eighth graders were proficient, down from 34 percent in 2019."[24] Among several minority communities, the results were even worse.[25]

Crime in America

The America of today is also experiencing a resurgence in crime. Crime increased in the twentieth century steadily. However, between the 1970s and the 1990s, while part of society focused on the plight of the criminal over that of the victims, crime rose significantly.[26] In response to that, the pendulum swung the other way, law enforcement increased, and crime statistics dropped. However, in the America of the 2020s, there has once again been a sharp increase as the enforcement of laws has taken a back seat to claims for social justice. The plight of America's largest cities such as New York, Los Angeles, San Francisco, Portland, Chicago, and others has become particularly dramatic in that timeframe. It became so bad that, in 2023, workers cited crime as the number one reason they did not want to return to the office in certain cities.[27] Of course, *the crime rates of the city have always been higher than the crime rates of the countryside. Proximity has always been a great incentive for mischief as it is for disease.*

Sexual Expression in America

The America of the early twenty-first century is also witness to considerable sexual experimentation and license, compared to the time of its founding. The 1960s was witness to a "sexual revolution." Within the twenty years before the writing of this book, gay marriage went from a minority view to the law of the land in 2015. In the wake of that change, sexual expression became emboldened to the point that transsexual rights became a major political and cultural issue in 2023.

Religion in America

Turning to religion, in this once-Christian nation, Christianity and especially the Catholic Church are increasingly under attack—physically and, in the media, rhetorically. One media outlet went so far as to claim that "the rosary has acquired a militaristic meaning for radical-traditional (or 'rad trad') Catholics."[28] Not to be outdone, it came to light in 2023 that the American FBI sought to spy on members of the American Catholic Church to identify "extremists." Of course, that is the same governmental activity that long ago provided part of the impetus for the founding of the American civilization.

Perhaps most tellingly, a 2023 *Wall Street Journal* poll found that just "39 percent of Americans say their religious faith is very important to them."[29] That percentage stood at 62 percent in 1998. The rapidity of that change likely can only be explained by the dynamic of that quickened pace of societal change mentioned above and, as the historian Victor Davis Hanson has opined, the Left's desire to "radically alter our customs and traditions."[30] Overall, what took wealth, science, and urbanization centuries to effect civilizations before is now happening right before the eyes of a wearied republic.

The danger, of course, is that no civilization has sustained itself without a moral code and no moral has lasted without religious and education institutions to buttress it.[31] Of course, in every era, there are those who claim that there is no god and religious institutions cause more trouble than good. Those voices increase with wealth and science and the growth of cities—right along with calls for socialism and communism. On that point, Will Durant noted, "Heaven and utopia are buckets in a well: when one goes down the other goes up; when religion declines Communism grows."[32] That dynamic is alive in the America of the 2020s as well.

Patriotism in America

That same *Wall Street Journal* poll cited in the previous section saw a precipitous drop in patriotism among respondents. In 1998, the figure stood at 70 percent. In 2023, that number dropped to just 38 percent.[33] What could cause such a rapid loss in belief in one's country? The answer again lies in the education system, which is often hostile to America's past, as well as the assault on the basic values and traditions of America by time and mass media critics. Add to that the general lack of historical perspective, and the reasons that America is in doubt become self-evident. Before leaving this topic, however, we should consider the debate, of sorts, that took place in America in the 2020s over nationalism.

Before the recent skeptics of American culture gained their voice, the simple dictionary definition of "nationalism" was the "identification with one's own nation and support for its interests, especially to the exclusion or detriment of the interests of other nations."[34] If we consider the whole of history, by now it should be apparent that a civilization could not come into being without a shared sense of self. It is the pervasiveness of that self, and a civilization's purpose, that defines it. Without that identity, a civilization cannot begin. Without nationalism, a nation cannot progress. Will Durant once asserted that national pride alone could be enough to make the difference in the competition among states. Consistent with that, we would do well to consider the words of Edward Gibbon:

> That public virtue, which among the ancients was denominated patriotism, is derived from a strong sense of our own interest in the preservation and prosperity of the free government of which we are members. Such a sentiment, which had rendered the legions of the [Roman] Republic almost invincible, could make but a very feeble impression on the mercenary servants of a despotic prince.[35]

The loss of the public virtue and patriotism, in Gibbon's eyes, was a clear factor in the decline and fall of the Roman Empire. In America, civic virtue is under attack as the popular culture derides the very founding of America for its start via "colonialism," its former slavery practices, and other practices that the cultural Left believes should have never occurred. In the end, they claim that despite a host of important historical firsts in America, the country is not exceptional. That view was not possible in early America among those who built this country and is not unlike the loss Gibbon noted about Rome. In my words, a people will do anything to survive and build a civilization. In the end, there will be those who seek to apologize for having done it. In many ways, that is the state of America today.

THE DIVIDED ERA REVISITED

Finally, we should consider the current status of America's body politic. I first referred to the state of American politics as the Divided Era in 2007 and published a book by the same name in 2015. Starting in the 1990s, the division along party lines became more pronounced with each passing year. America of the twenty-first century is now a country of Red and Blue states and Red and Blue counties within the states. While there have been defined parties in America for over two hundred years, perhaps only during the Civil War, Reconstruction, and America's Gilded Age have party differences been more defined than in this Divided Era.

Unlike those earlier periods, the reason for the current division today is quite plainly the massive size of American governments (local, state, and national). In politics, as in life, the greater the stakes, the greater the division. During the Civil War, when the stakes could not have been higher, America resolved its political differences with bullets more so than ballots. Afterward, during Reconstruction and the Gilded Age, the immense issues, such as the remaking of the South's governments, the nature of currency (gold, silver, or paper), the legality of political patronage, and other issues, separated Americans to a high degree as well. After those decisions and even the Civil War, the relatively small size of the American government (under 10 percent of the US economy in 1900) allowed most Americans to return to their lives largely unimpeded—with some notable exceptions like the aftermath of slavery. As they did, political tensions eased.

That dynamic may well no longer possible in America. *Every decision government makes results in a winner and a loser and finds someone to pay for it*. In the process, governments set off a competition for government spoils and another to avoid the taxes required to fund those government spoils. Simply stated, a government that decides and then funds one issue will encourage one set of combatants. The American governments that spend trillions of dollars and decide endless issues foster an endless set of political disagreement among a growing population of combatants. Along the way, the competition to be the political party that hands out that largess and determines those issues grows as well. Along the way, political centrists cannot find a home, such as during the run-up to America's Revolution after the failure of the Olive Branch Petition, and party discipline becomes paramount, such as during the run-up to the Civil War and Reconstruction, in an effort to secure political victory. Altogether, mathematically, with each dollar spent, political division rises.

As part and parcel of that existing division, the American media is greatly divided as well. Red and Blue voters maintain their preferred news sources and commentators, which often portray significantly different takes on the news of the days and their preferences for politicians. As technology further diversifies and multiplies the American media, rather than attempt to attract all consumers, most outlets have decided to focus on a partisan slice reminiscent of the party press era. As that process unfolds, division in America is increased.

That state of division is the America of the twenty-first century—the America of the Divided Era.

CHAPTER 12

The State of the American "Empire"

> *I saw the Emperor [Napoleon]—this world-soul—
> riding out of the city on reconnaissance. It is indeed
> a wonderful sensation to see such an individual, who,
> concentrated here at a single point, astride a horse,
> reaches out over the world and masters it.*
>
> —**G. W. F. Hegel,** letter to Friedrich Immanuel,
> October 13, 1806

The American civilization, as of the writing of this book, remains the most dominant civilization in the world. It has a combined worldwide military, corporate, and cultural reach beyond all others. But is it an empire, and if it is, is that empire ebbing?

The word "empire," in the classical sense, implies territorial hegemony over other people and lands. Often that mastery was gained through the ravages of wars designed to conquer those lands and subjugate its peoples. Any discussion of whether the American civilization was or is an empire should consider that question with reference to three distinct historical phases America has undergone, as well as one nonclassical consideration.

CONQUEST AND EXPANSION IN AMERICAN HISTORY

In the first stage of its existence, it could be said that the emerging American civilization eventually "conquered" the continent from sea to shining sea. However, the early Americans did so in an historically unorthodox fashion. They did not acquire all of its current land mass by invading the territories of the American continent with a large, centrally directed army led by an emperor or king. By contrast, the Kingdom of Macedon, under Alexander the Great, Rome under various emperors, and Genghis Kahn of the Mongol Empire led centrally directed armies into foreign territories to take their lands and subdue their people. Once they succeeded militarily, they claimed the land and set up military rule over their newly conquered subjects with the intent to incorporate the land into their empire.

The expansion of the American civilization was much less systematic. Yes, there was the French and Indian War by which the British acquired land. As we saw in chapter 3, there were also many wars with the Native Americans over territory. Those latter wars, however, were most often fought locally by colonists under the direction of their local leaders. For instance, the wars fought against Native Americans by colonists in Connecticut were not coordinated with the wars fought in the Southern colonies; nor did they have a single leader on the colonist side.

After the colonists won their freedom from England, the newly formed United States doubled its size not by a war fought with a centralized army but with the Louisiana Purchase.* Later, in the 1840s, President Polk attempted to purchase disputed territory from Mexico. When that failed, America went to war with Mexico and gained another huge swath of land all the way to California. Even with those gains, the United States government did not have a large military presence from the Atlantic to the Pacific to enforce and maintain its territorial claims. America was able to maintain it gains, with what could be considered a limited minimal military presence, because it benefited from its location far from Europe or other threatening powers. That too was quite different from Rome, Macedon, and the Mongol Empire when they were on the rise—none of which were territorially isolated. They required greater vigilance and men under arms to protect their gains.

After achieving territorial success in North America, in what can be considered the second stage of its existence, America became predominantly isolationist with respect to the rest of the world. That was in keeping with George Washington's desire for the young nation not to takes sides in the conflicts between European powers and later as part of the Monroe Doctrine. During that long stage, which lasted until 1917, America's territorial ambitions were limited and the country appeared largely satisfied with its geographical place in the world.

In its third stage, however, America was coaxed out of its isolationist policies to enter two world wars and the Korean War. As we know, America played a decisive role in those conflicts. However, despite its victories in conjunction with its allies, America's postwar actions were not classic empire-building ways. America did not claim permanent hegemony over land, people, or governments in Europe, despite having sufficient military resources to do so, including the world's first

---

* It remains true that Americans, even after the Louisiana Purchase, repeatedly fought Native Americans to gain control of the land. That process remained very different from the manner in which the Roman Empire was created or that of Macedon and others.

nuclear weapons. Departing from the empires of the past even further, after World War II, America developed the Marshall Plan, which taxed American citizens to help rebuild European infrastructure and even help the badly vanquished Germany. Further, after both World War I and World War II, America greatly reduced the size of its standing armies. The United States also promoted the League of Nations and then eventually the United Nations in an effort to reduce the possibility of future wars. In those ways and others, America did not act consistently with most of the great empires of the past.

On the other hand, America did project its power among after the World War II. It imposed conditions on Germany and Japan, which led to those countries becoming democracies. The United States also projected its power in the form of military bases. The United States has a military presence in over eighty countries worldwide. Those military installations form the backbone of America's putative desire to prevent another world war, as does the United States continuing to have the world's largest military budget. By contrast, China has but nine foreign military installations and bases, most of them in the Pacific. However, at the writing of this book, China and Cuba have established some form of joint military and intelligence activity within Cuba. For its part, Russia has over twenty military bases worldwide.

En route to US military dominance and might, the countries of the world took great notice of America. For American allies and foes, that took a form not unlike Georg Wilhelm Friedrich Hegel's description of his viewing of Napoleon: "It is indeed a wonderful sensation to see such an individual, who, concentrated here at a single point, astride a horse, reaches out over the world and masters it."[1] After World War II and Korea, in the eyes of many around the globe, America appeared to be the colossal astride the world stage and a force for good.

Even so, if we look back at the three stages, we can conclude that the American civilization has not been an empire in the classic, historical sense.

If we consider the reach of American culture, however, we may arrive at a slightly different conclusion.

American culture and, importantly, its founding purposes, have also been preeminent throughout the world. Prior to World War II, there were just six working democracies/republics in the world. That number has reached more than eighty in the years since. In 1945, when Ho Chi Minh proclaimed the independent Democratic Republic of Vietnam, he did so with these words:

> All men are created equal; they are endowed by their Creator with certain inalienable Rights; among them are Life, Liberty, and the pursuit of Happiness.
>
> This immortal statement was made in the Declaration of Independence of the United States of America in 1776. In a broader sense, this means: All the peoples on the earth are equal from birth, all the peoples have a right to live, to be happy and free.[2]

Although Vietnam was not in a position to sustain those ideals in practice, and most would say that was because Ho Chi Minh was not truly in favor of democracy, it nevertheless speaks volumes that a culture so unlike the United States of the West would cite American values.

As for the rest of American culture, it is perhaps even more dominant than its military. For instance, a 2008 survey found that "Canadians have a higher average percentage of correct scores on questions about America (47 percent) than they do on questions about Canada (42 percent)."[3] Meanwhile, a world away in remote Tibet, an American traveler, Max Perelman, spent time with Tibetans who had "apparently never traveled far from their village before" or "seen technology like Perelman's camera. Yet at some point in the conversation, one of the Tibetans turned to Perelman and asked: How is Michael Jordan doing?"[4] As the *New Republic* writer of those words points out, the Tibetan's knowledge of Michael Jordan "reveals a defining feature of the contemporary international order: The rest of the world is glued to the United States. Foreigners follow American news stories like their own, listen to American pop music, and watch copious amounts of American television and film."[5]

Beyond its culture and values, American business enterprises have become preeminent throughout the world. In chapter 10, we reviewed the sheer volume of major impacts American innovators have had on the world. Today, that trend continues with the enormous impacts Apple, Google (Alphabet), Tesla, Amazon, Facebook (Meta), and others are having on the world. In keeping with that, according to the World Economic Forum, at the outset of the 2020s, US companies "dominate[d] global markets." In 2023, American companies were 9 of the 10 largest companies in the world.[6] At the same time, foreign investments by US companies "grew from $580 billion [1982] to more than $6.4 trillion dollars" in 2021—a tenfold increase even after adjusting for inflation.[7] As a point of reference, if that amount of investment, $6.4 trillion, was that of a country, it would be the third largest economy in the world at that time.[8]

Beyond sheer size, America's "brand" is preeminent throughout the world as well. According to the 2020 Brand Origin Index Rankings, which measures "the connection between a nation and the popularity as well as preference of its products," America ranks in the top ten countries for all of the categories measured.[9] Similarly, the top four most valuable brands in the world belong to American companies.[10]

IS AMERICAN INFLUENCE EBBING?

The implied question posed at the outset of this chapter, however, was, what is the "state" of the American empire? As we answer that question, amid America's great power, we keep this quote in mind, which is attributed to Percy Bysshe Shelley, a British writer in the early 1800s who spent a considerable amount of time in Italy: "The Earth is littered with the ruins of empires that once believed they were eternal." Shelley's sentiment is plainly true. Given what we have discussed so far, is it also true that the American "empire" could be ebbing in several respects?

First, we must note that America's economy is growing at a significantly lower pace—below 2 percent a year on average—than in its earlier years. Meanwhile, government spending in America has exploded since the 1970s, and the national debt is now significantly larger than the size of the economy with no reasonable grounds to believe it will be reduced—let alone repaid. To the contrary, America seems not to care that it is running multitrillion-dollar deficits every year or that interest on the national debt now exceeds the defense budget—likely a telling sign of the decline of American power. We can add to that the fact that all of those military bases and activity around the globe, including foreign aid, has come at great expense. America's military budget is three times that of China and likely ten times that of Russia.[11]

Those should be of concern with respect to the American "empire" because, throughout history, there has been a self-limiting dynamic for empires in that they can only extend so far and last as long as their economy will permit. In the words of Paul M. Kennedy and Karin Schambach in their book *The Rise and Fall of the Great Powers*, "The history of the rise and later fall of the leading countries . . . shows a very significant correlation over the longer term between productive and revenue raising capacities on the one hand and military strength on the other."[12] Thus, while America today is able to sustain its military influence around the world, its ability to do so in the future is certainly in question if America continues to suffer from weak economic growth, a high tax burden, and an exploding national debt.

There is also the question of the American resolve with respect to its international role. Pacifism, defined as "the principle or policy that all differences among nations should be adjusted without recourse to war,"[13] is on the rise in America—as it usually is the farther away from its founding a civilization becomes. America is less stoic and more epicurean. In its culture today, masculinity is debated and in numerous circles masculinity decried. That is a far cry from the efforts of the colonists who, idealistically, took on a superpower and the efforts of the heroic young Americans to save the world from the likes of Hitler on the shores of Normandy, where they faced certain death—with no safe spaces to be found. Overall, Americans have passed from founding a nation in a war, to fighting to preserve their frontiers, to fighting world wars, to a significant percentage of Americans being morally opposed to wars.[†] Regardless of your view on the matter, that progression is in keeping with the historical dynamic that civilizations tend to be more martial in their beginning than toward their end.

Finally, we noted at the outset of the book that internal division can limit a civilization's progression if not prevent it altogether. America, as of the writing of this book, is deeply divided—beyond normal ideological bounds. The world is witness to the intense divisions in American politics today. The American states are divided between Red (Republican) states and Blue (Democratic) states. National elections are most often very close—decided by under 100,000 well placed votes across a country of over 360 million. Rarely do the parties compromise on legislation. Most recently, American politics has taken an ugly turn with the criminalization of political differences. This era of broad societal division is neither accidental nor temporary. Its root cause is simple but not easily remedied. America today is no longer a place of a largely singular cultural vision as it was for most of its history. It is now the home of widening and competing cultural views that play out in the massive size and scope of the federal, state, and local governments that we have created—and those differences and high-stakes competitions are driving Americans apart.

[†] While it was true America was isolationist early in its history, that was not the reflection of a weak martial spirit as much as it was a choice to not get involved in wars perceived as being outside America's national interest.

If we consider Lincoln's observation that "a house divided against itself cannot stand,"[14] given the level of division today in America, certainly there must be concern that America's ability to project its values across the world is in question. All combined, certainly there are warning signs about the state of the American "empire."

CHAPTER 13

Ten Vital Lessons of the American Civilization

In history, a great volume is unrolled for our instruction, drawing the materials of future wisdom from the past errors and infirmities of mankind.

—**Edmund Burke**, *Reflections on the Revolution in France*

Now that we have completed our survey of the American civilization, it is time for us to succinctly consider some of the more salient lessons of the American civilization. As we do so, we note that there has been much to absorb from those who landed on America's uncertain shores and started a new civilization amid great hardships. The same can be said about those Americans who revolted from the superpower that was England and wrote an unprecedented Constitution that proceeded from the principle of God-given rights of citizens and the consent of the governed—not the edicts of a monarch who claimed his own divine rights.

Americans fostered their own Industrial Revolution and now a worldwide technological revolution. They fought a civil war, two world wars, and numerous regional wars. Explorers, immigrants, patriots, politicians, artists, farmers, entrepreneurs, factory workers, individuals, families, and so many more created the rich fabric of America. From those varied lives, like so many civilizations before, the actions of Americans have been unique, but collectively, they have acted with some degree of regularity. From that regularity, we shall derive these lessons among others.

LESSON ONE: The American Story Shares Many Common Elements with Other Civilizations, Past and Present

We must start by recognizing that, as unique as the American civilization has been, from its start to today, America has progressed along a historical continuum shared by many civilizations of the past. America was born stoic. Its culture and economy moved from the farmlands to the city streets. The family gave way as the economic unit to the individual. Industrialization followed commercialism and great wealth was created. Governments started small and relentlessly grew.

The economy initially thrived under limited interference but has slowed with the growth of those governments and their mandates, regulations, and taxes. America extended its borders, projected its military might, and exported its goods, culture, and form of government. After obtaining great wealth, undergoing urbanization, and experiencing the progress of education and science, American values and culture changed. To a significant degree, America's morals have eased over time, and its once strongly and widely held beliefs, whether religious or about its basic purposes of opportunity and democratization, have become doubts—or, as Goethe would suggest, *unbelief.* In those ways and many others, the progression of America's civilization has been similar to that of ancient Greece, Rome, Venice, and many other places and times.

The first lesson, therefore, lies in answering our threshold question: *Does history repeat itself?* History does repeat itself. As Will Durant wrote, "History repeats itself, but only in outline and in the large . . . because human nature changes with geological leisureliness, and man is equipped to respond in stereotyped ways to frequently occurring situations and stimuli like hunger, danger, and sex."[1] We should add to that by noting that we may react to different degrees today because our means, especially in the age of tech, have grown and accelerated. When matched with the speed of technology, the pace at which civilizations rise and fall has been accelerated.

The fact that history does repeat itself, as a civilization progresses along its continuum, carries with it the one implication that can only be ignored with peril. *We can learn from the past* and immensely so. What seems new is often truly old. What is being tried likely was already tried—perhaps not in exact detail but generally. Billions of lives have come and gone and their wisdom, gained through so many varied experiences, is in fact the largest history lesson of all. We would do well to learn from the lessons of the past and be quite wary of those, often social engineers or proponents of ever more government, who say the past is not an essential guide for what lies ahead.

LESSON TWO: America Is Proof of How Capitalism Is Necessary for a Broad and Sustainable Democracy

Dissent is the mother of democracy—capitalism its father.

When capitalism is considered as a historical matter, most often it is a reference to it as an economic system that allows individuals the ability to produce goods and services and to create great wealth. Nearly as often, especially at the writing of this book, there are references to its effects on work conditions and the disparities in wealth. For our purposes, however, we shall concentrate on a more profound effect capitalism has had on history.

We must recall that, at the time the United States was founded, there was no working democracy or republic in the world. Despite no such working model, the Founders placed enormous power into the hands of its citizens. In significant part, *the United States succeeded because, at its founding, it had no existing class structure that simultaneously exercised the economic and political power of the day across the country*. That dynamic is in stark contrast to the history of the world. For most of world history, the owners of land, be it a king or feudal lord, had power over both the economy and the government. Under that system (serfdom), the masses had few possessions and, generation after generation, they were bound to poverty working on the lands of those feudal lords and kings. The masses, not surprisingly, had little to no political power.

In contrast, capitalism allowed for the creation of *new* wealth—one of money, goods, and services—not title to land. Over time, with that new wealth, which could be made virtually anywhere, came dispersed economic power—east, west, north and south. It was dispersed among countless participants. In America, it was dispersed among the thousands of family-owned farms and then to the developing commercial enterprises. Those countless participants included those from among the title-less masses and often did not include the landed aristocracy or nobility.

Throughout history, as developing economic (usually commercial) classes have matured, the owners of that new wealth have turned their attention to politics. Not only did they want a say in how their enterprises were treated by government, but as their economic power grew, they also would seek greater control over government at large. Often they seek that participation peacefully—other times only to a breaking point. Indeed, countless times the frustrated have used violent means to wrestle power away from their rulers. History is littered with such revolutions, including our own.

Ultimately, and most importantly, capitalism fostered the dispersement of economic and political power among many more people than had ever occurred under the previous centuries of feudal and monarchial systems. There remained a few kings and many feudal lords—but there were countless more cobblers, blacksmiths, doctors, lawyers, teachers, bakers and so on—many of whom participated in local politics. Among those many, the newly dispersed economic and political power became the foundation on which freely elected governments were born and the only lasting foundation on which they can survive.

So, in Florence, early capitalism preceded the founding of its Republic. It brought to power a merchant class where Florence, and its surrounding countryside, had been ruled by feudal lords and nobles for centuries. Once in power, those commercial interests, who were creating jobs within the city for those in the countryside, could abolish serfdom (1287). With that, they freed the masses from the centuries of generational poverty they endured at the hands of those feudal lords and nobles. From there, following the official overthrow of the noble class (1293), a Florentine constitution could begin to take form, in fits and starts, paving the way for Florence to become a republic and among the richest city-states of the Renaissance. We must also note that the separation of economic and political power, in the Florence of the 1300s and 1400s, was still not broad enough or sustainable enough within that small city-state for a true democracy/republic to be maintained. Instead, Florentine democracy would succumb, to varying degrees, into a republic influenced heavily by an oligarchy (rule by a few)—most prominently by the Medici.

A sustainable republic* would have to wait until America became history's greatest example of how a republic or democracy, with a broad

---

* Recall that France has had five republics during roughly the same time period as the single American Republic.

franchise, can succeed—if economic and political power are sufficiently separated for a long enough period. The America born in 1776 had no powerful, centralized government and no ruling class. Its economic power was dispersed over thirteen colonies, and so too was its political power—powers that were not, by all historical comparisons, in the same hands as the economically powerful, as was prevalent in most of Europe at the time. *That separation of economic and political powers, made possible by capitalism, is the most important benefit of capitalism—more so than the riches, goods, and services that flow from capitalism.*

Even so, and despite the efforts of the Founders to create a limited government, in America today, that hard-won separation of economic and political power is diminishing rapidly and much to the Republic's peril. Huge corporations, with the help of the governments they lobby and donations they make to politicians, obtain preferential laws and regulations, not to mention government contracts. In the modern vernacular, that dynamic is referred to as "crony capitalism"—in essence, a system in which economic decisions are the result of government favoritism as opposed to market forces[2]—a process that stands in contrast to "free enterprise," whereby the market has a greater say than the government and large special interests. As that process intensifies, those special interests are empowered to determine even the most consequential public policies to a far greater degree than voters or even elected officials. That dynamic is inherent to all large governments, which by their nature decide countless issues and whose politicians grant access to the interested not to mention accept their money.

Of the ancient Roman senators, it was said that the cost of a vote was well known. In the modern United States, the amount of money spent on lobbying has risen right along with the money spent by our governments. Those dynamics, however, stand in direct contrast to the original purposes of the American civilization: the broad democratization of power. If it is allowed to continue, it will undermine, if not threaten, the very viability of the American Republic.

LESSON THREE: America Is Exceptional Compared to All Other Civilizations

If we compare the American civilization to those before it, we find achievements and experiences unlike anywhere else in history. That is not to say America was ever perfect or without fault. We have seen some of those faults and, like all human experiences, some of those faults endure. It does mean, however, that by comparison, overall, it has had unparalleled successes.

We know that no other country was founded and sustained itself with such a broad array of rights for citizens. By comparison, the republics and democracies that came before the United States had more limited rights and often only for a select few. Since then, America has continued to build on those rights—albeit in fits and starts.

The American experience saw George Washington win a revolution, lay down his sword, and then relinquish his power. With that historic act, Americans could deviate from much of the world's known history and base their governments on God-given rights to their citizenry—not to a king. From there, Americans could authorize their governments to act only when citizenry permitted it to act. The magnitude of that precedent is lost on many today—but, in the annals of time, it was the foundational arch to the passageway of freedom for the masses.

Later, Americans made the decisive difference in two world wars and Korea, where freedom was at stake, but claimed, by all historical standards, title to no significant territory in return. Instead, consistent with their founding principles, they financed the recovery of citizens not governments in the form of the Marshall Plan for Europe and the reconstruction of Japan. No other civilization had done so before on such a grand scale.

Further, nowhere else has produced so many rags-to-riches stories, politically or economically—and still does. The American experience produced Abraham Lincoln, who changed the political history of the world, not from breeding and privilege, but from opportunity and perseverance.

In the private realm, John D. Rockefeller and Henry Ford, from humble beginnings, changed the economic history of the world through hard work, not inherited lands or important fathers. Hundreds of years later, America still produces enormously successful people who started from nothing, including Elon Musk, who came to America with little in his pocket and is now changing the world like few in history. Indeed, we have seen how so many of the world's inventions, which have become necessities in our lives, came from American entrepreneurs, not government. Along the way, the American system and its achievements lifted more people out of poverty than any system before or since, including by helping feed the disadvantaged overseas.

What makes the American civilization historically exceptional is that it has offered the greatest opportunity to the greatest number and most diverse set of people of any place on the globe for centuries—all the while giving them an unprecedented say in their government. That unique achievement was only possible because of the unique combination and degree of the economic freedom Americans enjoyed and the freedom from government that was the American experience for so many years. The historical dynamic, unlike any other system in history over centuries, allowed America to integrate tens of millions of diverse peoples who came and continue to come to its shores seeking opportunity. No other civilization in history has done that. To this day, and over 160 years later after President Lincoln's pronouncement, America still represents the world's last best hope for democracy. We must add the best hope for economic opportunity as well.

LESSON FOUR: It Remains the Natural Course of Events for Governments' Power to Centralize, and the America of Today Is Just Another Example

The American Founders studied ancient Greece and Rome in addition to living under the rule of King George. They saw the dangers centralized power presented. They also understood that the historical tendency is for power to centralize over time. In response, they considered Baron Montesquieu's model for a government of three completely autonomous branches of government and crafted a constitution, not with completely autonomous branches, but with a separation of powers.

It was the goal of the Founders *not* to have an efficient, powerful government. They wanted freedom to reign. They focused on restricting government growth and the centralization of power so as to preserve freedom—more so than any government that had existed before. That too was a unique achievement. Even so, and despite the Founders' genius, the law of history that power centralizes over time has overridden their best efforts and is now on stunning display in America.

Slowly at first, then spurred on by commercialization and urbanization, as well as crises after crises, government power has grown in America. Then, with the advent of television, we have seen how government spending and regulations have dramatically increased to nearly half the economy where just over one hundred years ago it was less than 10 percent. With each new dollar spent, American governments exercise greater power. The once small cabinet of President George Washington has become an executive branch spending trillions of dollars and proliferating countless regulations.

That growth, now combined with technological advances, has seen the expansion of the American surveillance state, whose growth and powers dwarf all prior abilities of governments to diminish the rights of citizens. It threatens the extinction of the Bill of Rights and provides another example of the growing and centralizing power of the federal government.

Overall, where once Americans lived nearly free of government influence let alone interference, and where once churches were at the center of its communities, American governments now exercise enormous power over nearly every activity Americans undertake. Whether it is the economy, the environment, schooling, healthcare, retirement, and now even speech, governments, and their ever-centralizing power are at the center of the American civilization.

LESSON FIVE: Centralized Power Is Antidemocratic and the Sworn Enemy of the Consent of the Governed

It is human nature, and therefore a law of history, for people to protect their own interests. When it comes to political power, that dynamic cannot be understated. That law of history applies to governments and their rulers as well. They often seek to protect their power from the governed or their rivals. So we find that history is littered with examples of those in power eliminating their opposition. King Herod, who became King of Judea through marriage, killed his wife he suspected of adultery and his two sons by her to secure his throne in the year 7 BC. After his return to Milan in 1479, Ludovico Sforza, perhaps more generously, used imprisonment and exile to ensure his rule, as did Ercole d'Este in Ferrara.[3] We saw at the height of the Venetian Republic that access to office was restricted in response to public dissent and a spy network was created in the form of the Council of Ten, which spied on the Venetian citizenry in the name of the stability of that republic.

Four centuries later, in America, the 1798 Sedition Act under John Adams jailed critics of Adams but permitted attacks on his opposition, then–vice president Thomas Jefferson.[†] The private acts of Rockefeller, Carnegie, and Morgan thwarted the populist influence on government in the late 1890s to maintain their hold on public policy. Woodrow Wilson's Sedition Act of 1918 curtailed dissent as well—by charging more than two thousand people and convicting more than one thousand. In California today, the Democratic Party in power has restricted the citizens' right to utilize the century old direct initiative process in an effort to limit their say in government.

---

† Note that in those early days, president and vice presidents did not run as aticket. The president was elected by winning the most electoral college votes and the vice president was elected by coming in second in the electoral college. That practice ended in 1804 with the ratification of the Twelfth Amendment in response to the Adams/Jefferson election.

That "protect the government from its citizenry" dynamic reached new heights with the 2016 election and coordination between the campaign of Hillary Clinton, the Obama administration, the FBI, and the Department of Justice. Together, pursuant to a partisan plan and a threadbare of information, they unleashed an investigation of their political opponent, Donald Trump, who was a direct threat to their power base, as signified by his call to "drain the swamp." The prosecutions of Donald Trump took that growing dynamic to a level never seen before. By the same token, the government protection of the Biden family from prosecution (2017–2023) was less about Joe Biden and more about the government supporting the proponents of government over those who would curtail it.

To what effect are such actions and this lesson?

History is rather clear on this point. *Dissent is the mother of democracy.* Therefore, it is often the target of those in power. America was founded by the likes of Samuel Adams and Patrick Henry, who stood in verbal defiance of government power. It was their early efforts that the idea of revolution took shape. As government power grows, the means and motives to squelch such dissent rises almost exponentially.

Further, *it is a tired refrain of history for those in power to claim that dissent is a threat to the stability of the government*—as they did in Venice and with the passing of the Sedition Acts referenced above. Really what those who exercised such powers were saying was that dissent is a threat to their power.

America today is witness to government interference with free speech, especially political speech, which was enshrined in the First Amendment. At the writing of this book, those in power arrogantly claim they do so in an effort to save democracy. In reality, like so many times before in history, it is an effort by those in power to maintain their power. It should be obvious that such interference and censorship are inimical to the founding purposes of the American civilization. It is also likely that it is only the beginning of their efforts, which efforts threaten the Republic and its citizens.

As for the American citizens, the French philosopher Voltaire would say, "it is dangerous to be right in matters where established men are wrong." That too is a lesson of history.

LESSON SIX: Growth in Government Reduces Economic Growth

One of the most fundamental laws of economics is the Law of Demand. That law "states that the quantity purchased varies inversely with price. In other words, the higher the price, the lower the quantity demanded."[4] Put another way, human beings are sensitive to price. Thus, Ford automobiles outsell Bentleys on price more than desirability. If two side-by-side stores were advertising the same pair of jeans, but one charged much more, the lower-priced store would garner more sales. That Law of Demand applies, almost without exception, to all things—cars, jeans, employees, and even income. When that Law of Demand is applied to the costs imposed by governments on the national economy, that law dictates that higher taxes and regulations operate to reduce economic activity as capital flows to more favorable environments.

In history, that has occurred precipitously at times, such as in 1330 Pisa, which after buying its freedom from the Holy Roman emperor Louis IV, was deeply in debt. In response, the Pisan government raised taxes, duties and fees significantly an in effort to refill the government coffers only to experience the opposite effect—a flight of capital, the departure of Florentine merchants and a steep economic decline.[5] In America, the steep rise of tax rates from 25 percent to 63 percent, in 1932, helped thwart the fledging recovery after the stock market crash of October 1929. That tax on the economy was a significant contributing factor in the Great Depression along with other government impositions on the economy such as the protectionist Smoot-Hawley Tariff Act, which set off a trade war.

In the words of Arthur B. Laffer, PhD, whose "Laffer curve" was premised on the foundational economic principles of the Law of Demand

and the negative effects tax-rate increases have on economic growth, and his colleagues in their work *Taxes Have Consequences*, the 125 percent tax increase came "at the worst time imaginable. The sensitivity of the economy to yet more shocks in the bitter early months of 1932—banks failing, life savings vanishing, breadlines winding—was exceptionally acute."[6] The results of the tax increase, the Tariff Act and the contraction of the money supply combined to reduce the US economy between 1929 and 1933. Predictably, as incentives to make income fell, along with the retroactive nature of the 1932 tax increase, "top income—the main target of the tax increase in the Revenue Act of 1932, went down by another 30 percent"[7] as part of the "catastrophic" results of government policy.

The costs of government, of course, are not limited to taxation. In the last hundred years, the American economy has been significantly burdened by government regulations. Indeed, at least one study has shown that "between 1949 and 2005 the accumulation of federal regulations slowed US economic growth by an average of 2 percent per year."[8] Compounded over decades, that has resulted in a huge reduction in economic activity. If we take a broader view, the comparative lower governmental costs of the 1800s fostered greater economic growth then when compared to the late 1900s and 2000s.

Indeed, the late 1800s saw US economic growth rates at their highest.[9] Today, American economic growth has slowed to under 2 percent on average. That rate is simply too low to support existing government spending and has resulted in huge government deficits, a national debt that greatly exceeds the size of the economy, and inflation. In 2024, "Bloomberg Economics ran a million forecast simulations on the US debt outlook. 88% of them show borrowing on an unsustainable path."[10] Raising the tax burden on the economy at this point to support more spending will only reduce economic growth further.

The problem reduced economic growth represents for the United States, however, is not just economic and lower standards of living. As we have seen, Americans' common DNA is economic opportunity among otherwise very different cultural groups. If economic growth continues to wane, the economic pie will have stopped expanding and become more fixed—like in Europe today where growth has slowed to nearly 0 percent over the last three decades. With a fixed pie, division in America will rise further as subgroups in America fight over political handouts versus the opportunities of the previous hundreds of years.

Given the level of division that already exists, in this Divided Era (see below), that mounting divide will threaten the social stability of the nation even further and pit differing cultural backgrounds against each other. Just as seriously, the consequence of a prolonged stagnating economy is the reduction of the once wide gulf between economic power and political power—again, threatening the American Republic.

LESSON SEVEN: Over Time, an Expanding Economy Provides the Greatest Possibility for Opportunity—More So Than Long-Term Government Actions

The sustained growth of the dynamic American economy not only produced unprecedented wealth for its time but also fostered the emergence of the largest middle class in history. As with other civilizations, urbanization, increasing wealth, commercialization, and industrialization have led to larger and more active governments. Part of that ever-growing and active governments includes the proliferation of programs purporting to end poverty and/or discrimination. Ever larger governments, however, have slowed economic growth in America and Europe.

That slower growth, as we have seen in chapter 11, has led to diminishing opportunity for many people—regardless of race or gender. In America, the response has been to double down on government programs in an effort to "help" people—even though government dependence has risen significantly in the process. Consider the history of the Great Society, which not only has failed to "end" poverty but has also caused enormous dependency on government.

In plain terms, laws imposed on static economies have never proven in history to either end discrimination or produce opportunity let alone prosperity. The United States should look back on its own history or the history of Singapore to take stock of how a dynamic economy can integrate people of so many different cultures.

LESSON EIGHT: America's Ever-Growing Government Is Fostering Dangerous Division

Throughout history, a people have most often divided politically into two groups. For instance, most of the medieval Italian city-states divided themselves among the Ghibellines (supporters of the Holy Roman emperor/king of Germany who viewed their power as an inheritance from ancient Rome) and the Papacy (whose greatest power arose after the Fall of Rome). In Tuscany, when the Guelphs finally triumphed over the Ghibellines (1289), the natural inclination of men took over again, and infighting became the order of the day in places like Florence. So much so that the Florentines divided themselves among the *Black* Guelphs, the strict supporters of the Papacy, and the *White* Guelphs, who otherwise remained averse to the Ghibellines but were dramatically opposed to Pope Boniface VIII.

Such black-and-white divisions found their way to America in the form of the Federalists and the Anti-Federalists—the two political groups that fought over whether power should centralize in what became the US Constitution. Their fight was quite bitter, engendering such comments from George Washington that either the Constitution must be adopted or the next "would be drawn in blood."[11] After the Constitution was adopted, despite the presence of two parties of two different political philosophies,[12] the division of the day largely receded. It did so because Americans, living mostly in the dominant countryside, could return to their lives largely free of their very small governments.

That dynamic could well be no more.

America, as of the writing of this book, is deeply divided—beyond normal ideological bounds. As I explore at great length in my earlier book, *The Divided Era*, every decision government makes picks a winner and a loser and someone to pay for it. With each such decision, governments foster a competition between Americans (and their corporations and special interests) to get the spoils of government and another competition as to who is to pay for it. Each such government decision also increases the natural competition among political parties to be the party that hands out those government spoils. That dynamic is intensified when the stakes are higher, such as with the issue of slavery.

Further, that competition, and therefore our divisions, also increase with every new dollar spent by our governments. It does so almost mathematically. Indeed, a government that does a dozen things will find a competition for those dozen programs. The American governments (state, local, and federal) that now spend, tax, and regulate over $10 trillion per year correspondingly find innumerable such competitions. That ever-growing competition among Americans and their political parties has become the prominent source of much of the division in America today.

In the final analysis, *the more government decides, the more it divides*. Enlarging government, therefore, only increases our divisions. Given the current rate of the expansion of our governments, America is headed to even more divisive times unless it changes course and limits government once again.

LESSON NINE: Class Division Is One of the Most Dangerous Divisions in History

At America's founding, its economic conditions (exclusive of indentured servitude and the horror of slavery) were comparatively equal among Americans for several reasons. Most prominently, we have seen how when the American civilization started, it was a nation of farms—mostly family farms. Boston, the largest city in 1700, had fewer than seven thousand people, while London had nearly six hundred thousand. Those American family farms were remarkably self-sufficient and there was, by historic standards, a remarkably even distribution of wealth. That dynamic was reinforced by the fact that America also did not have the class structures of the Old World.

Among commercializing societies, and certainly those followed by industrialization, enormous wealth can be made, which is often distributed as unevenly as the abilities among their people. Nevertheless, if economic growth is sustained for a sufficient period of time, dynamic economies create a middle class where precapitalist and socialist systems have not and cannot. Indeed, middle classes did not exist prior to the emergence of capitalism.

We also must recall what we noted in chapter 10, that dynamic economies also produce a fluidity that allows many to move up and down the economic ladders. Stagnant economies do not. Compare the last thirty years of Spain's economic history, or all of Cuba's or Russia's economic history, with that of the United States or Singapore. Again, at the end of the 1900s, 25 percent of America's richest top 20 percent fell out of the top quartile in income, over a fifteen-year period. Meanwhile, of those in the lower quartile, 32 percent moved up. Despite the changes of who is at the bottom and at the top of the economy, the glare of inequality always gives rise to the ambitions of politicians and cries of injustice. That dynamic has been playing itself out in America for 150 years or more. Today, it has reached dangerous levels in the United States.

Like Rome and ancient Greece before it, America has fallen into a class warfare whose flames are fanned by ambitious politicians and media. The Republic that was Rome and the direct democracy that was Greece ended among their deadly class warfare. Much of that class warfare found fodder, as it does today in America, amid the weak economic conditions of the day or the lack of opportunity for many of the lower economic classes. Of course, those weak economic conditions are the predictable result of burdensome government policies that were often the ideas of those who seek an ever-broader role of government.

America today is witness to a shrinking middle class—a by-product of weak economic growth of 2 percent instead of the higher growth of the late 1800s and early 1900s. America would be wise to understand that no socialist or semi-socialist government in history has significantly raised the standards of living of its people. Instead, those governments have reduced economic output to the point of economic stagnation, resulting in government dependence, as in America today, among a huge percentage of the population. If America is to avoid the fate of Rome and Greece, not to mention the economic and political results or Venezuela, it would be wise to adopt policies that foster economic growth, not political division.

LESSON TEN: The Cultural Breakdown in America Has Had Its Consequences

America over the last 140 years, consistent with historical norms, has witnessed the societal upheaval that is the transition from an agrarian-based civilization to one living in urban settings. With that, the patriarchal family as the economic and cultural foundation of America has given way to the individual as the economic unit and, consequentially, resulted in a dramatic reduction in the size and number of families. At the same time, growing wealth and expanding scientific knowledge have diminished religious devotion and loosened morals—as did the transition from the relatively poor medieval Italy to the far richer Italy of the Renaissance and in so many other places in history.

Adding to the American dynamic has been the fundamental change in its education system. In America, education, here defined as Durant would define it—the transmission of traditions and culture from one generation to the next—originally was the domain of families and school systems based in religious and/or private institutions. Jointly, they reinforced America's founding purposes of the democratization of freedom and opportunity. Over the last hundred years, however, government schools have supplanted private schools and even the traditional roles of the family.‡ With increasing frequency, those government institutions have not been teaching America's founding principles and purposes. Quite the opposite, they have become increasingly opposed to, if not hostile to, America's founding purposes and to the traditional family unit and traditional values. Indeed, one can safely make the argument that America's youth are not being taught the values or the purposes of the American civilization to any significant degree. Again, what is not taught in the schools is forgotten in the culture.

Beyond that, American children are being taught that nearly anything can be appropriate. Under such circumstances, when a young mind is taught that anything goes, no one should be surprised when it does. Nor can we be surprised under such circumstances that human life becomes devalued and crime without consequences rises. At the same time, the work ethic, patriotism, and resolve of the nation's youth has diminished with the accumulation of wealth and changing educational priorities. Consider the difference between the youthful soldiers who stormed the beaches of Normandy in World War II, facing near certain death, and the rise of "safe spaces" for American youth today.

According to Durant, writing in 1968, "As the sanity of the individual lies in the continuity of his memories, so the sanity of a group lies in the continuity of its traditions; in either case a break in the chain invites a neurotic reaction, as in the Paris massacres of September, 1792."[13] Tellingly, Victor Davis Hanson recently wrote of the American "Jacobian Revolution," describing the frantic assault on American traditions also by referring to the excesses of the French Revolution. We have discussed the

---

‡ Consider the 2023 fight in California whether schools can withhold informtion from parents related to a child's gender.

impact technology has on accelerating that process. We must also conclude, as Durant and others have concluded, that no civilization can sustain itself without a moral code and no moral code has lasted without the support of religious and educational institutions. Further, history has no working example of a civilization that did not suffer severe consequences from the breakdown of the family unit—let alone the manner in which it is occurring in America at the writing of this book. The speed at which traditions are being challenged and discarded is likely too fast for any one civilization to endure.

Worse yet, in that frenzy new norms go well beyond *voluntary* beliefs. Instead, this mistaken popular culturalism demands adherence to views however transitory or new. In the America of the 2020s, the dangerous realm of forced beliefs has taken hold, and with that come dangerous challenges to American freedoms.

One historical definition of tyranny is that of forced beliefs. One of America's primary founding purposes was to end such practices. If Americans do not see this dynamic in context, if they ignore Plato's warning that unmitigated democracy, here meaning immediate action by transient popular demand, leads to tyranny or unjust rule by despots, or they ignore Durant's and Hanson's warnings, then the American experiment with freedom will surely come to an end.

★ ★ ★

With those lessons of the American civilization, let us now consider what lies ahead.

EPILOGUE

What Lies Ahead

I do not believe that civilizations have to die because civilization is not an organism. It is a product of wills.

—**Attributed to Arnold J. Toynbee**

So, what does the future hold for the American civilization? Will America go the way of the republic that was Ancient Rome? Will America be surpassed by a rising civilization, China for example, while America luxuriates in its riches and the protections afforded it by two oceans and its weaponry? Will it continue to lead the Free World? Or will some other fate await the centuries-old American civilization that achieved unprecedented dominance?

A FUTURE AND A HOPE

As we consider those questions, let me repeat what I stated at the outset of this work that *history is no more a straight line than the emotions of our days.*

Just as tomorrow is guaranteed to no one, there is also no required timely end to a civilization, as the quote at the beginning of this chapter from Toynbee counsels us. Among other factors, the fate of America still lies in the hands of Americans and their combined wills. Even so, human nature being what it is, as we look to the future, we must do so with an eye to how humans acted in the past. We also cannot overlook one other lesson of history—mankind's ability to adapt and improve.

Consider, if you will, the fate of Japan after World War II. Centuries ago, it would have been a likely outcome for Japan, after losing the war so dramatically, that a victorious country and its army would have permanently occupied, if not annexed, the vanquished country—altering the Japanese civilization indelibly.

However, at the end of World War II, despite its defeat, Japan was not annexed by the United States and its allies. In what can be considered a more enlightened outcome than the fate of those occupied by the Soviets, Japan was temporarily occupied but not annexed. It was required by those victorious allies to become a parliamentary democracy. In time, those allies withdrew and the trajectory of the Japanese civilization ascended to a new peak of prosperity and culture nearly unrecognizable from the country that bombed Pearl Harbor. Indeed, by the end of the 1900s, Japan had the world's second-largest economy. Similarly, the democracy and economic powerhouse that is the Germany of the twenty-first century resembles not at all the country or the leadership that prosecuted two world wars.

Let us consider another example—the fate of Italy. Figure E.1 is a map of the Holy Roman Empire, circa 1181. The emperor at the time was Frederick Barbarossa. He became the ruler of what is now Germany in 1152 and later the Holy Roman emperor. Note how deeply, into what is now Italy, Barbarossa's empire extended at that time. Between inheritances and victories, Barbarossa annexed lands, thereby expanding his empire. How different the world history would have been if Italy had remained part of the Holy Roman Empire.

Epilogue: What Lies Ahead

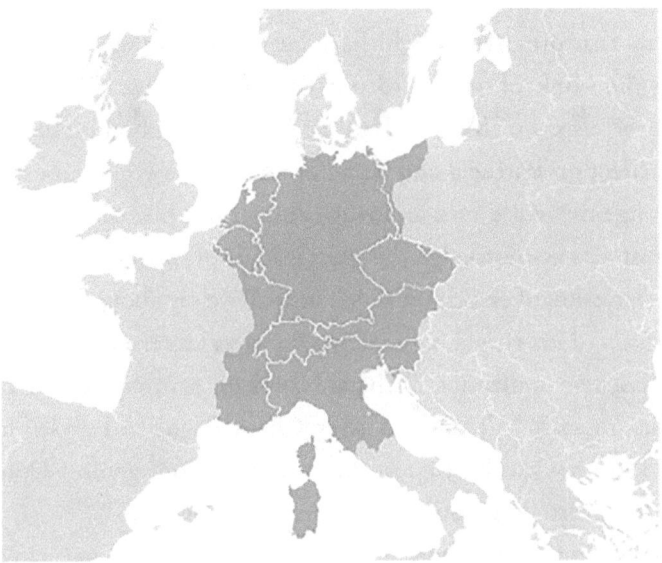

Figure E.1. Holy Roman Empire, circa 1181. (Source: "Holy Roman Empire Lessons for Kids: Timeline and Facts," Study.com, accessed March 29, 2024, https://study.com/academy/lesson/holy-roman-empire-lesson-for-kids-timeline-facts.html.)

Before then, the seminal Battle of Tours took place in 732 AD. Charles Martel's forces defeated the Muslim invaders of France. If Martel's forces had lost, the history of Western Europe would have been much different as well.

Such dramatic changes in the trajectory of a civilization are not limited to the effects of war. For instance, Portugal's successful sea-faring navigation around the Cape of Good Hope (Southern Africa) in 1488 changed the world dramatically. Prior to that, the trade routes to the Far East were dominated for centuries by the Republic of Venice of the Mediterranean Sea. Portugal's circumnavigation, however, more directly connected Atlantic trade with Far Eastern trade and forever diminished the importance of the Mediterranean Sea and its civilizations, including Italy. Now consider the technological advancements of the last seventy years that ignore sea routes altogether. For decades, planes have brought products on rather direct routes to their destinations. Then, with the advent of email, documents that otherwise might have been sent overnight by plane now arrive in the blink of an eye to our handheld devices. We also cannot discount the effects of Mother Nature. The 1755 Lisbon earthquake had a lasting effect on Portugal and its ambitions. Meanwhile, super volcanos could plunge the world into an ice age and write a history not yet known.

We must also acknowledge the great leaders of history and their effects on the progression of civilizations. What shall we say about the impact that Jesus Christ and his gospel has had on countless leaders and everyday lives over the last two millennia? Perhaps Napoleon summarized part of that effect when he said, "Alexander, Cæsar, Charlemagne and myself founded empires. But on what did we rest the creations of our genius? Upon sheer force. Jesus Christ alone founded His empire upon love."[1]

Greece's Solon, at the start of the sixth century BC, navigated bitter Greek divisions between rich and poor with economic reforms that set Greece on the path to its democracy. We could ask whether the Roman Republic would have emerged if democracy had not been allowed to develop in Greece. Centuries later, Charlemagne, after becoming king of the Franks in 771 AD, then king of the Lombards, and then ruler of the Holy Roman Empire, brought order to the wilderness that was Europe after the fall of Rome through force, administrative reforms, and his alliance with the Pope—thereby spreading Christianity across Europe. He succeeded in such efforts where others had failed before him.

Later, Napoleon, for a time, remade the map of Europe. Joan of Arc inspired the French nation with her courage at the Battle of Orleans centuries before Napoleon and changed the course of France's Hundred Years' War with England. We have seen how George Washington handed back his powers to Congress after his Revolutionary War victory, thereby giving birth to American democracy. What would the world look like today if he chose to be a king like some suggested and many others expected? The world also knows of Abraham Lincoln's resolve that kept America together. What if he had accepted the South's argument that the Constitution was a voluntary pact and allowed the South to simply secede, leaving the

American continent with two diverging civilizations? If he had, would America have been the world's "last best hope" or just another historical example of how internal division can limit a civilization?

VIGILANCE IN THE FACE OF UNCERTAINTY

As we reflect on those giants of history, we may find that no final answer to the age-old question—*Do men make the times or times make the men?*—is possible. Even so, history has been diverted, and substantially so at times, by leaders of great resolve and vision. Even amid the difficulty most find today in the world, perhaps we shall find ourselves again just one great leader away from changing the course of history.

If we consider all of that, we must conclude that a certain level of unpredictability is also a lesson of history. At any time, the winds of change can alter the fate of millions. America in the years ahead may just gain, or suffer, one or more of the fates referenced here or possibly others.

With that in mind, can we be more precise as to what does lie head?

First, we cannot discount the possibility of a significant war, conventional, cyber or otherwise, especially given that technology makes easier, and increases, our capacities to do harm to each other. That is especially true with respect to the prospects that future warfare will be in the cybersphere and the coming technological leap known as quantum computing. If America endures to such an attack, it may well be because its leaders failed to meet that challenge of upgrading its infrastructure in favor of other domestic spending they thought would garner more immediate accolades. History is littered with examples of the failure of leaders to meet the long-term needs of society in favor of their own short-term gains.

In the last millennium armies pillaged the economic capacity of their adversaries by burning fields, businesses, and towns. With cyber warfare, combatants will cripple economic capacity electronically by targeting private and government infrastructure. In 2024, that prospect was also raised with the fear that Russia's Putin would put a nuclear weapon in space—and with that, once again, what appears to be new is, in fact, a variance of what is really old. Despite the passage of time, it may be that we differ in our capacities but our motives remain stubbornly the same.

No nation should discount the stated intentions of others—such as those of China globally and locally with respect to Taiwan. All should be mindful of Iran's threats to Israel in the dangerous region of the Middle East or the ambitions of Russia to restore its prominence in Europe. If we consider nuclear weapons, which present a serious danger (to be surpassed by some technology of the future), we should also note that nuclear weapons—and America's enormous military might—have guaranteed more borders and reduced the number of wars after their use in World War II. Consider the sheer number of wars in the hundred years before America's bombing of Japan versus the years afterward.

Even so, the cautious reader notes that many wars are started by miscalculations that can proliferate out of control. The badly mistaken "peace in our time" assessment of Hitler in 1938 by the British Prime Minister Neville Chamberlain helped foster World War II. In 1950, US Secretary of State Dean Acheson's very public statement that the American "defensive perimeter" in the Pacific did not include that the Republic of Korea proved dangerous. Just six months later, the world was engulfed in the Korean War. If history teaches us anything, it certainly reminds us that peace can never be assured, especially when vigilance is neglected.

As we look to the future, there is the question of space. The world's borders have remained relatively stable for some time, but space offers no such certainty. Some fifty years ago, a NASA scientist, Donald J. Kessler, warned that the overcrowding of low-Earth orbit, with satellites and the like, would lead to collisions in space at an accelerating rate.[2] It may be that the rush to space will resemble the dynamics of early capitalism whereby the rush to succeed outpaces safety concerns. So, while the heavens may well be abundant in minerals and energy, given the competitive nature of humans, individually and played out among nations, beyond security threats in the form of weapons, we can expect friction or worse as we look to colonize the heavens.

Absent some cataclysmic event, let us start by stating that the territorial integrity of the United States is quite likely to endure for an untold number of years—again, in significant part, because of two oceans, docile neighbors, and America's nuclear arsenal. If that is so, then it is more likely than not that the current domestic trends affecting the American civilization will continue.

There is good cause to believe that the American civilization, comprising so many, will continue to innovate and produce riches—assuming the absence of serious foreign interference. The reasons America out-produces Europe and other more centralized economies remain and likely will for decades to come. However, the American governments' trend toward European-style social democracies will reduce prosperity from where it could have been. The Law of Demand, and its simple notion that the more something costs, the less of it you demand, will endure. It applies to the US economy as a whole and the American economy has become beset by more costs, taxes, and regulations than ever in its history. Given the ascent of those costs since the 1970s, with occasional reductions or limitations (for example, tax reforms in the 1980s, 2000s, and 2017), the current weak economic growth of 2 percent or lower can be expected to continue unless America learns from history and changes course.

Nevertheless, amid America's twenty-first-century luxury, it is also likely that America's skepticism and arc of moral easing shall continue. Stated simply, there is no significant historical example of a civilization that retrieved its religious fervor or moral standing for very long absent a dramatic loss in wealth or security. For instance, ancient Rome began more stoic and religious than it ended. After its fall, which featured a great loss in territorial security and prosperity throughout the European continent, the extended Middle Ages/medieval period featured a religious revival across Europe. When prosperity returned to some with the Renaissance, we saw religious fervor wane once again in many areas of Europe—as we do today in America. However, if the future holds with it a breakdown of society caused by war or technological change, then expect a return of religious fervor as people seek comfort in an uncertain world.

There is also little reason to believe that growth in governments, so evident in America today, won't continue. That will lead to the growth in debt and the inflationary pressures on the US economy as central bankers print money and devalue currency to keep up with the spending of politicians. It is possible that the size of the United States' national debt will restrict spending growth to some degree or another. On the other hand, the Great Depression and the COVID pandemic demonstrated that in difficult economic times, politicians and their voters support higher spending—dramatically so at times.

History also cautions us that Americans should be concerned about increases in societal division as well. We have noted how internal division can have a negative effect on a nation. America, as of the writing of this book, is becoming divided at an accelerating pace along cultural lines as well as political lines. As the American economy slows under the weight of government spending, taxes, and regulations, economic opportunity will correspondingly diminish and stagnant economies will become even more prevalent, leading to friction between economic and political subgroups in America. Moreover, with each increase in government power, personal freedom is diminished. If those economic conditions prevail long enough and the federal government continues to reduce personal freedoms, discontent will rise as has occurred countless times in history.

The question then will be what form that discontent will take. Protests already have become commonplace in America. Some have warned that those protests could grow in intensity and nature. That too has occurred in history. America also has a history of states refusing to comply with the actions of the federal government. The historical term for that is "nullification." In 1798, Thomas Jefferson anonymously wrote the Kentucky Resolutions, which declared the Alien and Sedition Acts "altogether void and of no force" in that state.[3] That Sedition Act dramatically reduced freedom of speech rights and led some, including Jefferson, to wonder if the American experiment in freedom was coming to an end. Later, the Nullification Crisis of 1832–1833 saw South Carolina declare the Federal Tariff of 1832, which the South characterized as the Tariff of Abominations because it disproportionately affected the South, "null, void, and no law."[4]

In the years leading up to this book, states have chosen to fight federal impositions by suing the federal government, with increasing frequency, on issues such as immigration policy, government regulations, and transgender issues, to name a few. In years past, Americans might have expected the Supreme Court to resolve those disputes. However, even its judgments have come under increasing political attacks, if not administratively ignored in what may be considered a different form of nullification.

If those dynamics continue, perhaps states will once again question whether the US Constitution truly requires state compliance or whether states will seek to change the nature of their obligations to the federal government, if not get behind secession movements, like have recently occurred in Alberta, Canada, and Venice, Italy. Meanwhile, the movement within states for areas to secede from states and become part of other states has gained momentum as well. That too is a modern form of nullification.

On a grander scale, we can note that in the last fifteen hundred years, the West has oscillated between periods of rule by centralized governments followed by an easing of their rule if not outright freedom. There were the monarchs and feudal lords of the Middle Ages/medieval period (500 to 1400–1500 AD) that gave some ground to a period of intellectual awakening and glimpses of freedom during the Renaissance (1300 to 1600s). Thereafter, we find the Age of Absolutism (1650 to 1789) and its excesses give way to its intellectual antitheses, the Enlightenment (1685–1815). Beginning with the American Revolution, a foundation for liberty was established, which would flourish until well after World War II, when the number of elected governments would quickly rise from just six to over eighty and an even greater number today. Despite the spread of that freedom, however, more recently we have seen another swing of the pendulum toward centralized governments with the aid of technology and the ease with which governments can keep track of the citizens they threaten to turn into subjects.

Given that latest dynamic, who is to say when the human urge will reverse the pendulum and another Spirit of 1776 will take place somewhere in the world. As for America, in 2023, the United States Supreme Court, in keeping with the Founders' First Amendment, strongly affirmed that US citizens cannot be made to parrot the dictates of governments. Only time will tell if that is but a flare in the night or the torch of a new generation.

As troubling as the recent trends may appear to some, we must also note that America retains a unique place in history. Even amid the difficulties we have noted, so much of the world still regards the United States as the place with the greatest opportunity on earth and a place where nearly anyone can not only economically succeed but also politically succeed. America remains the destination of immigrants in comparison to China or Russia or Venezuela. The continued influx of so many seeking that opportunity continues to renew the American spirit just as it did in the late 1800s, when the Statue of Liberty was dedicated. Those seeking opportunity also are taking historic leads in industry, such as Elon Musk, and in fighting for free speech.

In other words, after the passage of nearly six American centuries, America's twin purposes of democratization and opportunity are still at work. If that is to remain so, Americans shall have to heed Benjamin Franklin's prescient words. James McHenry, a Maryland delegate to the Constitutional Convention, noted that "a lady asked Dr. Franklin, 'Well Doctor, what have we got, a republic or a monarchy?' Franklin responded, 'A republic if you can keep it.'"[5]

It is more than important to note that Franklin, who was among the most learned of his time, did not say "if your leaders can keep it." No, he told the woman, "if *you* can keep it." Given that the American civilization was started by individuals facing great and lonely odds, Franklin could say no less—and that may be the single greatest lesson of the American civilization.

APPENDIX

Key Points from the Book

ON THE FOUNDING OF AMERICA

1. The American civilization is unique to history. Never before, and not since, has a nation of its size been born of such fresh ground and cultivated so deliberately by ideals.

2. The early American immigrants did not have a common DNA or a single culture. What most of those immigrants did share, at the outset of the founding of America, were complementary purposes. Those purposes were the free exercise of religion and opportunity—and ultimately, the democratization of rights—economic and political.

ON THE HISTORIC BENEFITS OF CAPITALISM

1. There can be no sustainable democracy where economic and political power are controlled by the same elites. Capitalism fostered the disbursement of economic power among many more people than had ever occurred under the previous centuries of feudal and monarchial systems. That separation of economic and political powers made it possible for true democracies to emerge for the first time in history and likely is the most important benefit of capitalism—more so than the riches, goods, and services that flow from capitalism.

2. Equality in history has been limited to poverty for the masses in economies prior to commercialization or in economies owned or dictated by monarchs or other authoritarian governments.

3. Capitalism fostered the dispersement of economic and political power among many more people than had ever occurred under the previous centuries of feudal and monarchial systems. Until the free markets of capitalism emerged, the lifting of the poor into a dynamic middle class had never occurred.

4. A sustainable republic would have to wait until America became history's greatest example of how a republic or democracy, with a broad franchise, can succeed—if economic and political power are sufficiently separated for a long enough period.

ON AMERICA'S EXCEPTIONALISM

1. If we compare the American civilization to those before it, we find achievements and experiences unlike anywhere else in history. That is not to say America was ever perfect or without fault. It does

mean, however, that by comparison, overall, it has had unparalleled successes.

2. What makes the American civilization historically exceptional is that it has offered the greatest opportunity to the greatest number and most diverse set of people of any place on the globe for centuries—all the while giving them an unprecedented say in their government.

3. Even though the Founders "democratized" government in ways untried and even unfathomed by those who went before it, their work was not a finished product any more than the foundation of the house is the only work necessary to create a home that could endure centuries of weather.

ON THE CENTRALIZATION OF POWER

1. Always and everywhere, power tends to centralize over time—especially in the hands of politicians. Despite the Founders' genius, the law of history that power centralizes over time has overridden their best efforts and is now on stunning display in America.

2. Limited government has always been more plausible in the simplicity and self-responsibility of the countryside than in the complexity of large cities.

3. It was the goal of the Founders *not* to have an efficient, powerful government.

4. The more money big business obtains from government, the less democratic the government—that is, the less voice average citizens will have in their government.

5. Dissent is the mother of democracy—capitalism its father.

6. It is a tired refrain of history for those in power to claim that dissent is a threat to the stability of the government.

7. History has shown time and again that the limiting of dissent is a signpost along the road to the demise of a free society.

ON AMERICA'S DIVIDED ERA

1. Every decision government makes picks a winner and a loser and someone to pay for it.

2. The more government decides, the more it divides.

3. Like Rome and ancient Greece before it, America has fallen into a class warfare whose flames are fanned by ambitious politicians and media.

ON AMERICA TODAY

1. At the beginning of a civilization's government, particularly if it is freely elected, there is a competition of ideas for the betterment of all. Toward the end, there is a competition for government spoils at the expense of those ideals and the less fortunate.

2. If the United States becomes a society of a nearly fixed economic pie, with its inhabitants dependent on government, it would no longer be a culture forged together by the pursuit of opportunity. If that cultural glue is lost, the signs of which we have seen since 2010 in the form of dissent between recent immigrants and the older populations, America's melting pot could well become a place of

different cultures fighting each other politically instead of enriching themselves economically.

ON THE WARNING SIGNS OF DECLINE

1. What marks the rise of any one civilization is the great level of consensus for its founding principles and purposes. Conversely, what marks a decline is a substantial growth in the level of dissent and doubt about those founding principles and purposes.
2. What isn't taught in the schools of a nation's youth eventually becomes forgotten in its culture.
3. At the beginning of a civilization a people will do anything to survive. Toward the end, they apologize for doing it.
4. Between the end of the North Korean and the Vietnam War, America had crossed the bridge between assurance and doubt.
5. We would do well to learn from the lessons of the past and be quite wary of those, often social engineers or proponents of ever more government, who say the past is not an essential guide for what lies ahead.

ON WHAT LIES AHEAD FOR AMERICA

1. History is no more a straight line than the emotions of our days. No civilization has an expiration date.
2. Despite the spread of freedom, more recently we have seen another swing of the pendulum toward centralized governments with the aid of technology and the ease with which governments can keep track of their citizens, threatening to turn them into subjects.

3. In the last millennium, armies pillaged the economic capacity of their adversaries by burning fields, businesses, and towns. With cyber warfare, combatants will cripple economic capacity electronically by targeting private and government infrastructure.

4. After the passage of nearly six American centuries, America's twin purposes of democratization and opportunity are still at work.

5. The fate of America still lies in the hands of Americans and their combined wills.

Notes

INTRODUCTION

1. Will and Ariel Durant, *The Lessons of History* (New York: Simon and Schuster, 1968), 12–13.
2. Oswald Spengler, *The Decline of the West* (New York: Vintage Books, 2006), 26.

CHAPTER 1

1. Will Durant, "Invitation to History: The Map of Human Character," remarks on WGN, Chicago, November 18, 1945, https://www.will-durant.com/invitation.htm.
2. G. W. F. Hegel, *Lectures on the Philosophy of History*, trans. J. Sibree (London: George Bell, 1894), 6.
3. George Santayana, *The Life of Reason*, vol. 1, *Reason in Common Sense* (London: Constable, 1905), 172.
4. See Virgil, "Ecolgue IV: The Golden Age," in *The Eclogues*, trans. A. S. Kline, 2001, https://www.poetryintranslation.com/PITBR/Latin/VirgilEclogues.php.
5. Giambattista Vico, *The New Science* (London: Penguin, 2001), §915.
6. Hegel, *Lectures on the Philosophy of History*, 63–64.

7. Oswald Spengler, *The Decline of the West* (New York: Vintage Books, 2006), 24.
8. Vico, *The New Science*, §915.
9. Will and Ariel Durant, *The Lessons of History* (New York: Simon and Schuster, 1968), 88.
10. Hegel, *Lectures on the Philosophy of History*, 78.
11. Hill Shine, *Carlyle and the Saint-Simonians* (New York: Octagon Books, 1971), 11.
12. Plato, *Republic*, bk. 4.
13. Albert J. Toynbee, *A Study of History* (New York: Dell, 1946), 1:197.
14. Toynbee, *A Study of History*, 1:286.
15. Toynbee, *A Study of History*, 1:414.
16. Durant, *The Lessons of History*, 90.
17. Quoted in Durant, *The Lessons of History*, 89.
18. Quoted in Durant, *The Lessons of History*, 89.
19. Quoted in Shine, *Carlyle and the Saint-Simonians*, 24n78.
20. Quoted in Shine, *Carlyle and the Saint-Simonians*, 26.
21. Thomas Carlyle, "Characteristics," *Edinburgh Review* 54 (December 1831), https://cruel.org/econthought/texts/carlyle/carlchar.html.
22. Hegel, *Lectures on the Philosophy of History*, 77.
23. Quoted in Durant, *The Lessons of History*, 89.
24. Quoted in Shine, *Carlyle and the Saint-Simonians*, 27.
25. *Merriam-Webster*, s.v. "nationalism," accessed March 19, 2024, https://www.merriam-webster.com/dictionary/nationalism.
26. Edward Gibbon, *The Decline and Fall of the Roman Empire* (New York: Modern Library, 2003), 15.
27. Quoted in John Burrow, *A History of Histories* (New York: Borzoi Books/Alfred A. Knopf, 2007), 84.
28. Susan Wise Bauer, *The History of the Ancient World* (New York: W. W. Norton, 2007), 668.
29. Charles Mann, *1491: New Revelations of the Americas before Columbus*, 2nd ed. (New York: Vintage Books, 2011).
30. Durant, *The Lessons of History*, 93–94.

CHAPTER 2

1. Kenneth R. Bartlett, "The Italians before Italy: Conflict and Competition in the Mediterranean," Great Courses, accessed April 16. 2024, https://www.thegreatcourses.com/courses/italians-before-italy-conflict-and-competition-in-the-mediterranean.
2. Quoted in Durant, *The Lessons of History*, 89.
3. G. W. F. Hegel, *Lectures on the Philosophy of History*, trans. J. Sibree (London: George Bell, 1894), 77.
4. Jonathan Sarna and Joellyn Zollman, "Jewish Immigration to America," *My Jewish Learning*, accessed April 16, 2024, https://www.myjewishlearning.com/article/jewish-immigration-to-america-three-waves/.
5. Hegel, *Lectures on the Philosophy of History*, 77.
6. Hegel, *Lectures on the Philosophy of History*, 64.
7. Quoted in Durant, *The Lessons of History*, 89.
8. Quoted in Hill Shine, *Carlyle and the Saint-Simonians* (New York: Octagon Books, 1971), 27.

CHAPTER 3

1. Will Durant, *Our Oriental Heritage* (New York: Simon and Schuster, 1935), 259.
2. *Oxford Learner's Dictionaries*, s.v. "stoic," accessed April 16, 2024, https://www.oxfordlearnersdictionaries.com/us/definition/english/stoic_1.
3. "Stoicism," *Stanford Encyclopedia of Philosophy*, January 20, 2023, https://plato.stanford.edu/entries/stoicism/.
4. Nathaniel Philbrick, *Mayflower* (New York: Viking Penguin, 2006), 4. See also John T. Wheelwright, *The Mayflower Pilgrims* (Boston: McGrath-Sherril Press, 1921), 8–9.
5. Philbrick, *Mayflower*, 27.
6. Wheelwright, *The Mayflower Pilgrims*, 12.
7. Philbrick, *Mayflower*, 23.
8. Philbrick, *Mayflower*, 25.
9. Philbrick, *Mayflower*, 26.
10. Robert Baird, *Religion in America* (Glasgow: Blackie and Son, 1844), 100.

11. Philbrick, *Mayflower*, 68; Bernard Bailyn, *The Barbarous Years* (New York: Vintage, 2012), 326.
12. Philbrick, *Mayflower*, 87–97; Bailyn, *The Barbarous Years*, 336–337.
13. Quoted in Bailyn, *The Barbarous Years*, 61.
14. Bailyn, *The Barbarous Years*, 170.
15. Bailyn, *The Barbarous Years*.
16. Bailyn, *The Barbarous Years*, 60.
17. Richard H. Dillon, *North American Indian Wars* (New York: Gallery Books, 1983), 19.
18. Dillon, *North American Indian Wars*, 20.
19. John Tebbel and Keith Jennison, *The American Indian Wars* (Edison, NJ: Castle Books, 2003), 1.
20. Anton Treuer, *The Indian Wars* (Washington, DC: National Geographic Books), 34; Baird, Religion in America, 113–114.
21. Tebbel and Jennison, *The American Indian Wars*, 31–34.
22. Treuer, *The Indian Wars*, 42.
23. Treuer, *The Indian Wars*, 43.
24. Treuer, *The Indian Wars*, 50.
25. Treuer, *The Indian Wars*, 55.
26. Digital History, "Childbirth in Early America," accessed April 16, 2024, https://www.digitalhistory.uh.edu/topic_display.cfm?tcid=70.
27. James Shepherd and Gary Walton, *Shipping, Maritime Trade, and the Economic Development of the Colonial North America* (Cambridge: Cambridge University Press, 1972), 34.
28. Steven Mintz, "Historical Context: Facts about the Slave Trade and Slavery," Gilder Lehrman Institute of American History, accessed April 16, 2024, https://www.gilderlehrman.org/history-resources/teacher-resources/historical-context-facts-about-slave-trade-and-slavery.
29. Bailyn, *The Barbarous Years*, 165.
30. David Jaffee, "Religion and Culture in North America, 1600–1700," Metropolitan Museum of Art, October 2004, http://www.metmuseum.org/toah/hd/recu/hd_recu.htm.
31. Bailyn, *The Barbarous Years*, 81–83.
32. Lyon Gardiner Tyler, "The F. F. V.'s of Virginia," *William and Mary College Quarterly Historical Magazine*, April 1915, p. 277.

33. Tyler, "The F. F. V.'s of Virginia," 277.
34. Thomas L. Purvis, "First Families of Virginia," in *A Dictionary of American History* (Malden, MA: Blackwell, 1997), 136.
35. Gordon S. Wood, *The Radicalism of the American Revolution* (New York: Knopf Doubleday, 2011), 113.
36. Will and Ariel Durant, *The Lessons of History* (New York: Simon and Schuster, 1968), 55.
37. Elvin F. Frolik, "The History of Agriculture in the United States Beginning with the Seventeenth Century," *Transactions of the Nebraska Academy of Sciences and Affiliated Societies* 453 (1977), https://digitalcommons.unl.edu/cgi/viewcontent.cgi?article=1456&context=tnas.
38. Richard Lyman Bushman, *The American Farmer in the Eighteenth Century* (New Haven, CT: Yale University Press, 2018), 10; Shepherd and Walton, *Shipping, Maritime Trade*, 37.
39. Bushman, *The American Farmer*, 3.
40. Mary Kelty, *Life in Early America* (Boston: Ginn, 1941), 207.
41. Bushman, *The American Farmer*, 7.
42. Bushman, *The American Farmer*, 10.
43. Kelty, *Life in Early America*, 254.
44. Bushman, *The American Farmer*, 10.
45. Bushman, *The American Farmer*, 12. See also Joseph M. Hawes and Elizabeth I. Nybakken, *Family and Society in American History* (Champaign: University of Illinois Press, 2001), 37.
46. Hawes and Nybakken, *Family and Society in American History*, 37.
47. Kelty, *Life in Early America*, 230.
48. T. H. Breen, "Back to Sweat and Toil: Suggestions for the Study of Agricultural Work in Early America," *Pennsylvania History* 49, no. 4 (1982): 247.
49. Bailyn, *The Barbarous Years*, 163.
50. Breen, "Back to Sweat and Toil," 252.
51. Shepherd and Walton, *Shipping, Maritime Trade*, 45.
52. Shepherd and Walton, *Shipping, Maritime Trade*, 37.
53. Shepherd and Walton, *Shipping, Maritime Trade*, 38.
54. Shepherd and Walton, *Shipping, Maritime Trade*, 38.
55. Shepherd and Walton, *Shipping, Maritime Trade*, 44.

56. Shepherd and Walton, *Shipping, Maritime Trade*, 113.
57. Benjamin Franklin, "A Proposal for Promoting Useful Knowledge among the British Plantations in America," National Archives, May 14, 1743, https://founders.archives.gov/documents/Franklin/01-02-02-0092.

CHAPTER 4

1. Quoted in Will and Ariel Durant, *The Lessons of History* (New York: Simon and Schuster, 1968), 89.
2. See also Durant, *Lessons of History*, 38.
3. Sydney H. Ahlstrom, *A Religious History of the American People* (New Haven, CT: Yale University Press, 2017), 350.
4. Robert Baird, *Religion in America* (Glasgow: Blackie and Son, 1844), 179.
5. Dorsey Armstrong, "Years That Changed History: 1215," Great Courses, accessed April 17, 2024, https://www.thegreatcourses.com/courses/years-that-changed-history-1215.
6. Peter Marshall, *Heretics and Believers* (New Haven, CT: Yale University Press, 2017), xi.
7. Marshall, *Heretics and Believers*, xiii.
8. Richard Bevan, "How Many People Did Henry VIII Execute?" History, accessed April 17, 2024, https://www.history.co.uk/article/the-killer-king-how-many-people-did-henry-viii-execute.
9. University of Notre Dame, "Martyrs of the English Reformation," accessed April 17, 2024, https://faith.nd.edu/s/1210/faith/interioraspx?sid=1210&gid=609&pgid9742&cid=38977&ecid=38977&crid=0&calpgid=10817&calcid=24284.
10. Baird, *Religion in America*, 91.
11. Jenna Weissman Joselit, *Immigration and American Religion* (New York: Oxford University Press, 2001), 19.
12. Joselit, *Immigration and American Religion*, 21.
13. Joselit, *Immigration and American Religion*, 26.
14. Baird, *Religion in America*, 113.
15. Baird, *Religion in America*, 118.
16. Baird, *Religion in America*, 130.

17. Baird, *Religion in America*, 133.
18. Sydney H. Ahlstrom, *A Religious History of the American People* (New York: Doubleday, 1975), 1:197.
19. Facing History and Ourselves, "Religion in Colonial America: Trends, Regulations, and Beliefs," March 14, 2016, https://www.facinghistory.org/resource-library/religion-colonial-america-trends-regulations-and-beliefs. See also Baird, *Religion in America*, 196, and David W. Beggs and R. Bruce McQuigg, eds., *America's Schools and Churches* (Bloomington: Indiana University Press, 1965), 38.
20. Library of Congress, "Religion and the Founding of the American Republic," accessed April 17, 2024, https://www.loc.gov/exhibits/religion/rel01.html.
21. Brent Tarter, "Lawes Divine, Morall and Martiall," *Encyclopedia Virginia*, December 7, 2020, https://encyclopediavirginia.org/entries/lawes-divine-morall-and-martiall/.
22. Facing History and Ourselves, "Religion in Colonial America."
23. Baird, *Religion in America*, 118.
24. Richard P. Hallowell, *The Quaker Invasion of Massachusetts* (Boston: Houghton Mifflin, 1887), 6.
25. Baird, *Religion in America*, 127.
26. Beggs and McQuigg, *America's Schools and Churches*, 38.
27. Commonwealth of Massachusetts, "Massachusetts Constitution," March 2, 1780, https://malegislature.gov/Laws/Constitution.
28. Baird, *Religion in America*, 128.
29. John Vile, "Established Churches in Early America," Free Speech Center, February 18, 2024, https://www.mtsu.edu/first-amendment/article/801/established-churches-in-early-america.
30. Torcaso v. Watkins, 367 US 488 (1961).
31. Ralph Walker, *Old Readers* (Gettysburg, PA: Early American Society, 1980), 54.
32. Robert A. Peterson, "Education in Colonial America," Foundation for Economic Education, September 1, 1983, https://fee.org/articles/education-in-colonial-america/; Beggs and McQuigg, *America's Schools and Churches*, 39–40.

33. Lawrence A. Cremin, *American Education: The Colonial Experience*, 1607–1789 (New York: Harper and Row, 1970), 40.
34. Beggs and McQuigg, *America's Schools and Churches*, 40.
35. Ahlstrom, *A Religious History of the American People*, 1:413, 416, 483, 493, 509, 516, 555, 584, 636.
36. Ahlstrom, *A Religious History of the American People*, 1:355.
37. Thomas Jefferson, *Notes on the State of Virginia* (Philadelphia: Prichard and Hall, 1788), 175.
38. Edwin J. Perkins, *The Economy of Colonial America* (New York: Columbia University Press, 1988), 116.
39. Thomas Doerflinger, *A Vigorous Spirit of Enterprise* (Chapel Hill: University of North Carolina Press, 1986), 16.
40. Doerflinger, *A Vigorous Spirit of Enterprise*, 5.
41. Harlow Giles Unger, *Lion of Liberty: Patrick Henry and the Call to a New Nation* (Cambridge, MA: Da Capo Press, 2010), 32–33.

CHAPTER 5

1. Gordon S. Wood, *The Idea of America* (New York: Penguin, 2011), 191.
2. Brutus, "Brutus, No. 1," October 18, 1787, in *The Complete Anti-Federalist*, vol. 1, ed. Herbert J. Storing (Chicago: University of Chicago Press, 1981), https://minio.la.utexas.edu/webeditor-files/coretexts/pdf/178720brutus201.pdf.
3. John Locke, *Second Treatise of Government* (London: A. Millar, 1763), https://www.gutenberg.org/files/7370/7370-h/7370-h.htm.
4. Wood, *The Idea of America*, 325.
5. Jean-Jacques Rousseau, *Discourse on the Origin of Inequality*, trans. G. D. H. Cole (Stillwell, KS: Digireads, 2018), 6.
6. Will and Ariel Durant, *The Lessons of History* (New York: Simon and Schuster, 1968), 91.
7. Maryland State House, "George Washington's Resignation," 2022, https://msa.maryland.gov/msa/mdstatehouse/html/gwresignation.html.

CHAPTER 6

1. H. W. Brands, *American Colossus: The Triumph of Capitalism, 1865–1900* (New York: Doubleday, 2010).
2. Gotham Center for New York City History, "Robert R. Livingston Papers," accessed April 17, 2024, https://www.gothamcenter.org/robert-livingston-papers.
3. Anders Stephanson, *Manifest Destiny: American Expansionism and the Empire of Right* (New York: Hill and Wang, 1995), 17.
4. Stephanson, *Manifest Destiny*, 18.
5. Johnson v. McIntosh, 21 US (8 Wheat.) 543 (1823).
6. James Monroe, "Seventh Annual Message," December 2, 1823, American Presidency Project, https://www.presidency.ucsb.edu/documents/seventh-annual-message-1.
7. Ancestry, "U.S. Immigration in the 1800s," accessed April 17, 2024, https://www.ancestry.com/c/family-history-learning-hub/1800-us-immigration.
8. Ancestry, "U.S. Immigration in the 1800s."
9. US Census Bureau, "Urban and Rural Areas," December 14, 2023, https://www.census.gov/history/www/programs/geography/urban_and_rural_areas.html.
10. Adam Smith, *An Inquiry into the Nature and Causes of the Wealth of Nations* (Chicago: Encyclopedia Britannica, 1952), 246.
11. Edwin J. Perkins, *The Economy of Colonial America* (New York: Columbia University Press, 1988), 13.
12. Gary M. Walton and James F. Shepherd, *The Economic Rise of Early America* (Cambridge: Cambridge University Press, 1979), 200.
13. Library of Congress, "Work in the Late 19th Century," accessed April 17, 2024, https://www.loc.gov/classroom-materials/united-states-history-primary-source-timeline/rise-of-industrial-america-1876-1900/work-in-late-19th-century/.
14. Library of Congress, "Work in the Late 19th Century."
15. Legends of America, "The Industrial Revolution in America," accessed April 17, 2024, https://www.legendsofamerica.com/industrial-revolution/.
16. Brands, *American Colossus*, 7.
17. Brands, *American Colossus*, 6.

18. Thomas Weiss, "U.S. Labor Force Estimates and Economic Growth, 1800–1860," in *American Economic Growth* and *Standards of Living before the Civil War*, ed. Robert E. Gallman and John Joseph Wallis (Chicago: University of Chicago Press, 1992), 51.
19. John Adams, letter to Thomas Jefferson, August 24, 1815, National Archives, https://founders.archives.gov/documents/Jefferson/03-08-02-0560.
20. Sean Wilentz, *The Rise of American Democracy* (New York: W. W. Norton, 2005), 7 (emphasis added).
21. John Adams, letter to James Sullivan, May 26, 1776, https://userpages.umbc.edu/~bouton/History101/FoundersOnDemocracy.htm.
22. John Meacham, *Thomas Jefferson: The Art of Power* (New York: Random House, 2012), xx.
23. Charles W. Jones, *Address of Charles W. Jones: Life and Work of Thomas Jefferson* (Washington, DC: T. McGill, 1881), 6.
24. Thomas Jefferson, "First Inaugural Address," March 4, 1801, National Archives, https://founders.archives.gov/documents/Jefferson/01-33-02-0116-0004.
25. Wilentz, *Rise of American Democracy*, 138.
26. Wilentz, *Rise of American Democracy*, 138.
27. Meacham, *Thomas Jefferson*, xix.
28. Wilentz, *Rise of American Democracy*, 514.
29. Andrew Jackson, "First Annual Message," December 8, 1829, American Presidency Project, https://www.presidency.ucsb.edu/documents/first-annual-message-3.
30. William MacDonald, *Jacksonian Democracy* (New York: Harper, 1906), 312.

CHAPTER 7

1. Bruce Collins, *The Origins of America's Civil War* (New York: Holmes and Meier, 1981), 42.
2. Collins, *The Origins of America's Civil War*, 42.
3. Collins, *The Origins of America's Civil War*, 42.
4. Paul Johnson, *A History of the United States* (New York: HarperCollins, 1997), 435.

5. Thomas G. Del Beccaro, *The Divided Era: How We Got Here and the Keys to America's Reconciliation* (Austin, TX: Greenleaf Book Group Press, 2015), 173.
6. William B. Hesseltine, *The Tragic Conflict: The Civil War and Reconstruction* (New York: George Braziller, 1962), 114.
7. National Park Service, "Independence Hall and the American Civil War," accessed April 17, 2024, https://www.nps.gov/articles/000/independencehall-civilwar.htm.
8. Russell McClintock, *Lincoln and the Decision for War* (Chapel Hill: University of North Carolina Press, 2008), 17.
9. Bruce Levine, *The Fall of the House of Dixie* (New York: Random House, 2013), 17.
10. Paul Johnson, *A History of the American People* (New York: HarperCollins, 1997), 434.
11. Ira Berlin, *Slaves without Masters: The Free Negro in the Antebellum South* (New York: Pantheon Books, 1974), 176; James Malvin, *Questioning Slavery* (London: Routledge, 1996), 22.
12. Berlin, *Slaves without Masters*, 3–4.
13. Berlin, *Slaves without Masters*, 4.
14. Berlin, *Slaves without Masters*, 4.
15. Berlin, *Slaves without Masters*, 9, citing Allen D. Candler, ed., *The Colonial Records of the State of Georgia* (Atlanta: Chas. P. Byrd, 1910), 18:659, and Winthrop D. Jordan, "American Chiaroscuro: The Status and Definition of Mulattoes in the British Colonies," *William and Mary Quarterly* 19, no. 2 (1962), 186–187.
16. Zinn Education Project, "Black Abolitionists," 2014, https://www.zinnedproject.org/materials/black-abolitionists/.
17. Roger Anstey, *The Atlantic Slave Trade and British Abolition, 1760–1810* (Atlantic Highlands, NJ: Humanities Press, 1975), 3; James Malvin, *Slaves and Slavery: The British Colonial Experience* (Manchester, UK: Manchester University Press, 1991), 3.
18. Anstey, *The Atlantic Slave Trade*, 5.
19. Malvin, *Slaves and Slavery*, 2.
20. Digital History, "Slavery in the Ancient, Medieval, and Early Modern

Worlds," 2021, https://www.digitalhistory.uh.edu/disp_textbook.cfm?smtID=2&psid=3027.
21. Malvin, *Slaves and Slavery*, 1.
22. Charles Sumner, *White Slavery in the Barbary States: A Lecture before the Boston Mercantile Library Association, Feb. 17, 1847* (Boston: William D. Ticknor, 1847), 4.
23. Tom Pocock, *The Royal Navy's War against White Slavery* (London: Chatham, 2006), 1.
24. Digital History, "The Origins and Nature of New World Slavery," 2016, https://www.digitalhistory.uh.edu/disp_textbook_print.cfm?smtid=2&psid=3033.
25. Don Jordan and Michael Walsh, *White Cargo: The Forgotten History of Britain's White Slaves in America* (New York: NYU Press, 2007), 14.
26. Barbara Krauthamer, *Black Slaves, Indian Masters: Slavery, Emancipation, and Citizenship in the Native American South* (Chapel Hill: University of North Carolina Press, 2013).
27. Anton Treuer, *The Indian Wars* (Washington, DC: National Geographic Books), 34.
28. R. Halliburton Jr., "Free Black Owners of Slaves: A Reappraisal of the Woodson Thesis," *South Carolina Historical Magazine* 76, no. 3 (July 1975): 129.
29. Henry Louis Gates Jr., "Did Black People Own Slaves?" *The Root*, March 4, 2013, https://www.theroot.com/did-black-people-own-slaves-1790895436; D. G. Hewitt, "10 Black Slaveowners That Will Tear Apart Historical Perception," *History Collection*, May 17, 2018, https://historycollection.com/10-black-slaveowners-that-will-tear-apart-historical-perception/.
30. Benjamin Askew, "White Slavery," *Raleigh News*, July 20, 1876, https://archive.org/details/whiteslaverydegr00rale. The story adds, "The facts above stated were verified from the records of Jones County by Hon. Thomas J. Jarvis and Maj. J. A. Engelhard, in the presence of Jake Scott, the Republican member of Legislature, and a large crowd of Republicans and Democrats."
31. John Hope Franklin, *Slavery to Freedom*, 9th ed. (New York: McGraw-Hill, 2010), 173.
32. Malvin, *Slaves and Slavery*, 2.

33. Royal Museums Greenwich, "Atlantic Worlds: Enslavement and Resistance," accessed April 17, 2024, https://www.rmg.co.uk/stories/topics/history-transatlantic-slave-trade.
34. Digital History, "The Origins and Nature of New World Slavery."
35. Thomas Sowell, *The Thomas Sowell Reader* (New York: Basic Books, 2011), 18.
36. Voltaire, *The Works of M. de Voltaire*, trans. T. Smollett and T. Franklin (London: J. Newbery, 1761), 9:145.
37. George Washington, untitled article, *Pennsylvania Journal and Weekly Advertiser*, November 14, 1787, p. 3.
38. Gary M. Walton and James F. Shepherd, *The Economic Rise of Early America* (Cambridge: Cambridge University Press, 1979), 143–144.
39. Bruce Levine, *The Fall of the House of Dixie* (New York: Random House, 2013), 4.
40. Richard Sylla, "Financial Foundations: Public Credit, the National Bank, and Securities Markets," paper presented at NBER Conference "Founding Choices: American Economic Policy in the 1790s," Dartmouth College, Hanover, NH, May 7–9, 2009, https://www.nber.org/system/files/chapters/c11737/revisions/c11737.rev1.pdf.
41. Mark J. Perry, "Thomas Sowell on Slavery and This Fact—There Are More Slaves Today Than Were Seized from Africa in Four Centuries," American Enterprise Institute, October 18, 2107, https://www.aei.org/carpe-diem/thomas-sowell-on-slavery-and-this-fact-there-are-more-slaves-today-than-were-seized-from-africa-in-four-centuries/.
42. Louis Charbonneau, "UN Member Countries Condemn China's Crimes against Humanity," Human Rights Watch, October 23, 2023, https://www.hrw.org/news/2023/10/23/un-member-countries-condemn-chinas-crimes-against-humanity.
43. Robert Kuttner, "Biden's Bind on Solar," *American Prospect*, May 15, 2023, https://prospect.org/blogs-and-newsletters/tap/2023-05-15-bidens-bind-on-solar/.
44. US House of Representatives, "'The Fifteenth Amendment in Flesh and Blood': 1870–1901," accessed April 17, 2024, https://history.house.gov/Exhibitions-and-Publications/BAIC/Historical-Essays/Fifteenth-Amendment/Introduction/.
45. Martin Luther King Jr., "I Have a Dream" speech, Washington, DC,

August 28, 1963, https://www.npr.org/2010/01/18/122701268/
i-have-a-dream-speech-in-its-entirety.

CHAPTER 8

1. US Department of Labor, "100 Years of U.S. Consumer Spending: Data for the Nation, New York City, and Boston," May 2006, https://www.bls.gov/opub/100-years-of-u-s-consumer-spending.pdf.
2. Theresa Huntley, *Women in the Renaissance* (New York: Crabtree, 2010), 18.
3. Monica Chojnacka, *Working Women of Early Modern Venice* (Baltimore: Johns Hopkins University Press, 2001), 86.
4. Venezia Autentica, "What It Was Like to Be a Woman in Venice at the Time of the Republic," accessed April 17, 2024, https://veneziautentica.com/woman-during-republic-venice/.
5. Charles L. Babcock, "The Early Career of Fulvia," *American Journal of Philology* 86, no. 1 (1965): 1. The legendary Greek Middle Platonist philosopher and historian Plutarch gives Fulvia "a very strong character and considerable influence in the career of Antony" (19).
6. NGC Collectors Society, "The Roman Empire: Fulvia, with Marc Antony," accessed April 17, 2024, https://coins.www.collectors-society.com/wcm/CoinView.aspx?sc=359879.
7. Imperium Romanum, "Fulvia—First Roman Woman on Roman Coins," September 14, 2021, https://imperiumromanum.pl/en/article/fulvia-first-roman-woman-on-roman-coins/.
8. Margaret L. King, *Women of the Renaissance* (Chicago: University of Chicago Press, 1991), 195.
9. "Women in the Renaissance and Reformation," Encyclopedia.com, accessed April 17, 2024, https://www.encyclopedia.com/history/encyclopedias-almanacs-transcripts-and-maps/women-renaissance-and-reformation.
10. National Museum of Women in the Arts, *Italian Women Artists: From Renaissance to Baroque* (Milan: Skira Editore, 2007), 20.

11. Mrs. Ashton Dilke, "Women's Suffrage," in *Imperial Parliament*, vol. 5, ed. Sydney Buxton (London: Swan Sonnenschein, 1855), 19.
12. Patricia Grimshaw, *Women's Suffrage in New Zealand* (Aukland: Aukland University Press, 1972), v.
13. US Department of Labor, "100 Years of U.S. Consumer Spending."
14. Ben Wattenberg, "Education: Female Graduates," PBS, accessed April 17, 2024, https://www.pbs.org/fmc/book/3education2.htm.
15. US Department of Labor, "100 Years of U.S. Consumer Spending."
16. Robert Gordon, *The Rise and Fall of American Growth* (Princeton, NJ: Princeton University Press, 2016), 3.
17. Calvin Coolidge, speech to the American Society of Newspaper Editors, Washington, D.C., January 17, 1925, American Presidency Project, https://www.presidency.ucsb.edu/documents/address-the-american-society-newspaper-editors-washington-dc.
18. Mike Moffatt, "The American Economy in 2000," *ThoughtCo*, February 11, 2019, https://www.thoughtco.com/the-us-economy-at-the-end-of-the-20th-century-1146946.
19. Statista, "Exports of Goods and Services from the United States from 1990 to 2020, as a Percentage of Gross Domestic Product," May 2023, https://www.statista.com/statistics/258779/us-exports-as-a-percentage-of-gdp/.
20. Carolyn Dimitri, Anne Effland, and Neilson Conklin, "The 20th Century Transformation of US Agriculture and Farm Policy," USDA *Economic Information Bulletin*, no. 3 (June 2005), https://www.ers.usda.gov/webdocs/publications/44197/13566_eib3_1_.pdf.
21. Will and Ariel Durant, *The Lessons of History* (New York: Simon and Schuster, 1968), 22.
22. George Washington, "Farewell Address," September 19, 1796, National Archives, https://founders.archives.gov/documents/Washington/05-20-02-0440-0002.
23. Woodrow Wilson, "Joint Address to Congress Leading to a Declaration of War against Germany," April 2, 1917, National Archives, https://www.archives.gov/milestone-documents/address-to-congress-declaration-of-war-against-germany.
24. Library of Congress, "The American Expeditionary Forces," accessed

April 17, 2024, https://www.loc.gov/collections/stars-and-stripes/articles-and-essays/a-world-at-war/american-expeditionary-forces/.

25. Library of Congress, "The American Expeditionary Forces."
26. Garry L. Thompson, "Army Downsizing Following World War I, World War II, Vietnam, and a Comparison to Recent Army Downsizing," master's thesis, US Army Command and General Staff College, 2002, p. 4.
27. National WWII Museum, "Research Starters: US Military by the Numbers," accessed April 17, 2024, http://www.nationalww2museum.org/learn/education/for-students/ww2-history/ww2-by-the-numbers/us-military.html.
28. PBS, "The War: War Production," accessed April 17, 2024, https://www.pbs.org/kenburns/the-war/war-production.
29. Lauren Monsen, "How Americans Observed V-E Day during World War II," US Embassy and Consulate in the United Kingdom, May 3, 2020, https://uk.usembassy.gov/how-americans-observed-v-e-day-during-world-war-ii/.
30. Richard W. Stewart, ed., *American Military History*, vol. 2, *The United States Army in a Global Era, 1917–2008* (Washington, DC: Center of Military History, 2010), https://www.history.army.mil/books/AMH/AMH-24.htm.
31. Harry Truman, "Radio Report to the American People on the Potsdam Conference," August 9, 1945, American Presidency Project, https://www.presidency.ucsb.edu/documents/radio-report-the-american-people-the-potsdam-conference.
32. "The Marshall Plan: Design, Accomplishments, and Significance," EveryCRSReport.com, January 18, 2018, https://www.everycrsreport.com/reports/R45079.html.
33. John F. Kennedy, "Special Message to the Congress on Foreign Aid," March 22, 1961, American Presidency Project, https://www.presidency.ucsb.edu/documents/special-message-the-congress-foreign-aid-1.
34. Will Durant, "What Is Civilization?," Will Durant Foundation, accessed April 21, 2024, https://www.will-durant.com/civilization.htm.
35. US Department of Labor, "100 Years of U.S. Consumer Spending."
36. Hans Hoegh-Guldberg, "Arts and Cultural GDP in the United States," Music in Australia Knowledge Base, October 27, 2015, https://www.musicinaustralia.org.au/arts-and-cultural-gdp-in-the-united-states/.

37. Paul Farhi and Megan Rosenfeld, "American Pop Penetrates Worldwide," *Washington Post*, October 25, 1998, https://www.washingtonpost.com/archive/politics/1998/10/25/american-pop-penetrates-worldwide/3416df02-7643-4894-9771-6dabd05f2bd1/.

38. Petra Goedde, "US Mass Culture and Consumption in a Global Context," in *The Cambridge History of America and the World*, vol. 4, *1945 to the Present*, ed. David C. Engerman, Max Paul Friedman, and Melani McAlister (Cambridge: Cambridge University Press, 2022), 281.

CHAPTER 9

1. Quoted in Hill Shine, *Carlyle and the Saint-Simonians* (New York: Octagon Books, 1971), 26.
2. Thomas Carlyle, "Characteristics," *Edinburgh Review* 54 (December 1831), https://cruel.org/econthought/texts/carlyle/carlchar.html.
3. Quoted in Will and Ariel Durant, *The Lessons of History* (New York: Simon and Schuster, 1968), 89 (emphasis added).
4. Quoted in Durant, *The Lessons of History*, 89.
5. Titus Livius (Livy), *The Early History of Rome*, trans. Aubrey de Sélincourt (New York: Penguin, 2002), 30.
6. Quoted in John Burrow, *A History of Histories* (New York: Borzoi Book/Alfred A. Knopf, 2007), 84.
7. Isocrates, *Antidosis*, 15:159–160.
8. Daryl Austin, "Anti-slavery Revolutionaries Who Practiced What They Preached," *The Hill*, July 10, 2020, https://thehill.com/changing-america/opinion/506782-anti-slavery-revolutionaries-who-practiced-what-they-preached/.
9. Alexander Lee, *The Ugly Renaissance: Sex, Greed, Violence, and Depravity in an Age of Beauty* (New York: Doubleday, 2013), 4.
10. Lee, *The Ugly Renaissance*, 27.
11. Robert S. Duplessis, *Transitions to Capitalism in Early Modern Europe* (Cambridge: Cambridge University Press, 2019), 3.
12. T. J. Stiles, *The First Tycoon: The Epic Life of Cornelius Vanderbilt* (New York: Vintage, 2010), 3–4.
13. Jared Blikre and Devan Burris, "How Rockefeller's Standard Oil Trust

Became Chevron, ExxonMobil, BP, and Marathon," *Yahoo! Finance*, June 6, 2022, https://finance.yahoo.com/news/how-rockefellers-standard-oil-trust-became-chevron-exxon-mobil-bp-and-marathon-204653351.html. See also Streetfins, "The Story of John D. Rockefeller: Racks on Racks," *StreetFins*, March 25, 2021, https://streetfins.com/the-story-of-john-d-rockefeller-racks-on-racks/.

14. William Jennings Bryan, "The Cross of Gold Speech," July 9, 1896, Teaching American History, https://teachingamericanhistory.org/document/the-cross-of-gold-speech/.

15. University of Illinois Urbana-Champaign, "American Newspapers, 1800–1860: An Introduction," accessed April 21, 2024, https://www.library.illinois.edu/hpnl/tutorials/antebellum-newspapers-introduction/.

16. University of Illinois Urbana-Champaign, "American Newspapers, 1800–1860."

17. Roger Schultz, "Christianity and the American University," *Liberty Journal*, February 26, 2019, https://www.liberty.edu/journal/article/christianity-and-the-american-university/.

18. Felicity Barringer, "The Mainstreaming of Marxism in U.S," *New York Times*, October 25, 1989, https://www.nytimes.com/1989/10/25/us/education-the-mainstreaming-of-marxism-in-us-colleges.html.

19. Cami Mondeaux, "Youngkin Criticizes Proposed Removal of Washington in Virginia Schools," *Washington Examiner*, August 17, 2022, https://www.washingtonexaminer.com/news/2877679/youngkin-criticizes-proposed-removal-of-washington-in-virginia-schools/.

20. Mondeaux, "Youngkin Criticizes Proposed Removal."

21. Mondeaux, "Youngkin Criticizes Proposed Removal."

22. "The 1619 Project," *New York Times Magazine*, August 14, 2019, https://www.nytimes.com/interactive/2019/08/14/magazine/1619-america-slavery.html.

23. Mandela Barnes, Twitter post, May 2, 2021, https://twitter.com/theothermandela/status/1388926771274436608?lang=ar.

24. *Merriam-Webster*, s.v. "nationalism," accessed March 19, 2024, https://www.merriam-webster.com/dictionary/nationalism.

25. Abraham Lincoln, "Annual Message to Congress—Concluding Remarks,"

December 1, 1862, Abraham Lincoln Online, https://www.abrahamlincolnonline.org/lincoln/speeches/congress.htm.

CHAPTER 10

1. "GDP Ranked by Country," *World Population Review*, accessed April 21, 2024, https://worldpopulationreview.com/countries/by-gdp.
2. Guy Sorman, "A Brief History of American Prosperity," *City Journal*, Autumn 2012, https://www.city-journal.org/html/brief-history-american-prosperity-13510.html.
3. Organisation for Economic Co-operation and Development, *Better Life Index*, 2013, https://stats.oecd.org/Index.aspx?DataSetCode=BLI2013.
4. US Bureau of Labor Statistics, "American Time Use Survey Summary," June 22, 2023, https://www.bls.gov/news.release/atus.nr0.htm.
5. Pew Research Center, "Mobile Fact Sheet," January 31, 2024, https://www.pewresearch.org/internet/fact-sheet/mobile/.
6. H. W. Brands, *American Colossus: The Triumph of Capitalism, 1865–1900* (New York: Doubleday, 2010), 6.
7. Rakesh Kochhar and Stella Sechopoulos, "How the American Middle Class Has Changed in the Past Five Decades," Pew Research Center, April 20, 2022, https://www.pewresearch.org/short-reads/2022/04/20/how-the-american-middle-class-has-changed-in-the-past-five-decades/.
8. US Department of Labor, "100 Years of U.S. Consumer Spending: Data for the Nation, New York City, and Boston," May 2006, https://www.bls.gov/opub/100-years-of-u-s-consumer-spending.pdf.
9. Jeffrey M. Jones, "Socialism, Capitalism Ratings in U.S. Unchanged," Gallup, December 6, 2021, https://news.gallup.com/poll/357755/socialism-capitalism-ratings-unchanged.aspx.
10. Stef W. Kight, "70 Percent of Millennials Say They'd Vote for a Socialist," *Axios*, October 28, 2019, https://www.axios.com/2019/10/28/millennials-vote-socialism-capitalism-decline.
11. John Bitzan, "2023 American College Student Freedom, Progress and Flourishing Survey," accessed April 21, 2024, https://www.ndsu.edu/fileadmin/challeyinstitute/Research_Briefs/American_College_Student_Freedom_Progress_and_Flourishing_Survey_2023.pdf.

12. Glenn C. Altschuler and David Wippman, "Getting to 'Yes' on Civics Education," *The Hill*, March 19, 2023, https://thehill.com/opinion/education/3907255-getting-to-yes-on-civics-education.
13. Keri D. Ingraham, "Students Exit the K–12 System with an Anti-American Worldview," Discovery Institute, September 28, 2022, https://www.discovery.org/education/2022/09/28/students-exit-the-k-12-system-with-an-anti-american-worldview/.
14. Karol Markowicz, "Why Schools Have Stopped Teaching American History," *New York Post*, January 22, 2017, https://nypost.com/2017/01/22/why-schools-have-stopped-teaching-american-history/.
15. Annenberg Public Policy Center, "Americans' Knowledge of the Branches of Government Is Declining," September 13, 2016, https://www.annenbergpublicpolicycenter.org/americans-knowledge-of-the-branches-of-government-is-declining/.
16. Ingraham, "Students Exit the K–12 System."
17. Chris Papst, "At 13 Baltimore City High Schools, Zero Students Tested Proficient on 2023 State Math Exam," *Fox News*, September 18, 2023, https://foxbaltimore.com/news/project-baltimore/at-13-baltimore-city-high-schools-zero-students-tested-proficient-on-2023-state-math-exam. Even "in Baltimore's top five performing high schools, only 11.4% of students scored proficient in math." Noah Webster Education Foundation, "Over a Dozen Baltimore Schools Don't Have Any Students Who Are Proficient in Math," September 26, 2023, https://nwef.org/2023/09/26/baltimore-schools-low-math-proficiency.
18. STEM Education Data, "How Proficient Are U.S. 12th Graders in Math and Science," accessed April 21, 2024, https://www.nsf.gov/nsb/sei/edTool/data/highschool-06.html.
19. Samuel J. Abrams and Amna Khalid, "Are Colleges and Universities Too Liberal? What the Research Says about the Political Composition of Campuses and Campus Climate," AEI, October 21, 2020, https://www.aei.org/articles/are-colleges-and-universities-too-liberal-what-the-research-says-about-the-political-composition-of-campuses-and-campus-climate/.
20. Gigi de la Torre, "96 Percent of Ivy League Political Donations Go to Democrats," *College Fix*, November 2, 2022, https://www.thecollegefix.com/97-percent-of-ivy-league-political-donations-go-to-democrats/.
21. Michael Gribbon, "An Overwhelming Majority of Campaign Donations

by USC Professors Go to Democrats," *USC Annenberg Media*, November 15, 2023, https://www.uscannenbergmedia.com/2023/11/15/an-overwhelming-majority-of-campaign-donations-by-usc-professors-go-to-democrats/.

22. Christian Schneider, "Democrats Collect Nearly All Swing-State College-Faculty Contributions," *National Review*, November 2020, https://www.nationalreview.com/2020/11/democrats-collect-nearly-all-swing-state-college-faculty-contributions/.

23. "Teachers Unions and an Indoctrination to Hate Capitalism," *New York Post*, May 4, 2023, https://nypost.com/2023/05/04/teachers-unions-and-a-lesson-in-capitalism-hatred/.

24. Steven M. Beaudoin, *Poverty in World History* (New York: Routledge, 2007), 17.

25. Beaudoin, *Poverty in World History*, 17.

26. Sakari Hakkinen, "Poverty in the First-Century Galilee," *HTS Theological Studies* 22, no 4 (2016), http://www.scielo.org.za/scielo.php?script=sci_arttext&pid=S0259-94222016000400046#top_fn7.

27. Dorsey Armstrong, "Years That Changed History: 1215," Great Courses, accessed April 17, 2024, https://www.thegreatcourses.com/courses/years-that-changed-history-1215.

28. Armstrong, "Years That Changed History."

29. Statista, "Monthly Length of the Average Working Week of All Employees in the United States from March 2022 to March 2024," April 2024, https://www.statista.com/statistics/215643/average-weekly-working-hours-of-all-employees-in-the-us-by-month/.

30. Stephanie Ferguson, "Understanding America's Labor Shortage," US Chamber of Commerce, February 13, 2024, https://www.uschamber.com/workforce/understanding-americas-labor-shortage.

31. Michael Schuman, "History of Child Labor in the United States—Part 2: The Reform Movement," *Monthly Labor Review*, January 2017, https://www.bls.gov/opub/mlr/2017/article/history-of-child-labor-in-the-united-states-part-2-the-reform-movement.htm.

32. Kathryn Reid, "Child Labor: Facts, FAQs, and How to Help," World Vision, January 25, 2024, https://www.worldvision.org/child-protection-news-stories/child-labor-facts.

33. International Labour Organization, "Child Labour in Africa," accessed April 21, 2024, https://www.ilo.org/africa/areas-of-work/child-labour/lang--en/index.htm. See also UNICEF, "Child Labour," June 2023, https://data.unicef.org/topic/child-protection/child-labour/.
34. William Bradford, *Of Plymouth Plantation, 1620–1647*, ed. Samuel Eliot Morison (New York: Modern Library, 1967), https://press-pubs.uchicago.edu/founders/documents/v1ch16s1.html.
35. Policy Circle, "Socialism: A Case Study on Venezuela," 2019, https://www.thepolicycircle.org/minibrief/socialism-a-case-study-on-venezuela/.
36. "Venezuela Crisis: Three in Four in Extreme Poverty, Study Says," *BBC*, September 30, 2021, https://www.bbc.com/news/world-latin-america-58743253.
37. Human Rights Watch, "Cuba: Events of 2022," 2023, https://www.hrw.org/world-report/2023/country-chapters/cuba.
38. David Filipov, "Here Are 10 Critics of Vladimir Putin Who Died Violently or in Suspicious Ways," *Washington Post*, March 23, 2017, https://www.washingtonpost.com/news/worldviews/wp/2017/03/23/here-are-ten-critics-of-vladimir-putin-who-died-violently-or-in-suspicious-ways/.
39. Ilya Somin, "Remembering the Biggest Mass Murder in the History of the World," *Washington Post*, August 3, 2016, https://www.washingtonpost.com/news/volokh-conspiracy/wp/2016/08/03/giving-historys-greatest-mass-murderer-his-due/.
40. Harlow Giles Unger, *Lion of Liberty: Patrick Henry and the Call to a New Nation* (Cambridge, MA: Da Capo Press, 2010), 32–33.
41. Daniel Webster, speech delivered at Niblo's Saloon, New York, March 15, 1837.
42. Gary Richardson and Tim Sablik, "Banking Panics of the Gilded Age," Federal Reserve History, December 4, 2015, https://www.federalreservehistory.org/essays/banking-panics-of-the-gilded-age.
43. Adam Carasso and Gene Steuerle, "A Brief History of the Top Tax Rate," Tax Policy Center, November 25, 2002, https://www.urban.org/sites/default/files/publication/59856/1000459-A-Brief-History-of-the-Top-Tax-Rate.PDF.
44. Gary Richardson, "The Great Depression," Federal Reserve History,

November 22, 2013, https://www.federalreservehistory.org/essays/great-depression.

45. Steven Horwitz, "Hoover's Economic Policies," *Econlib*, accessed April 24, 2024, https://www.econlib.org/library/Enc/HooversEconomicPolicies.html.

46. Franklin Delano Roosevelt, "Address on Constitution Day," September 17, 1937, American Presidency Project, https://www.presidency.ucsb.edu/documents/address-constitution-day-washington-dc.

47. Franklin D. Roosevelt, "Fireside Chat," March 9, 1937, American Presidency Project, https://www.presidency.ucsb.edu/documents/fireside-chat-17.

48. Board of Governors of the Federal Reserve System, "Distribution of Household Wealth in the U.S. since 1989," March 22, 2024, https://www.federalreserve.gov/releases/z1/dataviz/dfa/distribute/table/.

49. Edgar K. Browning, *Stealing from Each Other: How the Welfare State Robs Americans of Money and Spirit* (Westport, CT: Praeger, 2008), 25–27. "Among people who were 25 years old and older who filed income tax returns in 1996, and who were initially in the bottom 20 percent, their incomes had risen by 91 percent by 2005. Meanwhile, people of the same description whose incomes were in the top 1 percent in 1996 had a *drop* in income of 26 percent by 2005." Thomas Sowell, *Economic Facts and Fallacies,* 2nd ed. (New York: Basic Books, 2011), 152.

50. Browning, *Stealing from Each Other*, 25–27.

51. Robert Arnott, William Bernstein, and Lillian Wu, "The Myth of Dynastic Wealth: The Rich Get Poorer," *Cato Journal* 35, no. 3 (Fall 2015): 447–485.

52. Browning, *Stealing from Each Other*, 12–13.

53. Browning, *Stealing from Each Other*, 11.

54. Phil Gramm, Robert Ekelund, and John Early, *The Myth of American Inequality* (Lanham, MD: Rowman and Littlefield, 2022), 34.

55. Quentin R. Skrabec Jr., *William McKinley: Apostle of Protectionism* (New York: Algora, 2008), 195–196. "In general, the period from 1880 to 1910 saw one of the greatest growth rates for American industry ever" (195). "The U.S. gross national product grew from an estimated $11 billion in 1880 to $18.7 billion in 1890 to $35.3 billion in 1910" (196). See also Kevin Phillips, *William McKinley* (New York: Henry Holt, 2003), 115.

56. Trading Economics, "United States GDP Growth Rate," accessed April 24, 2024, https://tradingeconomics.com/united-states/gdp-growth.
57. Trading Economics, "Euro Area GDP Growth Rate," accessed April 24, 2024, https://tradingeconomics.com/euro-area/gdp-growth.
58. Trading Economics, "Spain Full Year GDP Growth," accessed April 16, 2024, https://tradingeconomics.com/spain/full-year-gdp-growth.
59. Hanan Morsy, "Scarred Generation," International Monetary Fund, March 2012, https://www.imf.org/external/pubs/ft/fandd/2012/03/morsy.htm.
60. Statista, "Spain: Youth Unemployment Rate from 2004 to 2023," March 2024, https://www.statista.com/statistics/813014/youth-unemployment-rate-in-spain/.
61. Steven A. Camarota and Karen Zeigler, "63% of Non-citizen Households Access Welfare Programs," Center for Immigration Studies, November 20, 2018, https://cis.org/Report/63-NonCitizen-Households-Access-Welfare-Programs.
62. Will Durant, *The Life of Greece* (New York: Simon and Schuster, 1939) 464–465.
63. Quoted in Will and Ariel Durant, *The Lessons of History* (New York: Simon and Schuster, 1968), 75.
64. Steve Forbes, "Welcome to the Unsustainable Folly of Modern Socialism," *Forbes*, March 28, 2023, https://www.forbes.com/sites/steveforbes/2023/03/28/welcome-to-the-unsustainable-folly-of-modern-socialism-steve-forbes-torches-bidens-ev-push/?sh=71af8a1d136d.
65. Committee on Oversight and Accountability, "The Cover Up: Big Tech, the Swamp, and Mainstream Media Coordinated to Censor Americans' Free Speech," February 8, 2023, https://oversight.house.gov/release/the-cover-up-big-tech-the-swamp-and-mainstream-media-coordinated-to-censor-americans-free-speech-%EF%BF%BC/; National Academies, "Censorship and the Right to Information during the Pandemic," September 29, 2022, https://www.nationalacademies.org/event/09-29-2022/censorship-and-the-right-to-information-during-the-pandemic.
66. "Twitter Suppressed Covid-19 Info, Suspended Top Experts, Allege Twitter Files," *Economic Times*, December 27, 2022, https://economictimes.indiatimes.com/tech/technology/twitter-suppressed-covid-19-info-suspended-top-experts-during-pandemic-twitter-files/articleshow/96545004.cms.

67. Thomas Del Beccaro, "Trump Raid Shows That FBI, Justice Department Want to Decide Who Can Be Our President," *Fox News*, August 16, 2022, https://www.foxnews.com/opinion/trump-raid-shows-fbi-justice-department-decide-who-our-president.
68. Edward Muir, *Civic Ritual in Renaissance Venice* (Princeton, NJ: Princeton University Press, 1981), 20.
69. Byron York, "Obama's Dissident Database Could Be Secret—and Permanent," *Washington Examiner*, August 5, 2009, https://www.washingtonexaminer.com/opinion/beltway-confidential/2409300/obamas-dissident-database-could-be-secret-and-permanent/.
70. Quoted in Jeorg Knipprath, "Daniel Webster (1782–1852)—Secretary of State, New Hampshire House and Senate Member, Known as the 'Great Orator,' Part 2," Constituting America, accessed April 21, 2024, https://constitutingamerica.org/daniel-webster-1782-1852-secretary-of-state-nh-house-senate-member-great-orator-part-2-guest-essayist-joerg-knipprath/.

CHAPTER 11

1. Wayne W. LaMorte, "What Is Culture?," Boston University School of Public Health, May 3, 2016, https://sphweb.bumc.bu.edu/otlt/mph-modules/PH/CulturalAwareness/CulturalAwareness2.html.
2. University of Michigan Center for Sustainable Systems, "U.S. Cities Factsheet," accessed April 21, 2024, https://css.umich.edu/publications/factsheets/built-environment/us-cities-factsheet.
3. Will Durant, *Our Oriental Heritage* (New York: Simon and Schuster, 1935), 259.
4. "Stoicism," *Stanford Encyclopedia of Philosophy*, January 20, 2023, https://plato.stanford.edu/entries/stoicism/.
5. "Epicurus," *Stanford Encyclopedia of Philosophy*, January 10, 2005, https://plato.stanford.edu/entries/epicurus/.
6. Donald L. Wasson, "Epicurus," *Work History Encyclopedia*, September 7, 2016, https://www.worldhistory.org/Epicurus.
7. "The historian records the exceptional because it is interesting—because it

is exceptional." Will and Ariel Durant, *The Lessons of History* (New York: Simon and Schuster, 1968), 41.

8. For a vivid reading on this subject, the reader is encouraged to listen to Kenneth R. Bartlett, "The Italians before Italy: Conflict and Competition in the Mediterranean," Great Courses, accessed April 16. 2024, https://www.thegreatcourses.com/courses/italians-before-italy-conflict-and-competition-in-the-mediterranean.

9. Archibald Dobbs, *Philosophy and Popular Morals in Ancient Greece* (London: Simpkin, Marshall, 1907), 226.

10. Dobbs, *Philosophy and Popular Morals in Ancient Greece*, 262.

11. Will Durant, *The Life of Ancient Greece* (New York: Simon and Schuster, 1939), 293.

12. Will and Ariel Durant, *The Renaissance* (New York: Simon and Schuster, 1953), 606.

13. Jacob Burckhardt, *The Civilisation of the Renaissance in Italy*, 9th ed. (New York: Macmillan, 1928), 487.

14. John M. Dillon, *Morality and Custom in Ancient Greece* (Indianapolis: Indiana University Press, 2004), 101.

15. Dillon, *Morality and Custom in Ancient Greece*, 101. See also Michael Rocke, *Forbidden Friendships, Homosexuality and Male Culture in Renaissance Florence* (New York: Oxford University Press, 1996), 112.

16. Cyril Bailey, *The Religion of Ancient Rome* (Chicago: Open Court, 1907), 104.

17. Robert Whaples, "Hours of Work in US History," Economic History Association, accessed April 21, 2024, https://eh.net/encyclopedia/hours-of-work-in-u-s-history/.

18. Whaples, "Hours of Work in US History."

19. US Bureau of Labor Statistics, "Civilian Labor Force Participation Rate," accessed April 21, 2024, https://www.bls.gov/charts/employment-situation/civilian-labor-force-participation-rate.htm.

20. Rachel Sheffield, "President Obama Admits Welfare Encourages Dependency," *Daily Signal*, July 9, 2011, https://www.dailysignal.com/2011/07/09/president-obama-admits-welfare-encourages-dependency/.

21. Jesse Washington, "Blacks Struggle with 72 Percent Unwed Mothers Rate," *NBC News*, November 7, 2010, https://www.nbcnews.com/id/wbna39993685.
22. "673 University Professors Sign Letter Opposing Courses on America's Founding, Constitution," *AllSides*, April 26, 2023, https://www.allsides.com/news/2023-04-26-0820/education-673-university-professors-sign-letter-opposing-courses-americas.
23. Neal McCluskey, "K–12 Education," Cato Institute, December 15, 2022, https://www.cato.org/publications/k-12-education.
24. "Math Scores Fell in Nearly Every State, and Reading Dipped on National Exam," *New York Times*, October 24, 2022, https://www.nytimes.com/2022/10/24/us/math-reading-scores-pandemic.html.
25. Sarah D. Sparks, "Two Decades of Progress, Nearly Gone: National Math, Reading Scores Hit Historic Lows," *Education Week*, October 24, 2022, https://www.edweek.org/leadership/two-decades-of-progress-nearly-gone-national-math-reading-scores-hit-historic-lows/2022/10.
26. Macrotrends, "US Crime Rate and Statistics, 1990–2023," accessed April 21, 2024, https://www.macrotrends.net/countries/USA/united-states/crime-rate-statistics.
27. Hanna Love and Tracy Hadden Loh, "The Geography of Crime in Four US Cities: Perceptions and Reality," Brookings, April 3, 2023, https://www.brookings.edu/research/the-geography-of-crime-in-four-u-s-cities-perceptions-and-reality/.
28. Daniel Panneton, "How Extremist Gun Culture Is Trying to Co-opt the Rosary," *The Atlantic*, August 2022, https://www.theatlantic.com/ideas/archive/2022/08/radical-traditionalist-catholic-christian-rosary-weapon/671122/.
29. Anders Hagstrom, "Importance of Traditional American Values Has Plummeted across US, Poll Shows," *Fox News*, March 27, 2023, https://www.foxnews.com/politics/importance-traditional-american-values-plummeted-us-poll-shows.
30. Victor Davis Hanson, "Our French Revolution," *Daily Caller*, April 6, 2023, https://dailycaller.com/2023/04/06/victor-davis-hanson-our-french-revolution/.
31. Durant, *Our Oriental Heritage*, 3.

32. Durant, *Lessons of History*, 43.
33. Hagstrom, "Importance of Traditional American Values."
34. University of Maryland Office of Diversity and Inclusion, "Key Terms and Definitions," May 5, 2022, https://diversity.umd.edu/resources/key-terms-definitions.
35. Edward Gibbon, *The Decline and Fall of the Roman Empire* (London: Frederick Warne, 1800), 1:23.

CHAPTER 12

1. Georg Wilhelm Friedrich Hegel, *Hegel: The Letters*, trans. Clark Butler and Christiane Seiler (Bloomington: Indiana University Press, 1985), 114.
2. Ho Chi Minh, *On Revolution: Selected Writings, 1920–66*, ed. Bernard B. Fall (New York: Frederick A. Praeger, 1967), 141.
3. Ipsos Reid, "O Canada: Our Home and Naïve Land," July 1, 2008, https://web.archive.org/web/20170323022225/http:/www.dominion.ca/CanadaDay.Survey.DominionInstitute.1July08.pdf.
4. Dexter Fergie, "How American Culture Ate the World," *New Republic*, March 24, 2022, https://newrepublic.com/article/165836/american-culture-ate-world-righteous-smokescreen-globalization-review.
5. Fergie, "How American Culture Ate the World."
6. "Top 10 Biggest Companies in the World Market Cap in 2024," *Forbes India*, March 19, 2024, https://www.forbesindia.com/article/explainers/top-10-largest-companies-world-market-cap/86341/1.
7. USAFacts, "Why Are US Companies Investing More Abroad," April 6, 2023, https://usafacts.org/articles/why-are-us-companies-investing-more-abroad/.
8. Caleb Silver, "The Top 25 Economies in the World," *Investopedia*, December 15, 2023, https://www.investopedia.com/insights/worlds-top-economies/.
9. Christina Lu, "Assessing the Power of the U.S. as a Brand," *U.S. News and World Report*, January 15, 2020, https://www.usnews.com/news/best-countries/articles/2020-01-15/assessing-the-power-of-the-us-as-a-brand.
10. Statista, "Leading Brands Worldwide in 2023, by Brand Value," November 2023, https://www.statista.com/statistics/264826/most-valuable-brands

-worldwide-in-2009/; Dorothy Neufeld, "The Top 100 Most Valuable Brands in 2024," *Visual Capitalist*, January 29, 2024, https://www.visualcapitalist.com/most-valuable-brands-in-2024/.

11. Subhayu Bandyopadhyay and Praew Grittayaphong, "Military Expenditures: How Do the Top-Spending Nations Compare?," Federal Reserve Bank of St. Louis, January 3, 2023, https://www.stlouisfed.org/on-the-economy/2023/jan/military-expenditures-how-top-spending-nations-compare; Katharina Buchholz, "China Steps Up Military Spending," Statista, March 11, 2024, https://www.statista.com/chart/16878/military-expenditure-by-the-us-china-and-russia/.

12. Paul M. Kennedy and Karin Schambach, *The Rise and Fall of the Great Powers: Economic Change and Military Conflict from 1500 to 2000* (New York: Random House, 1987), xvi.

13. *Dictionary.com*, s.v. "pacifism," https://www.dictionary.com/browse/pacifism.

14. Abraham Lincoln, "House Divided Speech," June 16, 1858, National Park Service, https://www.nps.gov/liho/learn/historyculture/housedivided.htm.

CHAPTER 13

1. Will and Ariel Durant, *The Lessons of History* (New York: Simon and Schuster, 1968), 88.

2. Paul H. Rubin, "Crony Capitalism," *Supreme Court Economic Review* 23 (2015), https://www.journals.uchicago.edu/doi/full/10.1086/686474?af=R&mobileUi=0.

3. Christine Shaw, *The Politics of Exile in Renaissance Italy* (Cambridge: Cambridge University Press, 2000).

4. Adam Hayes, "What Is the Law of Demand in Economics, and How Does It Work?," *Investopedia*, October 14, 2023, https://www.investopedia.com/terms/l/lawofdemand.asp.

5. Kenneth R. Bartlett, "The Italians before Italy: Conflict and Competition in the Mediterranean," Great Courses, accessed April 16. 2024, https://www.thegreatcourses.com/courses/italians-before-italy-conflict-and-competition-in-the-mediterranean.

6. Arthur B. Laffer, Brian Domitrovic, and Jeanne Cairns Sinquefield, *Taxes Have Consequences* (New York: Post Hill Press, 2022), 142.

7. Laffer, Domitrovic, and Sinquefield, *Taxes Have Consequences*, 143.
8. Patrick McLaughlin and Robert Greene, "The Unintended Consequences of Federal Regulatory Accumulation," Mercatus Center, May 8, 2014, https://www.mercatus.org/research/policy-briefs/unintended-consequences-federal-regulatory-accumulation.
9. Edward Chase Kirkland, *Industry Comes of Age: Business, Labor, and Public Policy, 1860–1897* (New York: Holt, Rinehart and Winston, 1961); US Bureau of the Census, "Historical Statistics of the United States, Colonial Times to 1970," September 1975, chapter F, https://www.census.gov/library/publications/1975/compendia/hist_stats_colonial-1970.html.
10. Bhargavi Sakthivel, Maeva Cousin, and David Wilcox, "A Million Simulations, One Verdict for US Economy: Debt Danger Ahead," *Bloomberg*, April 1, 2024, https://www.bloomberg.com/news/articles/2024-04-01/us-government-debt-risk-a-million-simulations-show-danger-ahead?embedded-checkout=true.
11. George Washington, untitled article, *Pennsylvania Journal and Weekly Advertiser*, November 14, 1787, p. 3.
12. Chief Justice John Marshall, in his five-volume work *The Life of George Washington*, first published in 1804, described a system resembling the Republican and Democratic parties of today: "At length, two great parties were formed in every state, which were distinctly marked, and which pursued distinct objects, with systematic arrangement." Marshall characterized them as follows: "The one struggled with unabated zeal for the exact observance of public and private engagements.... The distresses of individuals were, they thought, to be alleviated only by industry and frugality, not by a relaxation of the laws, or by a sacrifice of the rights of others.... The other party marked out for themselves a more indulgent course.... Viewing with extreme tenderness the case of the debtor, their efforts were unceasingly directed to his relief. To exact a faithful compliance with contracts was, in their opinion, a harsh measure ... which the people would not bear." John Marshall, *The Life of George Washington*, vol. 5 (Philadelphia: C. P. Wayne, 1807), 85, 86.
13. Durant, *The Lessons of History*, 88.

EPILOGUE

1. Clayton Kraby, "Napoleon Bonaparte's View of Jesus," *Reasonable Theology*, accessed April 24, 2024, https://reasonabletheology.org/napoleon-bonapartes-view-of-jesus/.
2. Donald J. Kessler and Burton G. Cour-Palais, "Collision Frequency of Artificial Satellites: The Creation of a Debris Belt," *Journal of Geophysical Research* 83, no A6 (1978), http://www.castor2.ca/07_News/headline_010216_files/Kessler_Collision_Frequency_1978.pdf.
3. Douglas C. Dow, "Virginia and Kentucky Resolutions of 1798," Free Speech Center, July 30, 2023, https://firstamendment.mtsu.edu/article/virginia-and-kentucky-resolutions-of-1798/.
4. "Nullification Crisis," *Britannica*, April 19, 2024, https://www.britannica.com/topic/nullification-crisis.
5. Julie Miller, "'A Republic If You Can Keep It': Elizabeth Willing Powel, Benjamin Franklin, and the James McHenry Journal," *Library of Congress Blogs*, January 6, 2022, https://blogs.loc.gov/manuscripts/2022/01/a-republic-if-you-can-keep-it-elizabeth-willing-powel-benjamin-franklin-and-the-james-mchenry-journal/.

Index

Page references in italics denote material in figures.

A

abortion, 83, 175
Acheson, Dean, 226
Adams, John, 54, 72, 84–86, 101–102, 129–130, 210
Adams, Samuel, 136, 211
Aeneid (Virgil), 12
Age of Absolutism, 61, 73, 229
agriculture, 40–44
    addressing world hunger, 2, 115–116
    agricultural, commercial, and industrial phases, 6, 14, 80, 147, 155–156
    centrality of, 2, 14, 16, 32, 40–41, 44, 55
    children and, 15, 41–42, 83, 155
    commerce in support of, 40–41
    loneliness in, 43
    number of farms and workers, 40, 82–83, 115
    production and consumption at home, 41
    reinforcement of faith, 12, 48, 56
    renewal and recurrence, 56
    self-sufficiency, 16, 90, 217
    southern plantation system versus northern family farms, 43, 90
    subsistence farming, 151
    working hours, 155

Ahlstrom, Sydney H., 49
Alexander the Great, 192
Amazon, 196
American civilization, lessons and key points from, 201–220, 231–236
    capitalism as father of democracy, 203, 233
    capitalism as necessary for democracy, 203–206
    centralization of power, 67, 70–71, 107, 154, 158–159, 161–163, 171–173, 206, 208–212, 215, 229–230, 233–235
    claim that dissent is threat to stability, 211, 234
    class warfare, 169–170, 217, 228, 234
    competition for ideas versus for government spoils, 18, 86, 189, 216, 234
    consequences of cultural breakdown, 218–220
    crossed bridge between assurance and doubt, 136, 235
    cyber warfare, 225, 236
    danger of class division, 216–218
    democratization and opportunity as still working, 230, 236

dispersed economic and political power, 109, 132–133, 154, 204–206, 232
dissent as mother of democracy, 203, 211, 233
equality in history limited to poverty, 150–152, 232
exceptionalism, 62, 126, 141–142, 187, 207–208, 232–233
expanding economy provides greatest opportunity, 214–215
fate of America still lies in hands of Americans and their combined wills, 222, 236
fixed economic pie and government dependency leading to cultural warfare, 168, 170, 213–214, 234–235
goal not to have efficient, powerful government, 209, 233
government decisions pick winners and losers, 188, 216, 234
government growth, 212–216
government money for big business means less democracy, 171–172, 233
government surveillance, 172–173, 186, 209
greatest opportunity to greatest and most diverse number, 208, 230, 233
history is no more a straight line than the emotions of our days, 5, 221–222, 235
immigrants' complementary purposes, 29–30, 32, 231
learning from history, 203, 235
level of consensus versus level of dissent and doubt, 126, 235
limited government, 16, 85, 87, 126, 135, 140, 143–144, 158–159, 163, 167, 206, 233
limiting of dissent, 157, 172–173, 210, 234
more government decisions lead to more divisions, 216, 234
separation of economic power from political power, 153, 171–172, 205–206, 232
shared elements with other civilizations, 202–203
survival and apology, 142, 175, 188, 235
sustainable republic, 87, 204–205, 232
unfinished product, 84, 233
uniqueness, 1, 3, 202, 208–209, 230–231
what isn't taught in schools becomes forgotten in culture, 16, 219, 235
American Colossus (Brands), 82
American flag, 141
American Indians. *See* Native Americans
American Samoa, 116
Anglicans, 50–51
Annenberg Public Policy Center, 149
Anstey, Roger, 95
Anthony, Susan B., 112
Antony, Mark, 112
Apple, 196
aristocracy. *See also* class
  cyclical progression of government, 18
  in England, 39–40, 68
  lack of, in America, 29, 68
  women in, 112
Aristotle, 65, 95
Armstrong, Dorsey, 10, 151
Arnott, Robert, 166
art, 17, 31, 112, 122–123, 137–138, 181
Articles of Confederation, 70–71, 80, 99, 160
Assyrian Empire, 14
atheism, 17
"Atlantic Worlds" (Royal Museums Greenwich), 98
Australia, 113, 116

B

Bacon, Francis, 72
Bailey, Cyril, 180
Bailyn, Bernard, 36, 43
Baird, Robert, 49
Bank of the United States, 161
Baptists, 51–52
Barbarossa, Frederick, 222
Barbary Wars, 116
Bartlett, Kenneth R., 27
Bauer, Susan Wise, 21–22

Index

BBC, 157
Beatrice d'Este, 30, 113
Beaudoin, Steven M., 150–151
Bell, Alexander Graham, 144–145
Bennet, Lerone, Jr., 97
Berlin, Ira, 93
Berra, Yogi, 120
Bezos, Jeff, 165
Biden, Joe, 104, 134, 172, 211
Bill of Rights, 49, 54, 71, 209
Bismarck, Otto von, 102
Black Americans. *See also* slavery
  abolitionists, 94
  elected officials, 94, 105
  prewar free Blacks, 28, 93–94
  1619 Project, 140
  slave ownership, 97–98
  voting rights, 86–87, 105, 129
  welfare and the family, 184
Black Slaves, Indian Masters (Krauthamer), 97
Bloomberg Economics, 213
Boniface VIII, 215
books, study of history through, 10
Boston University, 175
Bradford, William, 156
Brand Origin Index Rankings, 196
Brands, H. W., 82, 146
Breen, T. H., 43
Brown, William Wells, 94
Brutus, 62
Bryan, William Jennings, 133–134, 165, 172
Buffet, Warren, 166
Burckhardt, Jacob, 179
Burke, Edmund, 201
business. *See* capitalism and economics
Byzantine empire, 179

C

The Cambridge History of America and the World, 123
Canada, 195, 229
cancel culture, 140–142
capitalism and economics, 14–17, 30–32. *See also* agriculture
  accumulation of wealth, 15, 103, 110, 177, 183, 219
  agricultural, commercial, and industrial phases, 6, 14, 80, 147, 155–156
  art and science flourishing with commerce and wealth, 17
  average income, 132
  bank crises and failures, 161–162
  "bottom-up" economy, 134
  changing work habits, 182–183
  child labor, 41–42, 155–156
  class warfare, 169–170, 228
  commercialization, 41, 90, 102, 111–112, 114, 130–131, 152–156, 159, 165, 177, 202, 209, 214, 217
  commitment to success, 58
  consumerism, 122–123, 134–135, 144
  cultural warfare and, 168, 170, 214, 234–235
  democracy and, 152–154, 203–206
  depressions, 68–69, 110, 130, 139, 163, 212, 228
  dispersed economic power, 109, 132–133, 154, 204–206, 232
  doubts about capitalism, 130
  economic disparity and inequality, 40, 130, 132, 147, 152, 154, 156–157, 165–167, 204, 217
  economic freedom, 55–58, 131, 153
  economic growth, 80, 114–116, 144–146, 167–170, 197
  economic maturity, 62, 68–69, 94, 132, 153
  erosion of faith, 48, 180
  expanding economy provides greatest opportunity, 214–215
  exports, 44, 102, 115–116, 122–123
  family versus individual as center of economic activity, 14–15, 83, 111–112, 175, 218
  "free labor" versus slavery, 90–91
  government growth and power, 15, 161, 167–170, 212–214
  government money for big business, 171–172, 233
  "great capitalists," 82, 132
  industrialization, 15, 41, 48, 56, 80–81, 94, 103, 111, 114, 131–132, 146–147, 154–155, 159, 165, 183, 202, 214, 217

lack of class culture and aristocracy, 132–133
Law of Demand, 212, 227
middle class, 110, 132–133, 153, 167, 214, 217–218
mobility, 166
pervasive poverty, 150–152, 232
separation of economic power from political power, 153, 171–172, 205–206, 232
spending on nonessential items, 110, 122, 144, 146
stagnant economy and racism/division, 106–107
standard of living, 45, 82, 144–146, 176
stock market crash, 135, 162, 212
transition from rural to urban economy, 14–16, 81, 131
unions and guilds, 57, 154
wartime support from industry, *119*, 119–120
women in the workforce, 114
working from home, 145
working hours, 154–155, 182–183
world impact of American enterprises, 196
Capra, Frank, 120
Carlyle, Thomas, 3, 10, 19–20, 34, 48
Carnegie, Andrew, 82, 132, 147, 165, 210
Casablanca, 120
Catholics, 50–53, 185–186
Chamberlain, Neville, 226
Charlemagne, 224
Charles IX, 113
Chaucer, 137
Cherokee tribe, 97
Cheswell, Wentworth, 93
Chickasaw tribe, 97
children. *See also* education and schools; family
   agricultural work, 15, 41–42, 83, 155
   child labor, 41–42, 155–156
   child mortality, 38, 42
   cost of in urban settings, 15, 83
   family-based education, 148
   indentured servitude, 39

China, 14–15, 80, 103–104, 139, 157, 194, 226
Choctaw tribe, 36, 97
Christianity and Christians. *See* religion and faith; *names of specific denominations*
The Civilisation of the Renaissance in Italy (Burckhardt), 179
Civil War, 104, 136–137, 161–162, 173, 188. *See also* slavery
class
   class-based politics, 133–134
   class warfare, 169–170, 217, 228, 234
   dangers of class division, 216–218
   lack of class culture and aristocracy, 29, 56, 68, 132–133, 206
   middle class, 110, 132–133, 153, 167, 214, 217–218
   ruling classes, 18, 206
Clinton, Hillary, 211
Clodius Pulcher, Publius, 112
Columbus, Christopher, 26, 28
commerce. *See* capitalism and economics
communism, 121, 147, 152, 157, 186
Congregationalists, 54, 139
conservatism, 83–84, 149, 165
Constitution of the Athenians, 64–65
contraception, 83, 175
Coolidge, Calvin, 115
Copernicus, 30
Corsica, 113
COVID pandemic, 164, 171–172, 182–184, 228
Cox, James, 147
crime, 52, 71, 104, 131, 185, 219
Crusades, 16, 50
Cuba, 15, 157, 194, 217
culture, 122–123, 195–196. *See also* art
   cancel culture, 140
   defined, 175
   effects of societal change on, 182–188, 218–220
   export and dominance of, 2, 111, 195–196
   mass media and, 137
   religion and, 16
Curio, Gaius Scribonius, 112
cyber warfare, 225, 236

D

da Vinci, Leonardo, 31
Declaration of Independence, 63, 76, 104, 195
The Decline and Fall of the Roman Empire (Gibbon), 21
The Decline of the West (Spengler), 18
Deere, Donald, 166
Delian League Revolt, 18
de Sousa, Mathias, 94
d'Este, Ercole, 210
d'Este, Isabella, 30, 113
Dilke, Mrs. Ashton, 113
DiMaggio, Joe, 120
Diocletian, 152, 171
dissent and protest, 21, 135, 228–229
    level of consensus versus level of dissent and doubt, 126, 235
    limiting of dissent, 157, 172–173, 210, 234
    as mother of democracy, 203, 211, 233
    recent immigrants and, 170, 234
    religious dissent, 51–53
    tax revolts, 18
    as threat to stability, 211, 234
Divided Era, 188–189, 214, 234
The Divided Era (Del Beccaro), 216
Dobbs, Archibald, 178
Doerflinger, Thomas, 57–58
doubt, 4–5, 16, 125–142, 176, 181, 202. *See also* dissent and protest
    cancel culture, 140–142
    capitalism, 131–133
    class-based politics, 133–134
    defined, 47–48
    economic boom and bust, 134–135
    education, 138–140
    level of consensus versus level of dissent and doubt, 126, 235
    media and technology, 136–138
    origins and nature of, 129–130
    war, 135–136
    work in progress, 130
Douglass, Frederick, 94
Durant, Ariel, 6–7, 33, 72, 115–116
Durant, Will, 3, 5–7, 10, 19–20, 33–34, 50, 72, 85, 115–116, 122, 136, 169, 176–178, 187, 203, 218–220

E

Ecclesiastes, 12–13
The Economic Rise of Early America (Walton and Shepherd), 44
economics. *See* capitalism and economics
Economic Times, 172
Economist, 6
The Economy of Colonial Americas (Perkins), 57
Edison, Thomas, 145
education and schools, 138–140
    changing views toward capitalism and socialism, 148
    development of schooling in America, 148
    falling behind, 139, 149, 184
    history and civics, 148–149, 184
    moral structure, 218–220
    parental training, 55
    patriotism, 186
    political bias in, 149
    public schools, 139, 148, 184
    religion and, 55, 138–140, 184
    what isn't taught being forgotten, 16, 219, 235
Egypt, 152
Elizabeth I, 113
Emancipation Proclamation, 87
England. *See* Great Britain and England
Enlightenment, 61, 85, 229
Epicureanism, 176–181, 197
Epicurus, 177
Espinoza, Baruch, 1
Eturira, 15n
Euripides, 137
Europe. *See names of specific countries*
exceptionalism, 62, 126, 141–142, 187, 207–208, 232–233
expansionism, 15–16, 76–79, 77, 110, 116–117, 192–196

F

Fabius, 179
Facebook, 172, 196
Fair Labor Standards Act, 182
faith. *See* religion and faith; *names of specific denominations*

The Fall of the House of Dixie (Levine), 91–92
family, 14–17. *See also* children; moral structure; women
   as central unit in society, 14–16, 41–42, 83, 111–114, 175, 218
   childbirth and child mortality, 38, 42
   contraception and abortion, 83, 175
   decline in birth rates and size of, 83, 114
   decline of religion and, 16
   family versus individual as center of economic activity, 14–15, 83, 111–112, 175, 218
   homes and possessions, 42–43
   welfare and government dependence, 184
Father Knows Best (TV series), 138
FBI, 186
Federal Reserve, 162–163
Finland, 114
First Families of Virginia, 39–40
First Seminole War, 78
Florence, 58, 66–67, 112, 130–131, 153, 179, 205, 215
Forbes, 166
Forbes, Steve, 171
Ford, Henry, 145, 208
Foreign Policy, 6
1491 (Mann), 23
Fourth Eclogue (Virgil), 12
France, 16–17, 26–28, 30, 36, 64, 69–70, 72, 77, 101, 103, 111, 113–114, 116, 205, 219, 224
Francis I, 112
Francis II, 113
Franklin, Benjamin, 44, 72, 78, 136, 230
Freedom Journal, 94
Free Negro Owners of Slaves in the United States in 1830 (Woodson), 97
French and Indian Wars, 30, 36, 192
Fulvia, 112

G

Gable, Clarke, 120
Galenson, David W., 96
Gates, Bill, 165
Genghis Kahn, 192
Genoa, 14, 30
geographic expansion, 15–16, 76–79, *77*, 110, 116–117, 192–196
geographic remoteness, 26–27, 64, 70, 227
George III, 73, 136, 208
Germany, 16, 18, 26, 28, 80, 102, 114, 117–119, 157, 179, 194, 222
Ghibellines, 215
Gibbon, Edward, 21, 179, 187–188
Gilded Age, 167, 188
Goethe, Johann Wolfgang von, 3, 10, 18, 20–21, 32, 123, 202–203
Golden Age, 109–110
Google, 172, 196
Gordon, Robert, 114–115
government and politics, 17–21. *See also* capitalism and economics
   authoritarian versus elected, 17
   balance of power, 85–87, 160
   branches of, 64–66
   capitalism and democracy, 152–154
   centralization of power, 67, 70–71, 107, 154, 158–159, 161–163, 171–173, 206, 208–212, 215, 229–230, 233–235
   competition for ideas versus for government spoils, 18, 86, 189, 216, 234
   cyclical progression of, 18
   debt, 14, 17, 31, 69, 100, 103, 164, 197, 213, 228
   decentralized power, 14, 67, 70, 154
   dispersed political power, 205–206, 232
   Divided Era, 188–189, 214, 234
   divine right of kings, 4, 15, 63, 202
   Electoral College, 64, 86, 210
   Federalists versus Anti-Federalists, 85–86, 215
   foreign policy, 66, 70–71, 116–118, 121, 170
   forming in simplicity and growing in complexity, 17
   fostering economic growth, 114–115
   Founders' genius and intelligence, 72–73
   government by the people, 62–64

growth in size and power of, 15–17, 110, 167–170, 188, 228
intelligence services and surveillance, 172–173, 186, 209
limited government, 16, 85, 87, 126, 135, 140, 143–144, 158–159, 163, 167, 206, 233
limiting of dissent, 157, 172–173, 210, 234
minting coinage, 70–71
regulatory proliferation, cost, and complexity, 17, 148, 155, 158–159, 167–168, 171, 183, 202, 206, 209, 212–213, 216, 227–229
republics, 64–66, 204–205, 232
revolutionary success in America versus failure in Europe, 69–70
role in religiosity, 16–17
ruling classes, 18, 206
security from external threats, 13, 26–27, 64, 71, 100–101, 173
self-determination and self-governance, 49, 67–70, 87, 152–153
separation of economic power from political power, 153, 171–172, 205–206, 232
special interests and lobbying, 18, 87, 154, 206, 216
spending increases, 158, *159*, 164, 197
state constitutions, 62
taxation, 17–18, 67, 69–71, 114–115, 134, 161, 212, 216
voting rights, 85, 87, 105, 111, 113–114, 129–130
welfare state and dependence on benefits, 110, 158, 167, 169, 171, 183–184
Gracchus, Gaius, 170
Gracchus, Tiberius, 170
Great Britain and England, 17, 26–28, 58, 67–68, 76–77, 110, 116, 224
elected Black officials in, 94
exports to, 44
immigration from, 39–40
Industrial Revolution in, 82, 131
middle class, 153
Pilgrims and religious freedom, 31–32, 34
population of, 80
Reformation, 50–51
Renaissance, 179
Seven Years' War, 30
slavery in, 98
War of 1812, 71–72, 101
women's suffrage in, 114
Great Depression, 110, 130, 139, 163, 212, 228
Great Society, 164, 183, 214
Greece, 23, 33–34, 83, 110
art, 137
class warfare, 169–170, 217
democracy, 64–66, 95, 127–129, 224
moral easing and laxity, 180
on Stoicism–Epicureanism continuum, 178
tax revolts, 18
Grimes, Leonard, 94
Guam, 116
Guelphs, 215
Gutenberg, Johannes, 10

H

Hamilton, Alexander, 70, 72, 85, 100, 103, 116, 160
Hammurabi, 95
Hancock, John, 72
Hanson, Victor Davis, 186, 219–220
Harding, Warren G., 147
Harper, Frances Ellen Watkins, 94
Harvard University, 138–139
Hastie, William H., 89
Hegel, Georg Wilhelm Friedrich, 3, 10–11, 13, 19–21, 27, 29–30, 32, 34, 49, 191, 194
Hemingway, Ernest, 135
Henry, Patrick, 58, 72, 100, 160–161, 211
Henry II, 112
Henry III, 113
Henry VIII, 50–51
Heretics and Believers (Marshall), 50
Herod, 210
Hesseltine, William B., 91
historical philosophers and philosophy, 3–4, 6–7, 9–11, 13, 19, 34, 47,

125–126, 138. *See also names of specific philosophers*
history
  as a continuum, not a destination, 84
  as the exceptional recorded, 177
  lack of appeal versus allure of the present, 10
  learning from, 203, 235
  lessons and laws of history and its maxims, 2–3, 6
  men making the times versus times making the men, 225
  newness of the study of, 9–10
  as no more a straight line than the emotions of our days, 5, 221–222, 235
  as repeating itself, 3–5, 9–10, 12–14, 19, 203
  as unworthy of considerable study, 11
History of Slavery (Anstey), 95
The History of the Ancient World (Bauer), 21–22
History of the Decline and Fall of the Roman Empire (Gibbon), 179
Hitler, Adolf, 16, 118–119, 157, 198, 226
Hobbs, Thomas, 72
Ho Chi Minh, 195
Holland, 28, 34, 52, 58, 103
Holy Roman Empire, 215, 222–224, *223*
Homeland Security Department, 173
Hoover, Herbert, 163
Horace, 137
Huguenots, 51
Human Rights Watch, 157
Hume, David, 72
Hundred Years' War, 26, 224
Huston, John, 120

I

The Idea of America (Wood), 61–62
immigration, 2, 28–32, 36, 38–40, 112, 169
  commerce, 30, 32
  competitive dynamic, 30–31
  complementary purposes, 29–30, 231
  culturally distinct enclaves, 29
  dependence on government, 169
  dissent, 170, 234
  lack of class culture and aristocracy, 29
  opportunity, 30
  religion, 31–32
  through the 1800s, 80
  variety of origins and cultures, 28–29, 80
income. *See* capitalism and economics
indentured servitude, 29, 57, 96
The Indian Wars (Treuer), 97
Industrial Revolution, 2, 75, 81–82, 87, 137, 202
industry. *See* capitalism and economics
International Labour Organization, 155
Iran, 226
Iraq War, 136
Ireland, 80
Islam and Muslims, 50, 96, 223
Isocrates, 129, 169
isolationism, 110, 116–118, 193, 198
Israel, 226
Italy, 14, 16–18, 30–31, 95, 112, 118–119, 122, 127, 179, 218, 223. *See also names of specific city-states*

J

Jackson, Andrew, 78, 86–87, 92, 164
Jamestown, 28, 34–36, 52
Japan, 80, 118–120, 194, 222, 226
Jefferson, Thomas, 56, 72, 77–78, 84–86, 101, 116, 140, 161, 164, 210, 228–229
Jesus Christ, 224
Joan of Arc, 113, 224
Johnson, Andrew, 92
Johnson, Lyndon, 122, 135
Johnson, Paul, 92
Johnson v. M'Intosh, 79
Jordan, Don, 96–97
Jordan, Michael, 195–196
Judaism and Jews, 16, 29, 50, 133
Julius II, 30
The Jungle (Sinclair), 132

K

Kennedy, John, 121

Kennedy, Paul M., 197
Kentucky Resolutions, 228
Kessler, Donald J., 226
King, Martin Luther, 106
King Philip's War, 36–37
King William's War, 37
Korean War, 110, 120–121, 136, 193–194, 226, 235
Krauthamer, Barbara, 97

L

Laffer, Arthur B., 212–213
League of Nations, 118, 120, 194
Lectures on the Philosophy of History (Hegel), 11, 13
Lee, Alexander, 130–131
The Lessons of History (Durant and Durant), 7, 47, 72, 125
Levine, Bruce, 91–92
liberalism, 83–84, 141, 149, 165, 187
Lincoln, Abraham, 89, 91–92, 102, 104, 142, 153, 161, 173, 199, 207–208, 224–225
Lindbergh, Charles, 118
Lion of Liberty (Unger), 58, 160
literacy, 10
Little House on the Prairie (TV series), 138
Livingston, Robert, 77
Livy, 128
Locke, John, 63, 72
Louis IV, 212
Louisiana Purchase, 77, 79, 193
Luther, Martin, 179
The L Word (TV series), 138

M

MacDonald, William, 87
Macedon, 129, 170, 192–193
Machiavelli, 30
Madison, James, 72, 78, 101, 140
Magna Carta, 10, 50
Manifest Destiny, 2, 4, 75, 78
Manifest Destiny (Stephanson), 78
Mann, Charles, 23

Mao Zedong, 157
Marshall, John, 79
Marshall, Peter, 50
Marshall Plan, 121, 194
Martel, Charles, 223
mass media, 2, 136–138, 143, 182, 187, 189
Mayflower, 31, 34–35
McClintock, Russell, 91
McHenry, James, 230
Meacham, John, 86
Medici, Catherine de', 112–113
Medici, Cosimo de', 112
Medici, Lorenzo de', 112
Medici family, 30, 112–113, 152, 205
Mexican-American War, 78, 90, 193
Mexico, 193
Michelangelo, 30
military. *See also names of specific wars*
  budget, 197
  growth of superpower, 110, 115–121
  international installations/bases, 121, 194, 197
  militarism and pacifism, 6, 14, 177, 197
  postwar demilitarization, 118, 120, 194
Modern Family (TV series), 138
Mongols, 95, 192–193
Monroe, James, 72, 79, 116, 161
Monroe Doctrine, 79, 116, 193
Montesquieu, 63, 209
monuments, 127, 140
moral structure
  cultural breakdown, 218–220
  easing, laxity, and decline, 16–17, 83, 128, 177–179, 202, 218–220, 227
  religion and, 15, 32, 38, 53, 181, 186, 220
  retrieval of moral standing, 227
  sexual experimentation/expression, 180, 185
Morgan, J. P., 82, 132, 147, 153, 165, 210
Morse, Samuel, 144–145
Musk, Elon, 132, 165, 208, 230
"The Myth of Dynastic Wealth" (Arnott, Bernstein, and Wu), 166

N

Napoleon, 188–189, 194, 224
Narragansetts, 36
NASA, 226
Natchez, 36
National Assessment of Educational Progress, 149
National Defense Act, 118
National Education Association, 149
National Endowment for the Arts, 122
National Endowment for the Humanities, 122
National Geographic, 97
nationalism, 21–22, 141–142, 187
National Socialist Party, 157
Native Americans, 2, 23, 27–28, 30, 35–38, 80, 92, 97, 192–193
Nero, 179
Netherlands, 28, 34, 52, 58, 103
New Deal, 110, 122, 163–165
New Republic, 195
New York Democratic Review, 75
New York Times, 139
New Zealand, 113
Nicholas II, 69
9/11, 173
Nipmucks, 37
Nogarola, Isotta, 112
North Atlantic Treaty Organization (NATO), 121
Norway, 28, 80, 114
Notes on the State of Virginia (Jefferson), 56
nuclear weapons, 120, 194, 226
Nullification Crisis, 229

O

Obama, Barack, 134, 141–142, 173, 183, 211
Ocasio-Cortez, Alexandria, 141
OECD Better Life Index, 144
oligarchy, 18
Omar, Ilhan, 141
O'Sullivan, John, 75
Otis, James, 136
Ottoman Empire, 96

P

pacifism, 14, 177, 197–198
paganism, 17
Paine, Thomas, 72, 136
patent law, 144
patriotism, 21–22, 120, 186–188, 219
Paul, 95
Penn, William, 51
Pequot tribe, 36
Pequot War of Connecticut, 36
Percy, George, 36
Perelman, Max, 195
Perkins, Edwin J., 57, 81
Perusine War, 112
Pew Research, 147
Philippines, 116
Philip II, 129, 170
Phillips, Macon, 173
Philosophy and Popular Morals in Ancient Greece (Dobbs), 178
pilgrims, 31–32, 34–35, 156
Pisa, 212
Pitcairn Islands, 113
Plato, 3, 5–6, 18–19, 220
Pledge of Allegiance, 141
Pocock, Tom, 96
politics. *See* government and politics
Polk, James K., 193
Portugal, 223
Poverty in World History (Beaudoin), 150
Presbyterians, 51, 139
Presley, Elvis, 120
Pressley, Ayanna, 141
primogeniture, 40
Princeton University, 139
Prop 13, 18
protest. *See* dissent and protest
Protestant Work Ethic, 32, 59
Prussia, 80, 116
Ptolemaic dynasty, 152
public virtue, 21–22, 187
Puerto Rico, 116
Punic Wars, 178
Puritans, 34–35, 51, 138
Putin, Vladimir, 157, 226

Q

Qin Dynasty, 14
Quakers, 51–53
Quasi War, 101

R

The Radicalism of the American Revolution (Wood), 40
railroads, 81–82
Raleigh News, 98
Reconstruction, 105–106, 188
Reflections on the Revolution in France (Burke), 201
Reformation, 50–51
religion and faith, 14–17. *See also names of specific denominations*
  agriculture as reinforcing, 12, 48, 56
  belief/faith and unbelief/doubt periods, 4–5, 20–21, 125, 202–203
  commerce as eroding, 48, 180
  decline of family and, 16
  decreasing personal importance of, 186
  divine right of kings, 4, 15, 63, 202
  doubt, 16, 47–48
  education and, 55, 138–140, 148, 180, 184
  faith in purpose of civilization, 47–48
  increasing attack on, 185–186
  Middle Ages, 50
  mini-theocracies, 15, 31–32
  moral structure, 15–17, 32, 38, 53, 181, 186, 219–220
  official churches and related laws, 52–54
  outlawing religious persecution, 51
  Protestant Work Ethic, 32, 59
  pursuit and founding of "just societies," 49, 51–52
  religious freedom, 31–32, 34, 52, 54
  religious wars and strife, 50
  renewal and recurrence, 12, 56
  retrieval of religious fervor, 227–228
  science versus, 16, 176, 180
  separation between church and state, 52
  state indifference toward, 16
  state-sponsored attack and persecution, 16–17
Religion in the United States of America (Baird), 49
The Religion of Ancient Rome (Bailey), 180
A Religious History of the American People (Ahlstrom), 49
Renaissance, 14, 17, 30, 112–113, 122, 130–131, 179–181, 205, 218, 227, 229
Republic (Plato), 18
Rettenmaier, Andrew, 166
Revels, Hiram, 105
Revenue Act, 213
Revolutionary War, 18, 49, 61–62, 73, 84, 101, 103, 160, 189, 224, 229
The Rise and Fall of American Growth (Gordon), 114–115
rise and fall of civilizations, 3–4
  art, 17
  belief/faith and unbelief/doubt periods, 4–5, 20–21, 125, 202–203
  commerce, 14–17
  complete disappearance of civilizations, 23
  expiration date, 23
  external dangers and internal division, 13–14
  family, 14–17
  formation and progression of civilizations, 22–23
  government, 17–21
  historical philosophers' views, 19–22
  militarism and pacifism, 14
  organic/building and critical/destroying phases, 4, 21, 48, 118, 125–127, 142
  public virtue and nationalism, 21–22
  religion, 14–17
  renewal and recurrence, 12
  science, 16–17
  Stoicism–Epicureanism continuum, 177–181
  survival and apology, 142, 175, 187
  with traits similar to those of people, 19
  two broad phases of civilization, 19–21, 125–126
The Rise and Fall of the Great Powers (Kennedy and Schambach), 197

The Rise of American Democracy (Wilentz), 84–85
Roanoke, 28
Rockefeller, John D., 82, 132–133, 147, 165, 208, 210
Rome, 5, 12, 50, 84, 137, 206, 224, 227
   class warfare, 169–170, 217
   conquest and expansion, 192–193
   decline and fall of, 14, 23, 127–129
   democracy, 64–66
   moral easing and laxity, 179
   poverty, 151
   public virtue, 21, 187–188
   religion, 180
   slavery in, 95
   socialism, 152
   on Stoicism–Epicureanism continuum, 179
   wars, 26
   women, 112
Roosevelt, Franklin Delano, 93, 118, 122, 134, 163–165
Roosevelt, Theodore, 132
Rothschild family, 152
Rousseau, Jean-Jacques, 11, 70
The Royal Navy's War against White Slavery (Pocock), 96
Russia, 15, 69–70, 78, 95, 114, 116, 119, 157, 194, 217, 226

S

Saint-Simon, Claude Henri de Rouvroy, comte de, 3, 20–21, 27, 47–48, 123, 125, 127, 142
Sallust, 21, 128
Santayana, George, 11
Savonarola, Girolamo, 131, 179
Schambach, Karin, 197
science, 176–177, 180–181, 186, 202
   education, 184
   flourishing with commerce, 17
   religion versus, 16, 176, 180
Scienza Nuova (*The New Science*) (Vico), 3, 9, 13
Second Bank of the United States, 161
Sedition Acts, 210–211, 228–229

self-determination and self-governance, 49, 67–70, 87, 152–153
self-sufficiency and self-reliance, 16–17, 32, 40–44, 59, 69, 87, 107, 159, 217
serfdom, 204–205
Seven Years' War, 30
Sforza, Caterina, 113
Sforza, Ludovico, 210
Shakespeare, William, 137
Shelley, Percy Bysshe, 196–197
Shepherd, James F., 44, 81, 101–102
Sienna, 14
Sinclair, Upton, 132
Singapore, 106–107, 215, 217
1619 Project, 140
Slater, Samuel, 81
slavery, 4, 29, 81
   American Indians, 97
   ancient practice of, 95–96
   Black ownership of slaves, 97–98
   capitalism and abolition of, 153
   difference in the prevalence of, 90–91
   emancipation, 104–105
   implausibility of constitutional abolition, 100–103, 129
   judgment of history, 99
   legacy of racism, 106
   modern, 103–104
   northern abolition of, 90, 101, 129
   role of Africans in, 98
   seeds of doubt and dissent, 129–130
   1619 Project, 140
   white slavery and servitude, 96–97
Slaves and Slavery (Walvin), 96
Slaves without Masters (Berlin), 93
Smith, Adam, 72, 80–81, 86, 95
Smoot-Hawley Tariff Act, 162–163, 212–213
socialism
   changing views toward, 146–150, 158
   economic growth, 168–169
   examples of, 157
Solon, 5, 224
Songhai Empire, 95
Soviet Union, 15, 121, 152, 157, 222
Sowell, Thomas, 62, 96, 98, 103

space, 226–227
Spain, 26–28, 78, 168, 217
Speedwell, 34
Spengler, Oswald, 3–4, 18, 20, 22
Stalin, Joseph, 157
Statue of Liberty, 111, 230
Stephanson, Anders, 78
Stewart, Jimmy, 120
Stoicism, 33–34, 43, 138, 176–181, 197
The Story of Civilization (Durant and Durant), 7, 33
A Study of History (Toynbee), 19–20
Sullivan, John, 85
Sumner, Charles, 96
Supreme Court, 54, 79, 141, 161, 163, 229–230
Sweden, 28, 113
Swedish War of Liberation, 14

T

Taiwan, 226
Taxes Have Consequences (Laffer, Domitrovic, and Sinquefield), 213
Taylor, Alan, 35
Technological Revolution, 137–138, 145, 202
Tesla, 196
Thomas Jefferson: The Art of Power (Meacham), 86
Tibet, 195–196
timocracy, 18
Tlaib, Rashida, 141
Tocqueville, Alexis de, 17, 143
Townsend, James, 94
Toynbee, Arnold J., 3, 19–20, 22, 221–222
The Tragic Conflict (Hesseltine), 91
Truman, Harry, 120–121
Trump, Donald, 172–173, 211
Tubman, Harriet, 94
Tuscany, 113
Twitter, 172
tyranny, 18

U

The Ugly Renaissance (Lee), 130
understandings of time, 3, 6
Unger, Harlow Giles, 58, 160
United Nations, 120–121, 194
UN Office of the High Commissioner for Human Rights, 103
urbanization, 2, 41, 48, 76, 111, 114, 130–132, 156, 162, 174–177, 185–186, 202, 209, 214. *See also* agriculture
  colonial cities, 55–56, 80, 217
  cost of children in urban settings, 15, 83
  crime, 185
  equality of circumstances, 132
  industrialization and movement to cities, 131
  limited government, 16, 159, 233
  mass media, 136–137
  percentage living in urban areas, 174–175
  shift from family to individual as central economic unit, 83
  transition from rural to urban economy, 14–16, 81, 131
US Constitution, 49, 62, 65, 70–71, 80, 163
  First Amendment, 31, 54, 149, 211, 230
  Third Amendment, 71, 173
  Fourth Amendment, 71
  Twelfth Amendment, 210
  Thirteenth Amendment, 104, 106, 111
  Fourteenth Amendment, 54, 104–106, 111
  Fifteenth Amendment, 105–106, 111
  Nineteenth Amendment, 111, 114
  Article VI, 54
  Bill of Rights, 49, 54, 71, 209
  ratification of, 100
  slavery and, 99–103, 129
US Virgin Islands, 116

V

Vanderbilt, Cornelius, 132–133
Venezuela, 157, 218
Venice, 20, 30, 41, 58, 66, 112, 172, 178, 210–211, 223–224, 229
Verona, 112
Vico, Giambattista, 3, 9–10, 13, 18–19
Vietnam, 195
Vietnam War, 135, 137, 235
A Vigorous Spirit of Enterprise (Doerflinger), 57–58
Vikings, 26, 95
Virgil, 12
Voltaire, 99, 212

W

Wall Street Journal, 186
Walsh, Michael, 96–97
Walton, Gary M., 44, 81, 101–102
Walvin, James, 95–96
Wampanoag tribe, 37
War of 1812, 54, 71–72, 101
Washington, George, 26, 42, 54, 72–73, 78, 100–103, 116–117, 140, 160–161, 193, 207, 209, 215, 224
Washington, Martha Dandridge Custis, 42
Washington Post, 157
wealth. *See* capitalism and economics
Wealth of Nations (Smith), 80–81
Webster, Daniel, 160, 173
West, Benjamin, 73
White Cargo (Jordan and Walsh), 96–97
White Servitude in Colonial America (Galenson), 96
Whitney, Eli, 81
Wilentz, Sean, 84–86
Williams, Ted, 120
Wilson, Woodrow, 117, 147, 210
Winthrop, John, 51
women, 42. *See also* family
 aristocratic societies, 112
 childbirth and child mortality, 38
 nonagricultural workforce, 114
 Renaissance, 112–114
 suffrage, 85, 111–114, 130
Wood, Gordon S., 40, 61–62
Woodson, Carter G., 93, 97
World Economic Forum, 196
World Vision, 155
World War I, 110, 117–118, 135–136, 193–194
World War II, 110, 118–121, 135–136, 193–194, 219, 222, 226, 229
Wright brothers, 145

Y

Yale University, 139

Z

Zeno, 33
Zuckerberg, Mark, 133, 166

About the Author

TOM DEL BECCARO is an author, a speaker, and a political opinion columnist. In 2015, he released the Amazon bestseller *The Divided Era*, which defines our era and explains why "the more government decides, the more it divides."

Over the last eighteen years, Tom has made more than 4,100 radio and television appearances around the globe, from the Middle East to London to New York to Hawaii.

Tom's opinion pieces have appeared in *USA Today*, *Politico*, *Fox News*, *Fox Business*, *Newsmax*, the *Epoch Times*, *Forbes*, the *Daily Mail*, the *Telegraph*, the *Washington Examiner*, *Investor's Business Daily*, the *Washington Times*, *Real Clear Politics*, the *Weekly Standard*, the *Daily Caller*, and *Human Events*.

Recently, Tom made his major motion picture acting debut in the film *Sweetwater*.

www.ingramcontent.com/pod-product-compliance
Lightning Source LLC
Chambersburg PA
CBHW060515080526
44586CB00012B/492